Air and Dreams

The Bachelard Translation Series

Joanne H. Stroud, *Executive Editor*
Robert S. Dupree, *Translation Editor*

WATER AND DREAMS: AN ESSAY ON THE IMAGINATION OF MATTER
LAUTRÉAMONT
AIR AND DREAMS: AN ESSAY ON THE IMAGINATION OF MOVEMENT

Air and Dreams

An Essay on the Imagination of Movement

GASTON BACHELARD

translated from the French by Edith R. Farrell
and C. Frederick Farrell

THE BACHELARD TRANSLATIONS
THE DALLAS INSTITUTE PUBLICATIONS
THE DALLAS INSTITUTE OF HUMANITIES AND CULTURE
DALLAS

Originally published in 1943 as
L'Air et les songes, essai sur l'imagination du mouvement
Copyright 1943. Librairie José Corti, Paris
14th printing, copyright 1983

© 1988 by The Dallas Institute Publications

Cover: Drawing on paper of Gaston Bachelard by Robert Lapoujade;
collection Roger-Viollet
Design by Patricia Mora and Maribeth Lipscomb

LIBRARY OF CONGRESS CATALOGING-IN-PUBLICATION DATA

Bachelard, Gaston, 1884-1962
  Air and Dreams.

  Translation of: L'air et les songes.
  Includes bibliographical references and index.
  1. Imagination. 2. Air—Psychological aspects.
3. Dreams. 4. Movement, Psychology of. 5. Air in
literature. 6. Dreams in literature. I. Title
BF411.B2513 1988   153.3   88-25704
ISBN 0-911005-11-0 (alk. paper)

The Dallas Institute Publications, formerly known as The Pegasus Foundation, publishes works concerned with the imaginative, mythic, and symbolic
sources of culture. Publication efforts are centered at:
The Dallas Institute of Humanities and Culture
2719 Routh Street, Dallas, Texas 75201

Contents

Foreword

IN THIS PSYCHOLOGICAL and poetic study of *Air and Dreams* Gaston Bachelard again probes the multiple manifestations, magnificent or frightening, of commonplace matter. Like a verbal alchemist unveiling the nature of the material world, he teaches that spirit is the heart of matter; that matter is the ensoulment of spirit.

For Bachelard the objective world is more than an inert scientific sphere. It is alive and responsive. It challenges the human being to participate. Through interaction with the world we not only learn about our soul's desires, but also that nature mirrors our spiritual aspirations by engaging our imagination, seizing on images of matter, exploiting them to express innermost being. Not simply representations or reproductions of nature, these images are the reality we single out from all the multiple possibilities of animation surrounding us. Even the world of painting is helpful in understanding the link between the real and the irreal that this versatile philosopher of science unveils.

Art critic John Russell, explaining the methodology of the Surrealist painter Odilon Redon, writes: "Redon means us to watch until the image reveals itself, and he's not going to be hurried."[1] A like observation could be made of Bachelard, proceeding in his penetration or amplification of images at a pace that often seems maddeningly slow. How could empty, invisible air mask so many subtle yet distinctive qualities? In our century, as disciples of T. S. Eliot, we have become accustomed to swift shifts and sharp transitions in syntax. But contrarian Bachelard insists that one of his aims is "to school us in slowness."[2] According to Russell, Redon used visionary images as "a launching pad" from which to blast toward what he called "the unexpected, the imprecise, and the undefinable." Bachelard would only partially concur. He would say "yes" to the unexpected and "perhaps" to the imprecise; but he would argue vigorously, we can suppose, that images are "undefinable." Enigmatic,

1. *New York Times* (November 9, 1986).
2. Gaston Bachelard, *The Right to Dream*, trans. J. A. Underwood (New York, 1971), 131.

but still discernible, Bachelard's work focuses on proving that images have predictable patterns, provided one follows the logic of images rather than sequential, linear logic: "imaginary elements . . . have idealistic laws that are just as certain as experimental laws."[3] Images are never so opaque that they don't unfold themselves at least partially to loving, careful exploration: "the mobility of an image is not indeterminate" (2). He would surely applaud the aim of recovering the numinous quality of the image since: "The value of an image is measured by the extent of its *imaginary* aura" (1).

Yet Bachelard also holds that there is a darker side to images of matter which he, like Redon, wishes to expose: "Material imagination, which always has a demiurgic tonality, would create all white matter from dark matter and overcome the entire history of blackness."[4] In a letter to Emile Bernard, Redon wrote: "Black and white derives its source from the deepest recesses of our very being." Thus the attunement is further revealed between the painter and philosopher. Both are concerned with the elusive strength of the imaginary realm, how the imaginary is immanent in the real; both find the world of matter revelatory of the profound and subjective realms of experience.

In his prior work on the weird animal imagination of Isidore Ducasse, pseudonym Lautréamont, Bachelard pointed out the depth of the demiurgic function. After the verbal frenzies of that book, a return to the element of air may seem like the lift of a gentle breeze. But air, though paltry in its manifestations of cruelty, does display violence and determination as witnessed in the storm or the hurricane.

The study of air further reveals Bachelard's long involvement with the subject of will. Bachelard differs from other philosophers who give will a moral definition. For him will is provoked by engagement with the material world. *Air and Dreams*, published in 1943, continues his unique approach to the phenomenon of will that began with *Lautréamont* in 1939. Studies of the images of air, animal, and earth form an unexpected trilogy. In *Earth and Reveries of Will* (*La Terre et les rêveries de la volonté*, 1948) he concludes that: "Man is the

---

3. See below, p. 7. Subsequent references are cited in the text.
4. Bachelard, *On Poetic Imagination and Reverie*, trans. Colette Gaudin (Dallas, 1987), 9; from *La Terre et les rêveries du repos*, (Paris, 1965), 26.

indefatigable force standing against the universe, opposing the substance of things."[5]

For Bachelard the world is forever enticing human beings into an active relationship, contact or contest, resulting in exposure of our highest skills and strengths. This commingling with the world of matter furthers the future of both planes of being, human and material. Environmentalists might not always agree with this theory. With Bachelard's attitudes, however, it would be impossible to unconsciously abuse the environment. Robert Chapigny suggests that Bachelard's studies of material imagination demonstrate "a conversion to quality . . . Air is breathing rather than what a body breathes."[6]

Since, as Bachelard explains in his Introduction, air is "very thin matter" (8), he devotes more attention to its movement and dynamics than to an analysis of its material nature. Students of Bachelard will recognize that mobility is the liberating force, both the effect and cause of the exaltation of imagination which, by definition, is always active and dynamic. Because air doesn't have an inside and outside, aerial action takes place along the vertical axis, up and down. It is the vertical axis which links Olympus with Hades, the celestial with the infernal.

Chapter I, entitled "The Dream of Flight," indicates the direction of the first half of the book. Indeed only in Chapter III, "The Imaginary Fall," one of the shorter chapters, does he follow the downward dream, or nightmare, of falling. He believes that the falling dream is an outgrowth of melancholy, since imagination by its nature would prefer always to rise. Through Edgar Allan Poe's moody incantations, Bachelard illustrates the horrors of the unsupported fall. He perceptively demonstrates that Poe's poetic technique is most frightening because of the juxtaposition of the real with the imaginary: the fear of falling is intensified by the nightmare of falling.

Many of the early chapters are devoted to the joys of ascending, to what he called in an essay "The Painter Solicited by the Elements" the "naturally excessive character of the aerial element."[7] These

5. Bachelard, *Earth and Reveries of Will: An Essay on the Imagination of Forces*, trans. Liliana Zancu, University Microfilms (Ann Arbor, Michigan, 1975), 111.

6. Robert Chapigny, *Modern French Criticism*, ed. J. K. Simon (Chicago, 1972), 184.

7. Bachelard, *The Right to Dream*, 31.

transports are reminiscent of Matthew Arnold's depiction of cerebral life under the influence of Hellenism. This ideal is one of beauty and simplicity: "aerial ease, clearness, and radiancy."[8] It is easy, Bachelard posits, to be carried away by aerial ecstasies, to follow Apollonian wingedness to the windswept peaks of emotional experience, to desire the celestial of the Olympians. Each of the elements has particularized complexes. Bachelard stimulates our questioning: is the urge to explore space, to escape from the earth's atmosphere, which is such a part of the western imagination, a manifestation of an aerial complex?

In Chapter V, Bachelard draws upon Nietzsche to illustrate aerial ascendancy in one of its extreme forms, as a "complex of height." Nietzschean images depict the soaring parabola of a predatory bird in flight. Bachelard explains how Nietzsche is attracted to the pure freedom of cold, dry, empty air: "For Nietzsche, in fact, air is the very substance of our freedom, the substance of superhuman joy. Air is a kind of matter that has been mastered, just as Nietzschean joy is human joy that has been mastered" (136).

As opposed to Nietzsche's vision of will as will-power, Bachelard contrasts Schopenhauerian will which is substantive. But in each case, image provides the insight: " 'I want' and 'I fly' are both 'volo' in Latin. There is no way to investigate the psychology of will without going to the very root of imaginary flight" (156). In Chapter XI, Bachelard again uses an image drawn from the element to demonstrate how the material world reveals the nature of will and desire. In this instance it is the hurricane:

> With violent air, we can grasp elemental fury, which is entirely motion and nothing but motion. In it we can find some very important images in which *will* and *imagination* are united. On the one hand, a strong will that is attached to nothing, and on the other, an imagination with *no* shape sustain each other. Experiencing personally the images of the hurricane, we learn what furious and vain will is (225).

In this compelling work Bachelard provides a visionary meeting place for two traditional opponents, will and imagination. If he offers

8. Matthew Arnold, "Hebraism and Hellenism," in *The Portable Matthew Arnold*, ed. Lionel Trilling (New York, 1949), 563.

nothing else—an unlikely supposition—his map for the understanding of how these supposedly conflicting opposites are actually derivatives of each other, reinforcing and enriching each other, stamps *Air and Dreams: An Essay on the Imagination of Movement* as a unique and enduring work.

Air and Dreams

Introduction

Imagination and Mobility

> A philosopher who seeks to understand
> man should concentrate on studying
> poets.
>
> JOUBERT, *Pensées*

I

STUDIES OF THE IMAGINATION, like many inquiries into psychological problems, are confused by the deceptive light of etymology. We always think of the imagination as the faculty that *forms* images. On the contrary, it *deforms* what we perceive; it is, above all, the faculty that frees us from immediate images and *changes* them. If there is no change, or unexpected fusion of images, there is no imagination; there is no *imaginative act*. If the image that is *present* does not make us think of one that is *absent*, if an image does not determine an abundance—an explosion—of unusual images, then there is no imagination. There is only perception, the memory of a perception, a familiar memory, an habitual way of viewing form and color. The basic word in the lexicon of the imagination is not *image*, but *imaginary*. The value of an image is measured by the extent of its *imaginary* aura. Thanks to the *imaginary*, imagination is essentially *open* and *elusive*. It is the human psyche's experience of *openness* and *novelty*. More than any other power, it is what distinguishes the human psyche. As William Blake puts it: "The Imagination is not a State: it is the Human Existence itself.[1] We will be more easily convinced of the truth of this maxim if we study the literary imagination systematically, as I am going to do in this work. This verbalized imagination, because it depends on language, forms the temporal fabric of spirituality and is therefore not bounded by reality.

Conversely, an image that deserts its *imaginary* principle and

1. William Blake, "Milton," Plate 32, line 32, in *The Poetry and Prose of William Blake*, ed. David V. Erdman (Garden City, New York, 1965), 131.

becomes fixed in one definitive form, takes on little by little all the characteristics of immediate perception. Soon, instead of leading us to dream and speak, it causes us to act. We could say that a stable and completely realized image *clips the wings* of the imagination. It causes us to fall from the state of dreaming imagination that is not confined to image, and that we may call *imageless imagination*, just as we speak of *imageless thought*. In its prodigious life, the imaginary no doubt leaves behind some images, but it is always more than the sum of its images, always beyond them. The poem is essentially an *aspiration toward new images*. It corresponds to the essential need for novelty which characterizes the human psyche.

A psychology of the imagination that is concerned only with the *structure of images* ignores an essential and obvious characteristic that everyone recognizes: the *mobility of images*. Structure and mobility are opposites—in the realm of imagination as in so many others. It is easier to describe forms than motion, which is why psychology has begun with forms. Motion, however, is the more important. In a truly complete psychology, imagination is primarily a kind of spiritual mobility of the greatest, liveliest, and most exhilarating kind. To study a particular image, then, we must also investigate its mobility, productivity, and life.

It is possible to do so because the mobility of an image is not vague. A given image often has its own way of moving. A psychology of the imagination of movement, therefore, should define the mobility of images directly. It should bring us to the point where we can actually draw, for each image, an odograph which would summarize its kinetic activity. This book is a first attempt at such a study.

I shall not, therefore, consider established images, those stereotypes that have already become well defined. Nor shall I consider other clearly traditional images such as the many flower images found in poet's gardens. They are a conventional touch that serve to add color to literary descriptions but have lost their imaginative power. Other images are completely new, alive with the life of living language. We experience them as actively lyrical through their ability to renew our hearts and souls. These *literary images* add hope to a feeling, a special vigor to our decision to be a person, even have a tonic effect on our physique. The book that contains them suddenly becomes for us a personal letter. They play a role in our lives. They revitalize us.

Through them, words—speech, the written word, literature—are raised to the rank of creative imagination. Thought expressed by a new image is itself enriched as it enriches language. Being becomes speech. Speech appears at the psychic highpoint of being. Speech is revealed as the instant transformation of the human psyche.

How can we gauge this urge to live and to speak? Only by broadening our experience with literary figures and moving images; by restoring to each thing its own particular movement, as Nietzsche advises; by classifying and comparing the different movements that belong to images; and by counting the wealth of tropes that cluster around a word. Whenever we are struck by an image, we should ask ourselves what torrent of words this image unleashes within us. How can we detach it from the all too stable background of our familiar memories? To grasp the imagining role of language, we must patiently search out for every word its inclinations toward ambiguity, double meanings, metaphors. To put it in more general terms, we must take account of every urge to abandon what we see or what we say in favor of what we imagine. In this way we may be able to reinvest the imagination with its role as seducer. Imagination allows us to leave the ordinary course of things. Perceiving and imagining are as antithetical as presence and absence. To imagine is to absent oneself, to launch out toward a new life.

II

Often we have no guiding principle for our absence and do not persevere once we have set out. Reverie merely takes us elsewhere, without our really being able to live the images we encounter along the way. The dreamer is set adrift.

A true poet is not satisfied with this escapist imagination. He wants the imagination to be a *journey*. Every poet must give us his *invitation to journey*. Through this invitation, our inner being gets a gentle push which throws us off balance and sets in motion a healthy, really dynamic reverie. If the initial image is well chosen, it stimulates a well-defined poetic dream, an imaginary life that will have real laws governing successive images, a truly vital telos. The images which the *invitation to journey* arranges one after the other gain a special vitality from this careful disposition, allowing us to define a *movement of the imagination* for those instances that will be studied here at length.

This movement will not be a simple metaphor. We will really feel it within ourselves, most often as a release—as ease in imagining related images or desire to pursue a fascinating dream. A beautiful poem is a kind of opium or alcohol. It is refreshment that calms our nerves. It effects in us a dynamic induction. I shall try to elaborate all the possible meanings of Paul Valéry's profound remark: "The true poet is one who inspires." The poet of fire, of water, or of earth does not convey the same inspiration as does the poet of air.

This is why the meaning of the *imaginary journey* is very different for various poets. Some only bring their readers to the land of the picturesque. They want to find *elsewhere* what we see around us every day. They load, even overload, daily life with beauty. We should not scorn this *journey* to the land of the real that entertains us at little expense. A reality illuminated by a poet has at least the novelty of new light shed on it. Because the poet shows us a *fleeting* nuance, we learn to imagine every nuance as a *change*. Only the imagination can see nuances, grasping them *in transition* from one color to another. There are, then, in this old familiar world, flowers we have seen imperfectly! We have seen them imperfectly because we haven't seen them as they change. Flowering is a process of subtle changes; it is always motion filled with nuances. Anyone who watches the flowers in his garden as they open and take on color already has thousands of models at hand for the dynamics of images.

But real mobility, the very essence of motion, which is what *imagined* motion is, is not aroused by the description of reality, even when it describes the unfolding of reality. A true journey of the imagination is a journey to the land of the imaginary, into the very domain of the imaginary. By this I do not mean one of those utopias which reveals itself suddenly as heaven or hell, Atlantis or Thebes. It is the journey that should interest us, yet it is the sojourn that gets described. What I would actually like to examine in this work is how the imaginary is immanent in the real, how a *continuous* path leads from the real to the imaginary. Rarely does anyone live out the gradual imaginary deformation that the imagination obtains from perceptions or achieve the fluid state of the imagining psyche. If we could multiply our experiences of image transformation, then we would understand the profundity of Benjamin Fondane's remark: "First of all, an object is not real, but *a good carrier* of what is real."[2] The poetic object, rendered duly dynamic by the rich resonances of a name, will be, I maintain, a good carrier of the imagining psyche. To achieve this *conduction*, we must call the poetic object by its name, by its old name, giving it its proper oral value and allowing it to resonate, to awaken adjectives which will prolong its cadence and temporal life. Did Rilke not say: "In order to write a single verse, one must see many cities, and men and things; one must get to know animals and the flight of birds, and the gestures that the little flowers make when they open out to the morning."[3] Every object that is contemplated, every exalted name that is whispered is the starting point for a dream and a poem; it is a creative linguistic movement. How many times, at the edge of a well, with its old stone covered with wild sorrel and fern, have I murmured the names of distant waters, the name of a world buried in water . . . And how many times has that world suddenly answered me . . . O my things! What conversations we have had!

Finally, the journey to the far-away worlds of the imaginary does not really *channel* a dynamic psyche unless it takes the form of a journey to the land of the infinite. In the realm of the imagination transcendence is added to immanence. Going beyond thought is the very law of poetic expression. Of course, this transcendence often appears to be crude, artificial, or flawed. Sometimes, it happens too quickly and becomes illusory, impermanent, and diffused. The reflective person sees it as a mirage. But this mirage fascinates us. It brings with it a special dynamic, which is already an undeniable psychological reality. Poets, then, can be classified by their response to the question: "Tell me which infinity attracts you, and I will know the meaning of your world. Is it the infinity of the sea, or the sky, or the depths of the earth, or the one found in the pyre?" In the realm of the imagination, infinity is the place where the imagination asserts itself as pure imagination, where it is free and alone, vanquished and victorious, proud and trembling. Then images soar upward and vanish; they rise and are shattered by their very height. Then the realism of unreality is evident. Forms are understood through their transfiguration. Speech is prophecy. In this way, the imagination is indeed a way

2. Benjamin Fondane, *Faux traité d'esthétique* (Paris, 1938), 90.
3. Rainer Maria Rilke, *The Notebooks of Malte Laurids Brugge* (New York, 1949), 19.

of going beyond, psychologically. It takes on the appearance of a precursory psyche that *projects its being*. In *Water and Dreams*, I brought together many images in which the imagination projects its inner feelings on the outer world. As we study the aerial psyche in this book, we will find instances where the imagination projects the *whole being*. When we have come so far and so high, we will certainly find ourselves in a state of *open imagination*. Eager to experience the realities of the upper air, the imagination as a whole will double every impression by adding to it a new image. As Rilke put it, one feels as though he is on the verge of being written. "But this time I shall be written. I am the impression that will transform itself."[4] In this transposition, the imagination puts forth one of its Manichaean flowers that blurs the colors of good and evil, transgressing the most stable laws governing human values. We gather such flowers in the works of Novalis, Shelley, Edgar Allan Poe, Baudelaire, Rimbaud, and Nietzsche. By valuing them, we get the impression that the imagination is a form of human boldness. An innovative dynamism comes from them.

III

Our next step will be to make a positive contribution to the psychology of two different kinds of sublimation: discursive sublimation in search of a 'beyond' and dialectical sublimation in search of a 'beside.' Such studies are possible precisely because imaginary and infinite journeys are much more regular than might be thought. Modern archaeology has profited a great deal, as Fernand Chapouthier has noted, from the setting up of regular series of documents.[5] The slow pace of life that objects have led over the centuries allows us to make inferences about their origin. In the same way, when we examine carefully selected series of psychological documents, we are surprised by the regularity of their filiation; and we better understand their unconscious dynamism. In the same way, too, the use of a new metaphor can shed light on the archaeology of language. In this study, I will examine the most wide-ranging *imaginary journeys*, the most unconventional stopovers, and frequently inconsistent images. In spite of everything, we will see that this

---

4. Rilke, *Notebooks*, 50.
5. Fernand Chapouthier, *Les Dioscures au service d'une déesse* (Paris, 1935), passim.

elusiveness, shifting, and inconsistency do not prevent there being a truly *regular* imaginative life. It even seems that this lack of coordination sometimes takes on an appearance so well-defined that it could serve as a schema for *coherence* based on mobility. In fact, the way in which we escape reality gives a clear indication of our inner reality. A person deprived of the *function of the unreal* is just as neurotic as the one deprived of the *reality function*. It could even be said that difficulties with the function of the unreal have repercussions for the reality function. If the imagination's function of *openness* is insufficient, then perception itself is blunted. We must find, then, a regular filiation between the real and the imaginary. All we need to do in order to live out this regular filiation is to classify the psychological inventory carefully.

This regularity is due to the fact that in our research on the imaginary we are *carried along* by *fundamental kinds of matter*, by imaginary elements which have idealistic laws that are just as certain as experimental laws. I might mention here a few short works in which I have recently examined, under the name of *material imagination*, the astonishing need for "penetration." Going beyond the seductive imagination of forms, it thinks matter, dreams matter, lives in matter, or—what amounts to the same thing—it materializes the imaginary. I felt justified in speaking of a law of the four material imaginations, a law that *necessarily* attributes to the creative imagination one of the four elements: fire, earth, air, or water. Several elements, of course, can intervene to constitute a particular image. There are *composite* images, but the life of images has a more demanding purity of filiations. The moment that images form a series, they designate a primary matter, a basic element. Even more than its anatomy, the physiology of the imagination obeys the law of the four elements.

Isn't there a contradiction between my earlier work and this one? If a law of the four material imaginations requires the imagination to fix on a single matter, won't the imagination take that as a justification for inflexibility and monotony? In that case, there would be no point in studying the mobility of images.

Such is not the case, because not one of the four elements is imagined as inert. On the contrary, each element is imagined with its own particular dynamism; it heads a series which then produces a certain type of filiation with the images that represent it. To use Fondane's marvelous expression once again, a material element is the principle of a *good conductor* that gives continuity to the imagining psyche. In addition, every element that the material imagination enthusiastically adopts prepares a special sublimation, a characteristic transcendence, for the dynamic imagination. Proofs of this will be furnished throughout this work as we follow the life of aerial images. We will see that aerial sublimation is the most typically discursive sublimation, the one whose stages are the clearest and the most regular. It is carried further by an easy, perhaps too easy, dialectical sublimation. It seems as though the flying creature goes beyond the very atmosphere in which he flies. It seems that there is always an ether to transcend the air, and that an absolute is the final stage of the consciousness of our freedom. Is it even necessary to point out that the adjective most closely associated with the noun *air* is *free?* Natural air is free air. Images of liberation present a problem if their different stages have not each been experienced. The same difficulty arises with truths imparted by free air, or a *liberating aerial motion* to which someone has given his adherence too quickly. We shall have to be very cautious in these cases. I will try to detail the psychology of air, as I did for the psychologies of fire and water. My search will be limited insofar as material imagination is concerned because air is very thin matter. On the other hand, air offers a distinct advantage when one comes to the dynamic imagination. With air, movement takes precedence over matter. In this case, where there is no movement there is no matter. The aerial psyche will allow us to develop the stages of sublimation.

IV

In order to understand the varying nuances of this active sublimation and particularly the radical difference between kinematic and truly dynamic sublimation, we must realize that movement perceived visually is not *dynamized.* Motion perceived visually remains purely kinematic. Because sight follows movement so effortlessly, it cannot help us to make that movement an integral part of our inner lives. The play of formal imagination and the intuitions that complete visual images orient us in exactly the opposite way from that required for substantial participation. Only a real feeling for a matter can determine truly active participation, which I would like to call *induc-*

tion, if the word had not already been reserved by the psychology of reasoning. It would be in the life of images, however, that a person could experience the will to lead. Only this material and dynamic induction, this "duction" by the inmost recesses of the real, can rouse our inner being. We will discover this by establishing a correspondence in materiality between things and ourselves. To do this we must venture into the realm that Raoul Ubac has very aptly called *counter-space*.

> To the organs' practical finalism demanded by the urgent necessity of immediate needs, there corresponds a poetic finalism that exists in the body as a potential . . .We must be convinced that an object can in turn change meaning and appearance depending on whether the poetic flame touches it, consumes it, or spares it.[6]

Putting into practice this inversion of subject and object, Ubac gives us, in *The Practice of Purity*, "the other side of the coin." He seems to discover in this way a correspondence between three-dimensional space and that inner space that Joé Bousquet has so aptly termed "non-dimensional space." When we have gained experience with the psychology of infinite air, we will better understand that in infinite air dimensions are obliterated and that we come in contact with a non-dimensional matter that gives us the impression of an absolute inner sublimation.

Thus we can see the advantages of a specialized *Einfühlung* and the benefits to be derived from our becoming one with a particular matter rather than extending ourselves throughout a differentiated universe. We will ask simultaneously of things, different kinds of matter, and "elements" their specific density of being and their exact energy potential for becoming. We will ask of phenomena advice on change and lessons in substantial mobility—in short, a detailed physics of the dynamic imagination. Aerial phenomena in particular will provide very general and important guidelines for rising, ascent, and sublimation. These guidelines must be considered fundamental principles of a psychology that I would more readily call *ascensional psychology*. The invitation to aerial travel, if it has the appropriate sense of rising, is always bound up with an impression of a gradual ascent.

6. Raoul Ubac, "Le contre-espace," in *Messages* (1942), Cahier I.

As the dynamic imagination helps us develop a feeling for aerial phenomena, we will feel that there is a mobility of images in proportion to the awareness within ourselves of a release, a gaiety, a lightness. Ascensional life will then be an inner reality. At the very heart of psychic phenomena there will be a real *verticality*. This verticality is no empty metaphor; it is a principle of order, a law governing filiation, a scale along which someone can experience the different degrees of a special sensibility. Finally, the life of the soul, all the delicate and discreet emotions, all the hopes and the fears, all the moral forces that are involved in one's future have a *vertical differential* in the full mathematical sense of the word. Bergson says in *The Creative Mind* that the idea of Leibnitzian differential, or rather the idea of Newtonian fluxion, was suggested by a philosophical intuition of change and movement. I think that this idea can be refined even further and that a carefully investigated vertical axis can help to determine human psychic evolution, the differential of human valorization.

If we want really to know how delicate emotions develop, the first thing to do, in my opinion, is to determine the extent to which they make us lighter or heavier. Their positive or negative *vertical differential* is what best designates their effectiveness, their psychic destiny. This, then, will be my formulation of the first principle of ascensional imagination: *of all metaphors, metaphors of height, elevation, depth, sinking, and the fall are the axiomatic metaphors par excellence.* Nothing explains them, and they explain everything. Put more simply, if a person is willing to live them, feel them, and above all compare them, he realizes that they have an essential quality and that they are more natural than all the others. They engage us more than visual metaphors do—more than any striking image can. And yet language is not particularly well-suited to them. Language, conditioned by forms, is not readily capable of making the dynamic images of height picturesque. Nevertheless, these images have amazing power: they govern the dialectic of enthusiasm and anguish. Vertical valorization is so essential, so sure—its superiority is so indisputable—that the mind cannot turn away from it once it has recognized its immediate and direct meaning. It is impossible to express moral values without reference to the vertical axis. When we better understand the importance of a physics of poetry and a physics of ethics, then we will be closer to the conviction that every valorization is a verticalization.

There is, naturally, *a journey downward*. The *fall*, even before any moral metaphor intervenes, is a constant psychic reality. This psychic fall can be investigated as an aspect of poetic and moral physics. The *psychic slope* changes constantly. The *general tonus*—that dynamic fact that every consciousness grasps at once—becomes *immediately a slope*. If the tonus increases, the man straightens up at once. It is in its traveling upward that the *élan vital*, the impulse of life, is the *humanizing impulse*. To put it another way, the paths to greatness form within us during this task of discursive sublimation. In man, says Ramon Gomèz de la Serna, everything is a path. We should add: every path encourages us to ascend. The positive dynamism of verticality is so clear that we can formulate this aphorism: what does not rise, falls. Man qua man cannot live horizontally. His rest, his sleep, is most often a fall. Those who rise up in their sleep are rare. They sleep an aerial sleep, a Shelleyan sleep in the intoxication of a poem. The theory of materiality as it is developed in Bergsonian philosophy could easily illustrate this aphorism of the primacy of ascent. Edouard Le Roy has developed Bergson's theory of matter in a number of ways. He has shown that habit is the inertia of psychic development. From my very particular point of view, habit is the exact antithesis of the creative imagination. The habitual image obstructs imaginative powers. An image learned in books, supervised and criticized by teachers, blocks the imagination. When it has been reduced to a form, an image is a poetic concept; it forms superficial links with other images, as one concept is linked to another. And this *continuity of images* to which the rhetoric teacher pays such careful attention often lacks the deep continuity that alone can bring forth material and dynamic imagination.

For this reason, I think I am justified in characterizing the four elements as the hormones of the imagination. They activate groups of images. They help in assimilating inwardly the reality that is dispersed among forms. They bring about the great syntheses that are capable of giving somewhat regular characteristics to the imaginary. Imaginary air, specifically, is the hormone that allows us to *grow* psychically.

I will, therefore, make every effort in this study of ascensional psychology, to measure images by their potential for *rising*. As to the words themselves, I will try to include the small amount of ascension that they are able to bring out. I am firmly convinced that if man lives his images and words sincerely, he receives from them a unique ontological benefit. The imagination given temporality by the word seems to me to be the humanizing faculty par excellence. In any case, the examination of individual images is the only way that I can go about this task. Therefore, I will always attempt to define vertical determination in its *differential* and never in its *integral* aspects. In other words, I will limit myself to examining very brief segments of verticality. We will never experience the full joy of integral transcendence that could transport us to a new world. On the other hand, my method will allow us to experience in its particularity the tonic quality of our aerial hopes, hopes which cannot let us down because they are not heavy. These hopes are associated with hopeful words, words that have an immediate future within us, and allow us suddenly to discover a new, exhilarating and lively idea, an idea that is our own, like a new treasure. Isn't a word our first joy? It has a tonic effect if it hopes. If it fears, it becomes blurred. Here, not elsewhere, while we are close to a poetic word, close to a word that is in the act of imagining, we must find a differential of psychic ascension.

If I sometimes seem to be placing my trust in images that are too immaterial, I ask the reader to bear with me. Air images are found along the road to dematerialized images. We will often have trouble in measuring air images exactly; too much matter or too little and the image will either remain inert or become too volatile: two different ways to make it ineffective. Moreover, personal factors intervene to make the scales tip one way or the other. The important thing to me is to show that a weight factor necessarily intervenes in the problem of dynamic imagination. I want to stress the necessity of weighing every word, in the full meaning of the term, by *weighing* the psyche that the words set in motion. I cannot produce a detailed psychology of this thrust toward what is higher without some *amplification*. When we have recognized all its characteristics in this way, then we can place the image on a real-life scale again. Thus the metaphysical psychologist has the task of placing in dynamic imagination a real amplifier of the ascensional psyche. To put it more precisely, the dynamic imagination is a *psychic amplifier*.

No one will have any trouble believing me if I state that I am aware of the difficulties of my subject. I often wondered whether I "had control of my subject." Can the study of *fleeting images* be a subject? Images of aerial imagination either evaporate or crystallize. We must seize them between the two poles of this constantly active ambivalence. I shall thus be reduced to demonstrating the double defeat of my own method: the reader will have to help me through his own personal meditation if, in the short interval between dream and thought or between image and work, he is to experience the dynamic word which both dreams and thinks. The words *wing* and *cloud* provide immediate proof of this ambivalence between the real and the imaginary. The reader can do what he likes with them: they can be a view or a vision, a sketch of something real or a movement that is dreamed. What I ask of the reader is not only that he live this dialectic, these alternating states, but that he connect them in an ambivalence whereby he can understand that reality is a potential for dreams and that dreams are reality. Alas, this ambivalence lasts only a moment. I must confess that very quickly we are either seeing or, just as quickly, dreaming. Then we become either a mirror for forms or the mute slave of an inert matter.

The decision to adopt a method that reduces our problems to an appearance of discursive sublimation, which depends on detail and plays constantly between impression and expression, places problems of religious ecstasy out of reach. These problems would no doubt be a part of a complete ascensional psychology. However, besides the fact that I am not qualified to deal with them, they correspond to experiences that are too rare to contribute to the general problem of poetic inspiration.[7]

Neither will this research extend to a study of the long history of *pneumatology*, which has played such a large role through the ages. I will have to leave out such documents since I am attempting to write as a psychologist and not as an historian. In this study, then, as in all of my other research on the psychology of the imagination, I shall draw from mythology and demonology only what is still capable of having an effect on a poet's soul and moving the spirit of a dreamer

---

7. A very complete discussion of the problem, along with a detailed bibliography may be found in Olivier Leroy's book *La Lévitation. Contribution historique et critique à l'étude du merveilleux* (Paris, 1928).

living far from books and faithful to the infinite dreams of natural elements.

As a counterpart to all these rigorous restrictions of method, I would ask my readers' permission to come back again and again to the one characteristic that I want to examine in aerial images: their mobility, comparing this external mobility to the mobilism that aerial images induce in us. To put it another way: images, to my way of thinking, are psychic realities. Both at the time of its birth and when it is in full flight, the image within us is the subject of the verb *to imagine*. It is not its direct object. In human reverie, the world imagines itself.

V

Here is a brief overview of my plan.

After this overly philosophical and abstract introduction, I will present in the first chapter as quickly as possible a very concrete example of dynamic oneirism. There I will study *the dream of flight*. It will seem, perhaps, that I am starting with a very specialized and rare experience. I will, however, undertake to show that this experience is far more widespread than is generally believed and that, at least for certain psyches, it leaves a profound impression on our conscious thought. I will even show that this impression explains the destiny of certain poetics. For example, very long series of images will be shown to have a clear, orderly, rapid pattern of growth and regular proliferation once I have demonstrated that the dream of flight is where they get their initial impulse. Specifically, images taken from such disparate works as those of a Shelley, a Balzac, or a Rilke, will demonstrate that the concrete psychology of the nocturnal dream of flight is what allows us to uncover what is concrete and universal in poems that are often obscure and hard to grasp.

When we have a firm basis in this natural psychology that does not rest on a priori constructions, we can go on in the second chapter to study *the poetics of wings*. Here, we will see a favorite image of the aerial imagination at work. From my previous remarks we will realize that the dynamic imagination provides us with the means to distinguish between artificial images and truly natural ones, between imitative poets and those inspired by the creative forces of the imagination.

At that point in the development of my thesis, I will have given enough images of *positive* ascensional psychology to be able to characterize all the metaphors of moral fall in their *negative* form. The third chapter will be given over to these metaphors. I will then have to answer many objections that will lead to my considering the experience of the imaginary fall as a first axiom of dynamic imagination. My answer will be very simple. I will give it here, since it sheds light on my general theses: the imaginary fall leads us to metaphors that are fundamental only to a *terrestrial* imagination. A long fall, a fall into black pits, the fall into the abyss are almost necessarily imaginary falls. They have affinities with an imagination of waters or—most especially—with an imagination of the black earth. To be able to categorize all the possible circumstances in which they occur, we must take into account the anguish of the *terrestrial being* who, during his troubled nights, struggles against the pit, actively digs his pit, and works with an axe and shovel, or with his hands and his teeth, in the depths of that imaginary mine where so many suffer their infernal nightmares. Such descents into hell cannot be described from the point of view of the poetic imagination, unless I find the strength one day to undertake the difficult and multifaceted psychology of the earth's material imagination. In the present work, devoted entirely to the material and dynamic imagination of aerial fluid, the imagination of the fall will be present only insofar as it is an inverted ascent. This indirect point of view—which is nevertheless very informative—is the one that will lead to the partial study suited to my present subject. Once the *psychological fall* has been studied in its simplified, dynamic form, I will have what I need to examine the dialectical play of vertigo and victory. We will measure the importance of a courage associated with attitude and stature, a courage to live in opposition to weight—to live "vertically." We will value the meaning of a healthy straightening up, growing tall, and carrying our heads high.

This health, this cure by means of imaginary verticality and altitudes, has already found its psychologist and its practitioner. In works that are not well enough known, Robert Desoille has tried with neurotic patients to reinforce the conditioned reflexes that cause us to make associations with values of elevation: height, light, and peace. I will take a special chapter to call attention to Desoille's work, which has been an invaluable help to me in many parts of my study.

In this chapter, as in others, I will not hesitate to use psychological observations as a pretext for developing my own theses on the metaphysics of the imagination—which remains my avowed aim throughout this work.

As I did for fire with Hoffmann, and for water with Poe and Swinburne, I have thought it possible with air to take a great thinker and a great poet as a fundamental type. It seemed to me that Nietzsche could be the representative for a *complex of height*. I have, then, undertaken in the fifth chapter to gather together all the symbols that group naturally—around the dynamics of ascension. We will see how naturally and easily a genius brings thought to imagination, how, for a genius, imagination produces thought—for it is far from true that thought goes looking for tinsel in some image shop. To use Milosz' startling ellipsis, I would say of Nietzsche: "Superior, he surmounts." He helps us to surmount because he obeys the dynamic imagination of height with marvelous fidelity.

When we have understood the dynamic meaning of an *invitation to travel* given by an aerial imagination to its fullest extent, and in all of its ramifications, then we can try to determine the imaginary vectors that can be attributed to various aerial objects and phenomena. In a series of short chapters I will show how much aerial imagination is involved in well-formed poetic images of the *blue sky*, the *constellations*, the *clouds*, and the *milky way*. I will speak at somewhat greater length in a later chapter devoted to the *aerial tree* to demonstrate how we can dream about a being of the Earth and still follow the principles of aerial participation.

As in my book *Water and Dreams*, where I pinpointed themes of violent water, I have provided some documents on violent Air—that is, on wrathful *winds*. I was greatly surprised that, in spite of fairly wide and varied readings, I was not able to find very many poetic documents on this subject. It seems that a poetics of the storm, which is basically a poetics of anger, requires forms more animalized than those of clouds driven by the hurricane. Violence, then, remains a characteristic that does not fit well into an aerial psychology.

Aerial dynamism, on the other hand, is more readily a dynamism of a gentle breath. Since I had taken almost all my examples from poets, I wanted to come back, in my last chapter, to the problem of poetic inspiration. For this reason, I set aside all the problems of actual breath and all the psychology of breathing that a psychology of air might very naturally consider. I therefore limited myself to the realm of imagination. Even with reference to prosody, I did not try to speak in a scientific way. Pius Servien's penetrating research has shown rather clearly the interrelationships of the variations of breath and style in this particular area. I felt, then, that I could adopt a resolutely metaphorical point of view and, in the chapter entitled *Silent Speech*, I have tried to show the stimulation received by someone who submits body and soul to the dominants of the aerial imagination.

After so many and diverse efforts, only the conclusion remained. I felt that I had to write not one but two concluding chapters.

The first summarizes my views—which are scattered throughout the work—on the truly particularized nature of the *literary image*. It aims at placing *literary imagination* among the natural activities that correspond to a *direct* action of the imagination upon language.

The second concluding chapter takes up a few philosophical views that I was unable to discuss with any continuity in the course of the work. It tries to assign literary images their rightful place as a source of philosophical intuition and to show that a philosophy of movement can gain by going to the school of poets.

1

The Dream of Flight

On my feet are four halcyon wings,
I have two on each heel, blue
And green, which over the salty sea
Can trace twisting flight.
GABRIELE D'ANNUNZIO, *Undulna*

I

CLASSICAL PSYCHOANALYSIS has often handled a knowledge of *symbols* as though they were concepts. It could even be said that psychoanalytic symbols are the fundamental concepts of psychoanalytic inquiry. Once a symbol has been interpreted, that is, once its "unconscious" meaning has been found, it becomes a mere instrument of analysis, and one no longer thinks that he need study it in its context or in its variations. That is how the *dream of flight* has become one of the most obvious symbols for classical psychoanalysis, one of the most common "explanatory concepts." It symbolizes, we are told, voluptuous desires. By means of it, innocent remarks made in confidence are suddenly stigmatized. It seems to be an absolutely reliable indicator. Since it is particularly straightforward and striking, and since its apparently innocent telling is not censured, the dream of flight will often be among the first signs deciphered in dream analysis. It will quickly shed light on a whole oneiric experience.[1]

Such a method, which assigns a definite meaning once and for all to a particular symbol, allows a lot of problems to go by unnoticed. In particular, it neglects the problem of the imagination, as though the imagination were unproductive time-off from a persistent, affective occupation. From at least two perspectives, classical psychoanalysis

1. The practice of psychoanalysis, of course, has contributed many nuances which complicate symbolization. Thus, Dr. René Allendy comments, with reference to the *dream of the staircase*, so closely associated with the dream of flight: "Man climbs the stairs (activity); woman comes down them (passivity)." Allendy notes, moreover, numerous inversions that further complicate this very simple dream. René Allendy, *Rêves expliqués* (Paris, 1938), 176.

fails in its duty to remain curious: it does not take into account the *aesthetic* nature of the dream of flight, and it ignores those efforts at *rationalizing* which work upon and distort the fundamental dream.

Let us agree for a moment with psychoanalysis that *oneiric pleasure* is satisfied by making the dreamer *fly*. How could this dull, confused, obscure impression take on the *graceful* images of flight? In its essential monotony, how could it become so picturesque as to provide endless stories about traveling on wings?

To answer these two seemingly specialized questions would be to make a contribution both to the aesthetics of love and to the rationalization of imaginary travels.

The first question allows for a new perspective on the aesthetics of grace. A visual description alone does not suffice for this aesthetics. Any Bergsonian can attest that a gracefully curved trajectory must be followed by a responsive inner movement. Every graceful line, then, discloses a kind of *linear hypnotism*: it guides our reverie by giving it the continuity of a line. But beyond the imitative intuition that obeys, there is always an impulse that commands. To one who contemplates a graceful line, dynamic imagination suggests a most unlikely substitution; you, dreamer, you are grace in motion. Feel *graceful power* within yourself. Become conscious of being a reservoir of grace, of being a potential for breaking into flight. Understand that within your will are scrolls coiled like the new leaf of a young fern. With whom, for whom, against whom are you graceful? Is your breaking into flight a deliverance or an abduction? Do you take pleasure in your goodness or your strength? In your dexterity or in your nature? When *flying*, voluptuousness is *beautiful*. The dream of flight is the dream of a *seductive* seducer. Love and its images cluster around this theme. By studying it we will see how love *produces* images.

To resolve the second question, we must pay attention to the ease with which the dream of flight can be rationalized. Even during the dream itself, this flight receives a tireless commentary from the dreamer's intelligence, explained in long speeches that the dreamer makes to himself. In the midst of his dream, a person who is flying declares himself the author of his flight. A clear awareness of being able to fly develops in the dreamer's soul. This is a wonderful opportunity to study the logical and objective images of a dream while in the very midst of it. Pursuing a dream as well defined as is the dream of flight, we begin to realize that it can have the "logical consistency of ideas" as well as the emotional obstinacy of its passionate love.

Even at this point, before I have presented my evidence, it should be clear that psychoanalysis has not said all there is to say when it attests to the voluptuous nature of oneiric flight. Like all psychological symbols, oneiric flight requires a multifaceted interpretation: an emotional, aesthetic, and finally rational and objective interpretation.

Explanations of an organic kind are, of course, even less capable of following all of the psychological details of the dream of flight. Isn't it amazing that a folklorist as learned as P. Saintyves is satisfied with such explanations? In his opinion, the dream of falling is linked with "very characteristic intestinal contractions" which we feel in daily life "when falling off ladders."[2] "Still," he writes, "in my adolescence, when I woke up in the middle of a dream of this kind (imaginary flight), I nearly always felt a sense of well-being connected with my breathing." A psychological analysis is required to understand this well-being. We must eventually reach a *direct psychology* of the imagination.

While examining the dream of flight, we will find still more evidence that a psychology of the imagination cannot be developed using *static forms*. It must be based on forms that are in the process of being deformed, and a great deal of importance must be placed on the dynamic principles of deformation. The psychology of air is the least "atomic" of the four psychologies that treat material imagination. It is essentially *vectorial*. Every aerial image is essentially *a future* with a vector for breaking into flight.

If there is a dream that is capable of showing the *vectorial* nature of the psyche, it is certainly the *dream of flight*. The reason is based not so much on its imagined movement as on its inner substantial nature. Through its *substance*, in fact, the dream of flight is subject to the dialectics of lightness and heaviness. From this fact alone, dreams of flight can be divided into two different kinds: light flights and heavy flights. Around these two kinds are grouped all the dialectics of joy and sorrow, release and fatigue, activity and passivity, hope and regret, good and evil. The most divergent activities that occur during

2. P. Saintyves, *En marge de la légende dorée* (Paris, 1930), 93.

flight will find their connecting principles in one instance or the other. As soon as we give attention to material and dynamic imagination, the psychic laws of substance and of becoming will prove superior to the laws of form: the elevated psyche can be differentiated from the faltering psyche in a dream as unvarying as the dream of flight. I will come back to this fundamental duality of oneiric flight after we have examined its varieties.

Before beginning this study, we should recognize that this special oneiric experience of flight can leave deep impressions on our conscious life. It is also, therefore, very common in both reveries and poems. In waking reverie, the dream of flight seems to be absolutely dependent on visual images. All these images of flying creatures provide ways of covering up the uniform symbolism maintained by psychoanalysis. It would in fact be a mistake to suspect that a hidden sensual pleasure is buried in some reveries or poems about Flight. The dynamic impression made by lightness or heaviness goes much deeper. It leaves a more indelible mark on a person than does a passing desire. Specifically, the ascensional psychology that I wish to set forth here seems more appropriate than psychoanalysis for examining the continuity of dream and reverie. Our oneiric being is *one*. During the day it carries on the experience of the night.

Ascensional psychology must also set up a whole metapoetics of flight, which will prove the aesthetic value of the dream of flight. Of course poets often copy from one another. An arsenal of ready-made metaphors is used to put wings everywhere—often every which way. But we will see that the method of referring systematically to *nocturnal experience* is the most reliable for distinguishing the superficial from the deeper image, for determining which image truly provides dynamic benefits.

Finally, let me point out one of the difficulties in this task, namely, the relatively small number of existing documents on the oneiric experience of flight. Yet this dream is very frequent, very common, and almost always very clear. Herbert Spencer mentions "that in a group of a dozen persons, three testified that in their lifetime they had had such vivid dreams of flying downstairs, and were so strongly impressed by the reality of the experience, that they actually made the attempt. One of them suffering from an injured ankle as a result." This fact, moreover, is very widely known. The dream of flight so easily leaves behind the memory of an ability to fly that we are surprised at not being able to do so during the day. Brillat-Savarin expressed his confidence in the reality of flight very clearly:

> I dreamed one night that I had found the secret for freeing myself from weight, so that once my body had become unconcerned with going up or coming down, I could do either one with equal ease, at will.
>
> This state of affairs delighted me: and perhaps many people have dreamed something very like it; but what made it even more special was that I remember that I explained to myself very lucidly (or at least so it seems to me) the means by which I had obtained this result; and these means seemed so simple that I was amazed that they had not been discovered sooner.
>
> When I woke up this explanatory part escaped me completely, but the conclusion remained; and, since that time, I am absolutely convinced that sooner or later, some more enlightened genius will make this discovery and so, as a precaution, I'm fixing the date.

Joseph de Maistre shows the same certainty:

> Young men, especially studious young men and even more especially those who had the good fortune to escape from certain dangers, are very inclined to dream, while they are asleep, that they are rising into the air and that they can move about at will; an extremely intelligent man . . . told me once that in his youth he had been visited so often by such dreams that he began to suspect that weight was not natural to man. As for me personally, I can assure you that this illusion was sometimes so strong that I had been awake for several seconds before being disabused.

Certain dreams of a *gliding* walk or of a *continuous* climbing must also be ascribed to dreams of oneiric flight. This seems to me to be the case in an account of an oneiric experience reported by Denis Saurat:

> A mountain that was neither steep nor covered with rock, but which we had been slowly climbing for a long time. . . . A long fairly regular, unbroken sweep—no physical discomfort; on the contrary a feeling of strength and well-being. . . . Short, rather sparse grass, then snow, then bare rock, but, above all, the wind that became stronger and stronger. We are walking against the wind; we are now at a stage where there is a very gentle descent before we

start up the major upward sweep again; we weren't disappointed; we already knew it.

I have omitted some notes that seem superfluous. But the dynamic unity of this account is sustained for four pages, and a reader can see in it the great simplicity and confidence of oneiric flight. Most often, however, we pay no attention to this account, because we think it merely a part of a more complicated dream. Always concerned about putting things in rational terms, we think of oneiric flight as though it were a means of getting to some goal. We do not see it as "journey for its own sake," an "imaginary journey" that is more real than any other since it involves the substance of our psyche. It *puts its imprint* deeply on our substantial psychic development. On the other hand, it may also be that psychological documents on oneiric flight are encumbered by irrelevant details. The psychologist of dynamic life, therefore, must undertake a special psychoanalysis to guard against overly explicit reasons as well as overly picturesque images.

By examining a few texts, I am going to make every effort to understand their dynamic roots, and thereby to define more precisely the deep, elemental, inner life of oneiric flight.

I am adopting in this work a psychological point of view and will therefore study psychological interpretations of this nocturnal experience. In his book *The World of Dreams*, Havelock Ellis devotes a chapter, entitled "Aviation and Dreams," to this experience. Ellis is particularly interested in the psychological conditions that produce this special dream. He speaks of "the objectification of the element and the rhythmic rising and falling of respiratory muscles—perhaps in dreams of the systole and diastole of the heart's muscles under the influence of some slight and unknown physical oppression." His long discussion, however, does not take into consideration the fact that the dream of flight is pleasurable—and often psychologically beneficial. It does not explain the very specific images that abound in the imagination. I will limit myself, then, to the psychological problem of images.

II

To set up the psychological problems of oneiric flight, I will start with a passage taken from Charles Nodier. Here is the question that

Nodier planned to submit to the Academy of Sciences if he ever became, as he says, "famous enough or rich enough, or important enough to be able to raise his voice sufficiently to be heard by them."

Why does a man who has never dreamed that he cut through the air with wings, like the other creatures of flight with which he is surrounded, dream so often that he rises and is buoyed up, like aerostats? And, since this dream is mentioned in all the ancient commentaries on dreams, why did he dream it long before aerostats were invented, if this ability to anticipate is not an indication of progress in his organic functions?

First, let us rid this document of any trace of rationalization. To do it, let us look at rationalization at work and see how reason operates on the dream. Or, to put it another way, since all of our faculties can be influenced by dream, we will examine *how reason dreams*.

At the beginning of the nineteenth century, when Nodier was writing, aerostats played the same *explanatory* role as did aviation at the beginning of the twentieth. Thanks to the aerostat, and to the airplane, human flight ceased to be an absurdity. In confirming our dreams, these means of flying have increased—if not the number of *effective* dreams of flight—at least the number of them that are *recounted*. Let us not forget that logic often likes to take advantage of preparation done in dreams, to the extent that thinkers like to present their dreams as "reasonable" expectations. Nodier's essay on "Human Regeneration and Resurrection" is very interesting from this point of view. The central argument is that since a human being experiences flight in a genuine nocturnal dream, and since, after long objective research, the conscious being succeeded in his experiments with aerostats, the philosopher ought to find a way of tying together the private dream and the objective experiment. To make this correlation, that is, to dream this correlation, Nodier imagines the "resurrectional being" who *will continue* and who will perfect man as a being endowed with aerostatic qualities. If this prediction seems a little quaint to us today, it is because we did not experience the *novelty* of aerostats. The inelegant "spherical" aerostat is an old, lifeless cliché for us, a concept that has been completely rationalized. Therefore this object has no great oneiric value today. But let us think back to the days of men like Montgolfier in order to understand Nodier's passage. Despite the literary effects which must always be taken into account with Nodier, we will quickly become aware of a sincere imagination behind the images, an imagination which naively follows the dynamics of its images. Here then is the aerostatic-man, the resurrectional man: he will have a vast, solid, enlarged torso, "the shell of an aerial ship." He will fly by creating "at will, a vacuum in his extensive lungs and by striking the earth with his foot, as the instinct arising in his developing organism teaches man to do in his dreams."

A rationalization that seems too blatantly artificial is, for this very reason, most appropriate for demonstrating how oneiric experience and real experience come together. When he has returned to a waking state, man rationalizes his dreams using concepts from his everyday life. He has a vague recollection of the dream images, and already distorts them by expressing them in the language of his waking life. He does not realize that through the dream in its pure form, we become completely involved with the material and the dynamic imagination and, conversely, detached from formal imagination. The most profound dream is essentially a phenomenon of visual and verbal *repose*. There are two principal kinds of insomnia: visual and verbal. Night and silence are the two great guardians of sleep; to sleep we must stop speaking and seeing. We must give ourselves over to an elemental life, that is, to our own particular elemental imagination. The *elemental* life avoids that swapping of picturesque impressions that constitutes language. Silence and night are two absolutes that we cannot attain completely even in our deepest sleep. At least we must feel that oneiric life is purer the more it frees us from the tyranny of forms, and restores us to substances and to the life of our own element.

Under these conditions, every addition of a form, however natural it may appear, risks obscuring an oneiric reality or causing a deviation within our profound oneiric life. Therefore, in order to enter into the essence of an oneiric reality as clear-cut as the dream of flight, we must, in my opinion, refrain from bringing in visual images. We must get as close to the essential experience as we can.

If I am right about the *hierarchical* role of the material imagination in opposition to the formal imagination, then I can formulate the following paradox: given the profound dynamic experience that is the dream of flight, *the wing is already a rationalization*. In the beginning of his work, before he set about playing with fantastic rationalizations, Nodier pointed out this great truth: *oneiric flight is never winged flight*. From this we can assume, I believe, that *when a wing appears in an account of a dream of flight, we must suspect that the account has been rationalized*. It is almost certain that the account is contaminated, either by images from conscious thought or by bookish inspiration.

The presence of wings in the *natural world* has nothing to do with it. The *naturalness* of the objective wing does not change the fact that wings are not a natural part of oneiric flight. In a word, the wing represents an *old rationalization* where oneiric flight is concerned. This *rationalization* is what has produced the *Icarus images*. In other words, Icarus images filled the same role for the ancients' poetics as does the aerostat, "the lung mechanism," in Nodier's ephemeral poetics; and the same role as the airplane for Gabriele d'Annunzio. Poets are not always able to remain faithful to the origin of their inspiration. They desert the profound and simple life. They *translate* the original word, without having read it carefully enough. Since ancient man did not have at his disposal an eminently rational reality for translating oneiric flight, that is, a reality constructed by reason, like the balloon or the airplane, he was forced to fall back on natural reality. He therefore created the image of a man in flight by making him a kind of bird.

I will, therefore, postulate as a principle that in the dream world we do not fly because we have wings; rather, we think we have wings because we have flown. Wings are a consequence. The principle of oneiric flight goes deeper. Dynamic aerial imagination must rediscover this principle.

III

Let us now refuse to acknowledge any rationalization and, in this spirit, go back to the fundamental experience of oneiric flight and consider it in accounts which are as purely dynamic as possible.

In this same book by Nodier, I shall take a very pure document, one that I have already used in my study on the imagination of water.[3] We shall see that the feeling is so clear that it moves the dreamer to try it out when awake.

3. Charles Nodier, *Rêveries, Les Feuilles vives* (Paris, 1979), 235.

One of the most clever and profound philosophers of our time . . . told me . . . that in his youth, after dreaming for several nights in a row that he had acquired the marvelous ability to hold himself up in the air and to move about, he could never rid himself of the feeling without trying it out whenever he came across a stream or a ditch.[4]

Havelock Ellis tells us that "Raffaeli, the eminent French painter, who is subject to floating in the air in his dreams, confesses that the experience is so real that he has jumped out of bed on waking and attempted to repeat it." Here, then, are very clear examples of a conviction formed during sleep—that is, during the unconscious but amazingly homogenous life of dreams—that seeks confirmation in everyday life. For certain people, intoxicated with dreams, days were created to explain nights.

An examination of such people can help us understand the dynamic psychology of the imagination. In order to provide a foundation for a psychology of the imagination, I propose to begin systematically with dreams and to reveal the true element and true movement of images, both of which precede their forms. I must, therefore, ask my readers to make the attempt to discover oneiric flight in its most dynamically pure form in their own nocturnal experiences. Anyone who has had this experience will recognize that the dominant oneiric impression is one of a really substantial lightness involving the whole being, a lightness in-itself that has no cause of which the dreamer is aware. Often the dreamer is filled with wonder, as if he had suddenly been given a gift. Only the *slightest impulse* is needed to activate this lightness that pervades his whole being. It is easy, and very simple: *striking the heel lightly* on the ground gives us the impression of being set free. This slight movement seems to free a potential for mobility in us that we had never known, but that our dreams revealed.

If we come back to earth during oneiric flight, another impetus immediately gives us back our aerial freeedom. We have no anxiety on that score. We feel secure. There is a force within us, and we know the secret that unleashes it. The return to earth is not a fall, because we

4. Cf. Jules Michelet: "it is in his best age . . . in his youthful dreams . . . that man has the good fortune to forget that he is . . . bound to the earth. Then he takes off and soars." *L'Oiseau* (Paris, 1961), 86.

are certain of our *buoyancy*. Everyone who dreams about oneiric flight knows this buoyancy. He also knows the feeling of the *pure leap*, one that is not goal-oriented, that has no end in sight. Coming back to earth, the dreamer, *a new Antaeus*, is once more filled with an easy, sure, and intoxicating energy. But it is not the earth that really nourishes his *élan*. If the myth of Antaeus is often interpreted as a myth of the maternal earth, it is only because the imagination of the terrestrial element is powerful and widespread. The aerial imagination on the other hand often lacks this power and clarity. Any psychologist of material and dynamic imagination, then, owes it to himself to separate out very carefully the mythical traces that persist in our dreams. Oneiric flight seems to offer evidence that the myth of Antaeus is a *myth about sleep* rather than a myth about life. Only in sleep can stamping a foot be enough to give us back our ethereal nature and allow us to participate in a surging life. This motion is truly, as Nodier says, the trace of an "instinct" for flight that survives or that awakens during our nocturnal life. I would rather say that it is the trace of an *instinct for lightness* which is one of the most profound instincts in life. Much of this book will be devoted to seeking the phenomena of this instinct for lightness. Because of its extreme simplicity, I believe that oneiric flight is a dream of the instinctive life. This explains why it is so little differentiated.

Under these conditions, if we want to reduce rationalization *to a minimum* in recapturing our memories of nocturnal aerial travel, where should we put wings? Nothing in our inmost nocturnal experience suggests that we put wings on our shoulders. Unless the imagination is especially contaminated, no dreamer lives a dream in which wings flap. Often a dream about flapping wings is no more than a dream about falling. We struggle against vertigo by flapping our arms, and this dynamic can produce wings on our shoulders. But natural oneiric flight, the positive flight that is our nocturnal activity, is not a rhythmic flight. It has the continuity and development of an *élan*; it is the swift creation of a *dynamized moment*. Here, in the realm of wing images, the only rationalization that is consistent with the primitive dynamic experience is *wings on the heels*. These are the small wings that are associated with Mercury, the nocturnal traveler.

Conversely, Mercury's small wings are themselves nothing but heels.

I would not hesitate to make these little wings the sign of a dreamer's sincerity. They are dynamically placed to symbolize the aerial dream, and they have no real visual significance. When a poet knows how to suggest these tiny wings in his images, then we can have some guarantee that his poem is linked to an *image that he has experienced dynamically.* It is therefore not uncommon to see in these images a special coherence not belonging to those brought together by fantasy. They are endowed with the greatest of poetic realities: *oneiric reality.* They induce natural reveries. It is not surprising, then, that wings on the heel are rediscovered in myths and tales from all parts of the world. Jules Duhem, in his thesis on the history of flight, points out that in Tibet "Buddhist saints travel through the air with the help of a kind of footwear called light feet," and he alludes to the tale of the flying slipper which is widespread in popular literatures of Europe and Asia. The *seven league boots* (in English tales, the "thousand-league boots") have their origin here.[5]

The man of letters will make this association instinctively. Flaubert, in the first version of *The Temptation of St. Anthony,* writes: "Here is the good god, Mercury, with his petasus in case of rain and his traveling boots." We may note in passing how the jocular tone ruins the oneirism of the image, an oneirism that is more faithfully observed in other passages of the *Temptation.* The power to fly lies in a dreamer's feet. Thus to avoid long explanations in my metapoetic study, I will simply refer to the wings on the heel as *oneiric wings.*

The eminently oneiric nature of the wings on the heel appears to have escaped the attention of classical archaeology. Salomon Reinach reduces them very quickly to a rationalistic element: "Hellenic rationalism always reasserts its rights. . . . Despite Hermes being a god, he attaches wings to his heels before taking off in flight: *primum pedibus talaria nectit/Aurea,* as Virgil puts it."[6] This commentary by

---

5. A surrealist, freeing himself from lengthy transitions, writes: "Walk, transparent seven league boots, toward the conquest of the world." LéoMalet, "Vie et survie du vampire," *Cahiers de poésie. Le Surréalisme encore et toujours* (August, 1943), 17. Classical criticism, thinking of policeman's boots, would laugh at these "transparent boots." In so doing, it would show its ignorance of the underlying dynamic imagination: everything that passes through air is dynamically and substantially aerial.

6. Salomon Reinach, *Cultes, mythes et réligions,* II:49.

Virgil does not replace oneiric archaeology, which would take the underlying feeling of *lightness* into account.

Of course, like all images, oneiric wings can be added artifically—as a veneer—onto accounts of very diverse types of dreams. In poetry they can result from copying a book image; they can be a superfluous allegory, a simple rhetorical habit. But then they are so lifeless, so useless, that a psychologist wanting to reflect on the axioms of dynamic imagination could not mistake them. He will always be able to recognize a properly dynamized heel. He will recognize it in its unconscious forms, slipped in surreptitiously by an unconscious that is sincerely faithful to oneirism. Thus in *Paradise Lost*, Milton speaks of an angel from heaven with six wings: "The third his feet/Shadowed from either heel with feathered mail,/a Sky-tinctured grain." The larger wings would not be enough, it seems, for imaginary flight; even an angel needs oneiric wings.

Looking at the problem another way, our survey of oneiric wings will allow us to critique the purity of certain documents. Let me first give an example of an account in which there are no oneiric wings.

Albert Béguin points out that among Jean-Paul's "elective dreams," which really resemble "poetic dreams," there appear dreams of flight. In his effort to produce and direct his dreams, Jean-Paul creates dreams of flight by *going back to sleep in the mornings.* These are not, therefore, strictly nocturnal dreams. He describes them in these terms:

> This flight, in which I am sometimes climbing and sometimes rising straight up with my arms beating like oars, is a real air and ether bath for the brain, voluptuous and restful—if it were not for the fact that the too rapid strokes of my arms in my dream make me feel dizzy and lead me to fear brain congestion. Truly happy, exalted in body and spirit, I have even risen straight up sometimes into the star-filled sky, greeting the structure of the universe with my songs. Absolutely certain, in the context of my dream, that I can do anything . . . I quickly scale walls that are as high as the sky, so that from this vantage point I can see an immense, luxuriant country-side beyond them; for (I say to myself) according to the laws of the representation and the desires of dream, the imagination must cover all the space around with mountains and prairies; and it does so every time. I climb up on the summits so I can throw myself off them just for the pleasure of it . . .

In these elective, or half-dreams, I always think about my dream theory. . . . Besides the lovely landscapes, I always look but always while flying (that is the sure characteristic of an elective dream) for beautiful figures to embrace. . . . Alas, I often have to fly a long ways looking for one. . . . (On occasion I have said) to figures that appeared to me: "I am going to wake up and you will be annihilated"; once I even stood in front of a mirror, saying with dread: "I want to *see* how I look with my eyes closed."[7]

It is not difficult to show that his text is *over-determined*: bringing in beating arms and oars in a single line destroys the dynamic unity of a dream of flight. We can connect two forms in one dream, but not two forces. Dynamic imagination has remarkable unity. We cannot fear a "brain congestion" and feel a "real ether bath, voluptuous and restful" in the same nocturnal experience. Moreover, the "brain" does not exist for a dreamer. On another point, the teleology of the dream is a construct that should be ascribed to a *dream account*. In dreams, no one flies in order to rise up into the skies; he *rises* into the skies because he is flying. Finally, the circumstances are too numerous and the means of rising too diverse. *Oneiric wings* are obliterated by the overload. I am now going to give a contrasting example where there will be nothing but oneiric wings.

IV

The following example is taken from the eleventh dream of Rilke, a very pure document from the point of view of the dynamic imagination, since the whole narrative takes a dynamic sense of lightness as its starting point.

Then there was a street. We were going down it together, keeping step, close to each other. Her arm was lying across my shoulders.

The street was wide, with the emptiness of morning, a boulevard slight downhill, sloping just so much as would be needed to take the little bit of weight from a child's step. She walked as if little wings were on her feet.

I was thinking of . . .[8]

7. Cited by Béguin in Jean-Paul Richter, *Choix de rêves*, pref. and trans. Albert Béguin (Paris, 1931, 1964), 52.
8. Rainer Maria Rilke, *Selected Works I: Prose*, trans. G. Craig Houston (New York, 1967), 24.

So it was a memory, and such a pleasant memory! A memory of sleeping forms, but one in which the certitude of happiness is indestructible. Do we not have here the great timeless memory of an aerial state, one in which everything is weightless, in which our very own matter is innately light? We feel uplifted and upraised by everything, even when we are going downward, "just so much as would be needed to take the little bit of weight from a child's step." Isn't this feeling of youthful lightness the sign of that confident strength that will let us leave the earth, that will let us believe that we can rise *naturally* toward the sky, with the wind, with a breath of air, carried *directly* by our feeling of ineffable happiness? If in your dynamic dreams you find that slight slope, the street that slants down just a little, so little that it is not noticeable to the eye, you will find wings growing, little wings on your feet; your heel will have just enough light, delicate effortless energy to let you fly. With a very simple movement, your heel will change the descent into an ascent, the walk into a soaring. You will have the experience of the "first thesis of Nietzschean Aesthetics": "What is good is light; whatever is divine moves on tender feet."[9]

Following *gentle slopes* in our dreams, we experience the way in which dreams help us rest. To cure a tired heart, there used to be a medical technique that prescribed a *walking cure*: it drew up a progressive list of controlled walks which were to restore eurythmy to a disrupted circulatory system. At night, when it is finally master of our integrated self, the unconscious also guides us in a kind of *imaginary walking cure*. Our heart, heavy with the burdens of the day, is cured during the night by the pleasantness and ease of oneiric flight. When a light rhythm is added to this flight, it is the rhythm of a calm heart. Isn't it in our very heart, then, that we feel the *joy of flying*? In the poems that Rilke wrote for Madame Lou Albert-Lasard, we read these verses:

> Through our hearts, which we keep open
> There passes a god, with wings on his heels.

Is it necessary to emphasize the fact that such lines cannot really be experienced without the aerial participation that I am suggesting?

9. Friedrich Nietzsche, *The Case of Wagner*, in *Basic Writings of Nietzsche*, trans. and ed. Walter Kaufmann (New York, 1968), 613.

Mercury's wings are the wings of human flight. They are so much a part of us that we can say that they make both flight and sky a part of us. It seems that we are in the very center of a universe in flight, or that the cosmos in flight becomes a reality in the depths of our being. This marvelous flight can be felt by meditating on a poem taken from the sketch book translated by Madame Lou Albert-Lasard.

> See, I knew they were real,
> the ones who never learned to walk,
> as men commonly do.
> For them, rising into the heavens
> suddenly spread out before them
> was the beginning. Flight . . .
> . . . .
> Do not ask
> how long they felt; how long
> they could still be seen. For invisible heavens
> indescribable heavens are
> above the inner landscape.

For a soul as sincere as Rilke's, oneiric incidents, however rare, are closely related to living substance. They are inscribed in the long dynamic past of our being. For isn't the purpose of oneiric flight to teach us to overcome our fear of falling? Doesn't that happiness carry the sign of our first successful attempts to conquer this primordial fear? What a role, then, it must have played in the consolations—the limited and rare consolations—of the Rilkean soul! For one who suffered from the noise of a pin falling on the floor and from the terrifying noise of leaves falling in the fateful symphony of the fall of everything, what a pleasant surprise it must have been to greet beings with little wings on their feet in his dreams. If we truly experience the frequent connection between flight and fall in our dreams, we see how fear can change into joy. That is really a *Rilkean turnabout*. The conclusion of the eleventh dream—which is so beautiful!—shows this very clearly: "Did you not know, then, that joy is, in reality, a terror whose outcome we don't fear? We go through terror from beginning to end, and that precisely is joy. A terror about which you know more than the beginning. A terror in which you have confidence." Oneiric flight, then, is a slow-motion fall, a fall from which you can get up easily with no damage done. Oneiric flight is the synthesis of

falling and rising. Only a soul as totally integrated as Rilke's can
retain in joy itself the terror that joy surmounts. Less integrated souls
have only memory at their disposal to bring opposites together, to
experience joy and pain in succession, as one causing the other. But
this is an important revelation that we already owe to the dream: it
shows us that terror can produce happiness. If, as I will show, one of
our first fears is the fear of falling; if the greatest human responsibility—both physical and moral—is the responsibility for our *verticality*, then think how much we owe to the dream that makes us more
erect, that makes us dynamically upright, that arches our body from
heels to neck, that rids us of our weight, that gives us our first and
only aerial experience! How salutary, comforting, marvelous, and
moving this dream must be! What memories it must leave in a soul
who knows how to make connections between nocturnal life and
daytime poetic reverie! Psychoanalysts will repeat that the dream of
flight is the symbol of voluptuousness, and that we pursue it, as Jean-
Paul says, "to embrace beautiful figures." If we need to love in order
to loosen the hold of stifling anguish, then yes, the dream of flight
can soothe at night an unhappy love. It can fulfill an impossible love
with nocturnal happiness. But the dream of flight has more immediate functions: it is a reality of the night, an autonomous nighttime
reality. If we approach it from the perspective of nocturnal realism,
we will find that a daytime love satisfied by oneiric flight appears to
be a special case of levitation. For certain souls whose nocturnal activity is very powerful, to love is to fly; oneiric levitation is a more
profound, more essential, less complicated psychic reality than love
itself. The need to become lighter, to be freed, to take great freedom
from the night, appears as a psychic destiny and as the very function
of normal nocturnal activity: of a restful night.

V

Those who study sleep, therefore, should pay attention to the nocturnal experience of oneiric flight. But do they only think about
teaching us to sleep well, and do the few remarks of an Aldous
Huxley on hypnopaedia extend beyond an Anglo-Saxon's fanciful
predictions?[10] From my personal experience, sleeping well means dis-

10. Aldous Huxley, *Brave New World* (New York, 1932, 1946).

covering the primary element of the unconscious. To put it more directly, we must all sleep *in* our own element. A good sleep is one in which we are rocked or carried, and the imagination is well aware that we are rocked and carried by something and not by someone. While asleep we inhabit a Cosmos; we are rocked by water; we are carried in the air and by the air—which we breathe according to the rhythm of our own breath. This is the sleep of childhood, or at least the peaceful sleep of youth when nocturnal life so often hears an invitation to travel, to undertake an infinite voyage. In his *Preface to the Comic History of the Countries and Kingdoms of the Sun*, Cyrano de Bergerac writes: "in my golden youth, it seemed to me that I became light as I slept and rose up into the clouds." He quite correctly uses positive psychological experience as the basis for his fiction—for how could we consider the nocturnal flight of our dream-filled youth as anything but positive? The mechanical elements of the Traveler to the Empires of the Sun and Moon were added after Cyrano had studied Cartesian mechanics. They too are mechanics tacked onto a living experience. That is why Cyrano's writings amuse us without moving us. They belong to the world of fantasy; they too quickly abandon the great land of the imagination.

Genuine hypnopaedia ought, then, to help us exteriorize the power of oneiric flight. Perhaps substantialist intuitions and even more basic alimentary intuitions can give us more powerful material images than those in which we must adjust wings, wheels, and levers. Who has not found himself dreaming when he saw the winged seed of a dandelion or a thistle flying in the summer sky? Jules Duhem reports that in Peru anyone who wishes *to fly* eats "a light seed that floats with the wind." Along these same lines, Joseph de Maistre tells us in *Les Soirées de Saint-Pétersbourg* that "Egyptian priests . . . during the time of their ritual purifications ate only the flesh of flying creatures, *because birds were the lightest of all the animals.*" An Arab naturalist (quoted by Giuseppe Boffito in *Library of Italian Aeronautics*) thinks of the bird as an animal that has been *made lighter.* "God made their body weight lighter by leaving out several parts . . . such as teeth, ears, ventricles, bladder, and backbone." Basically, to fly we need wings less than we need winged substance or wing-like food. To absorb *light* matter or to become conscious of an essential *lightness* is the same dream, expressed first by a materialist and then by an idealist. It is interesting, moreover, to read in a footnote a remark by the editor of *Les Soirées*: "It is superfluous to point out that this expression must be taken in its common meaning of *light meat*." The editor is making every effort to find a material meaning for a prescription that brings into play such obvious imaginary values. It is an excellent example of a rationalization that completely misunderstands psychological reality.

If we read the history of efforts to imitate Icarus, we will find many examples of materialistic thinkers who believe that participating in the nature of feathers is the same thing as participating in flight. For example, Father Damian, an Italian living at court in Scotland, tried to fly in 1507 using wings made out of feathers. He took off from the top of a tower, but fell and broke his legs. He attributed his fall to the fact that some rooster feathers had been used to make the wings. The rooster feathers showed their "natural affinity" for the barnyard despite the presence of truly *aerial* feathers which, if they alone had been used, would have guaranteed him success in flying up toward the sky.

In accordance with my method, let me follow these examples of materialism based on the cruder alimentary processes with a more literary, more refined example. It is one which, in my opinion, brings the same image into play. In *Paradise Lost*, Milton suggests a kind of vegetal sublimation which, throughout its development, prepares a series of progressively more ethereal foods.

> So from the root
> Springs lighter the green stalk, from thence the leaves
> More airy, last the bright consummate flow'r
> Spirits odorous breathes: flow'rs and their fruit,
> Man's nourishment, by gradual scale sublimed,
> To vital spirits aspire, to animal,
> To intellectual; give both life and sense,
> Fancy and understanding, whence the soul
> Reason receives . . .
> Time may come when men
> With angels may participate, and find
> No inconvenient diet, nor too light fare;
> And from these corporal nutriments perhaps
> Your bodies may at last turn all to spirit
> Improved by tract of time, and winged ascend
> Ethereal, as we . . .

Vico has said: "Every metaphor is a myth in miniature." Here we see that a metaphor may also be physics or biology, to say nothing of a dietary plan. Material imagination is truly the plastic mediator that joins literary images and substances. By expressing ourselves materially we can put all of life into poems.

VI

To prove that my seemingly very specific interpretation of oneiric flight can furnish a general thesis for elucidating certain works, I am going to take a quick look at Shelley's poetry from this point of view. I have no doubt that Shelley loved all of nature; he sang, better than any other, about the river and the sea. His tragic life binds him forever to the destiny of the waters. Nevertheless, the *aerial* character of his poetry seems to me to be most profound, and if we could have only one adjective to define his poetry, it would no doubt be easy to get everyone to agree that it is *aerial*. But this adjective, however accurate it may be, is not enough. I wish to prove that Shelley is materially and dynamically a poet of aerial substance. In his works, wind, odor, light, and formless aerial beings can act *directly*: "Wind, light, air, the odor of a flower stir violent emotions in me."[11] If we contemplate Shelley's work, we understand how certain personalities are affected by the *violence of gentleness*, to what extent they are sensitive to the weight of imponderables, and how they become dynamic as they are sublimated.

As we go on, we will find many proofs—direct and indirect—that Shelley's poetic reveries bear the mark of *oneiric sincerity*, which I have postulated as crucial from a poetic point of view. But to orient the discussion, we will first look at an obvious image of an "oneiric wing":

> Whence come ye, so wild and so fleet,
> For sandals of lightning are on your feet,
> And your wings are soft and swift as thought . . .

There is a slight shift in the images that detaches the wings from the sandals of lightning, but this shift cannot break the unity of the image. The image is a whole, and what is smooth and gentle is the movement, not the wing or the feathers of a wing that a dreamer's hand might caress. Let me say again that such an image rejects

11. Cited by Louis Cazamian in *Etudes de psychologie littéraire* (Paris, 1913), 52.

allegorical attributes. It must be understood by the delighted soul as an imaginary movement. I would even be willing to say that it is an act of the soul and that it can be understood if it is *undertaken*.

> An antelope,
> In the suspended impulse of its lightness,
> Were less aethereally light . . .

as Shelley says elsewhere. With this notion of the *suspended impulse*, Shelley gives us a hieroglyphic that the formal imagination would have a great deal of difficulty deciphering. Dynamic imagination gives us the key: the suspended impulse is itself *oneiric flight*. Only a poet can explain another poet. To this *suspended impulse* which leaves the impression of its flight within us, we could compare these three lines by Rilke:

> Where no path has been marked out
> we flew.
> The arc is still engraven in our minds.[12]

Now that we have recognized the principal characteristic of Shelley's poetry, we will delve further into its sources. Let us take, for example, his "Prometheus Unbound." We will quickly realize that this is an *aerial Prometheus*. The Titan is chained on top of a mountain so that he can breathe life from the air. He stretches toward the heights, *straining* against his bonds. His tension is the perfect dynamic of *aspiration*.

No doubt in his humanitarian aspirations, in his lucid reveries about a happier human race, Shelley saw in Prometheus one who sets man *up* in the face of Destiny, in the face of the gods themselves. All of Shelley's social claims are active in his poetry. But the means and movements of the imagination are totally independent of social passions. In fact, I believe that the true poetic power of "Prometheus Unbound" does not lie in any one of the elements borrowed from social symbolism. In certain souls, the imagination is more cosmic than social. Such is the case, in my opinion, with the Shelleyan imagination. The gods and demi-gods are less persons—more or less clear images of men—than *psychic forces* that will play a role in a Cosmos animated by a true psychic destiny. But we should not be too

12. Rilke, *Poèmes*, trans. Lou Albert-Lasard (Paris, 1937), 8.

quick to say that the characters are therefore *abstractions*, because the force of *psychic elevation*, which is the Promethean force par excellence, is eminently concrete. It corresponds to a psychic *operation*, which is very familiar to Shelley and which he wants to convey to his reader.

Let us not forget that "Prometheus Unbound" was written "upon the mountainous ruins of the Baths of Caracalla, among the flowery glades . . ." as he faced "dizzy arches suspended in the air." A *terrestrial imagination* would see its pillars; an *aerial imagination* sees only "arches *suspended in the air.*" More precisely, Shelley is not contemplating the *design* of arches, but rather, if I may put it this way, *vertigo*. With all his soul, Shelley lives in an aerial world, in the highest world. This world is dramatized by his vertigo, a vertigo that is brought on deliberately to savor the victory of rising above it. Thus, man pulls on his chains in order to know which *élan* will liberate him. But we must make no mistake here. Liberation is the positive function. It is what shows that the intuition of the air is superior to the solid terrestrial intuition of the chain. The surmounting of vertigo and the shaking of the chains from which the captive is struggling to get free are at the very heart of Promethean dynamics.

In his preface, Shelley explains the psychological meaning that is to be given to his Promethean images:

> The imagery which I have employed will be found, in many instances, to have been drawn from the operations of the human mind, or from those external actions by which they are expressed. This is unusual in modern poetry, although Dante and Shakespeare are full of instances of the same kind: Dante indeed more than any other poet, and with greater success.[13]

Thus is "Prometheus Unbound" placed under the aegis of Dante, the poet most attracted to verticality. He has explored the two verticals: Paradise and Hell. For Shelley, every image is an *operation*, an operation of the human mind. This operation is characterized by an inner spiritual principle, even though some may believe it to be a mere reflection of the exterior world. Therefore, when Shelley tells us that "poetry is a mimetic art," we must understand that it imitates what

13. Shelley, "Prometheus Unbound," preface, in *The Complete Poetical Works of Percy Bysshe Shelley*, ed. Thomas Hutchinson (London, 1905), 205.

we cannot see: profound human life. It imitates strength rather than movement. Prose is enough to tell us about life as we see it and move-ment as it unfolds. But only poems can bring to light the hidden forces of spiritual life. They are, in the Schopenhauerian sense of the word, the phenomena of these psychic forces. All truly poetic images seem to be a *spiritual operation of the mind.* To understand a poet in the Shelleyan sense, then, it is not a question, as might be thought from a hasty reading of the preface of "Prometheus Unbound," of analyzing the "operations of the human mind," as Condillac did. The poet's task is to extend the images a little to be sure that the human quality of the mind is operating in them, to be sure that they are human images, images that humanize the forces of the cosmos. Then we are led to a cosmology of what is human. Instead of experiencing a naive anthropomorphism, we turn man over to elemental and deeply rooted forces.

Spiritual life is characterized by a dominant function: it wants to grow, it wants to rise. It instinctively tends toward *height.* For Shelley, then, poetic images are all *agents of elevation.* In other words, poetic images are *operations* of the human mind insofar as they make us lighter, raise us or elevate us. They have only one referential axis: a vertical one. They are essentially aerial. If there is one image in a poem that fails to fulfill this function of making us lighter, the poem fails: man is once again enslaved, and his chains hurt him. Shelley, with a total lack of conscious effort—which is the mark of genius—succeeds in avoiding unintended images of weight in his poetics and gathers into one well-made bouquet all the flowers sug-gesting upward movement. He seems to be able, with his delicate touch, to gauge the upward thrust of every flower's floral spike. Reading him, we understand the profound remark of Masson-Oursel: "The height of spiritual life resembles taxis."[14] One touches the grow-ing height. Shelley's dynamic images operate in this high realm of the spiritual life.

We can easily understand that images whose polarity is so strongly oriented toward *height* can easily take on social, moral, and Pro-methean valorizations. But these valorizations are not sought after; they are not a part of the poet's purpose. The dynamic image is

14. Masson-Oursel, *Le Fait métaphysique* (Paris, 1941), 49.

revealed, behind the social metaphors, as a primary psychic value. Love for others, by putting us on a higher plane, merely supplies additional support to the person who constantly strives to live on a higher plane, at the heights of being. Imaginary levitation thus assimilates all the metaphors of human greatness. But the psychic realism of levitation has its own inner thrust. It is the dynamic realism of an aerial psyche.

I have examined the poetic themes of the bark in my book *Water and Dreams*. There I showed that these themes are very powerful because implicit in them is the unconscious memory of the *joy of rocking*, the memory of the cradle in which people experience in every fiber of their being a joy that knows no bounds. I indicated that for some dreamers the dream bark that rocks on the waves imperceptibly leaves the water for the sky. Only a theory of dynamic imagination can take into account the *continuity* of such images, which neither formal realism nor any experience in our waking moments can justify. The principle of continuity in the dynamic images of water and air is none other than *oneiric flight*. Therefore, once we have grasped the profound meaning of the joy of rocking and once we have compared it to the gentleness of oneiric travel, then aerial travel may be seen as a readily attained transcendence of travel over the waves: one who was rocked in his cradle, on the earth, is now rocked in maternal arms. He experiences the highest form of the joy of rocking, that is, the joy of being carried. Given this, we can conclude that all images of aerial travel are pleasant ones. If voluptuousness enters in at all, it is gentle, vague and remote. An aerial dreamer is never tormented by passion, nor is he ever carried away by tempests and north winds. At the least, he always feels himself in safe hands, in protective arms.

Shelley has frequently stepped into the aerial bark. He has truly lived in the *wind's cradle*. In "Epipsychidion" he says:

> Our bark is as an albatross, whose nest
> Is a far Eden of the purple East;
> And we between her wings will sit, while Night,
> And Day, and Storm, and Calm, pursue their flight.[15]

If we were to associate images according to their appearance, there

15. Shelley, "Epipsychidion," lines 416-19, 420.

would be no hope of uniting a bark and an albatross or of ever seeing a nest resting on the horizontal rays of dawn. But dynamic imagination has another power. George Sand, a writer whose rationalism often prevents her from dreaming, included in *The Wings of Courage* a bird that lays its eggs on the clouds where they are hatched by the wind. But Sand never really experiences the image, nor is she capable of letting us participate in aerial life and travels, as Shelley does.[16]

Just as with the bark, the *floating island*—that enchanting image that so frequently comes to the psyche whose element is water—is transformed, for the aerial psyche, into a *suspended island*. In Shelley's poetics, the land of choice is really "an isle 'twixt Heaven, Air, Earth, and Sea,/Cradled, and hung in clear tranquility." Clearly, then, it is because the poet imagines or experiences a gentle rocking motion that he *sees* the celestial island. The movement creates the vision. As the movement is experienced, it carries with it the balm that soothes as no merely intellectualized movement could ever do. How often the poet has found rest "upon those wandering isles of aëry dew."

In the infinite space of the skies, Shelley inhabits a palace made of "fragments of the day's intense serene" with "moonlight patches." When we have examined the imaginary union of what enlightens and what elevates, when we can show that it is the same "operation of the human mind" that attracts us to both light and height, we can then come back to this desire to build with diaphanous material, this opaline solidification of everything in the insubstantial ether that we so dearly love. From this point on, I want to create the impression that it is light itself that carries and cradles the dreamer. In the realm of dynamic imagination, this is one of the roles played by abundant light filled with round, mobile shapes, where there is nothing that can pierce or cut. Then light, the true sister of shade, carries shade in its arms.

> And, day and night, aloof, from the high towers
> And terraces, the Earth and Ocean seem
> To sleep in one another's arms, and dream

16. Cf. Pierre Guéguen:
> They will bloom from a huge cloud egg
> In the forget-me-not's heavenly nest.

from *Jeux cosmiques: "Sur la montagne"* (Paris, 1929), 57.

> Of waves, flowers, clouds, woods, rocks, and all that we
> Read in their smiles, and call reality.[17]

On the *suspended island*, all the imaginary elements—water, earth, fire
and wind—mingle their flowers by means of aerial transfiguration.
The island is suspended in the sky, a physical sky; its flowers are the
Platonic ideas of Earthly flowers. They are the most *real* of all of the
Platonic Ideas that a poet has ever contemplated. If we really want to
live the aerial idealism of images, we must recognize, when listening
to Shelley's poems, that it is more than the idealization of what can
be seen on Earth. Aerial life is real life: earthly life, on the other
hand, is an imaginary, ephemeral and distant life. Woods and rock
are indeterminate, fleeting, dull objects. Life's true home is the blue
sky; gentle breezes and perfumes *nourish* the world. How well Shelley
would have understood this Rilkean image:

> As seen by angels, the tree's crowns perhaps
> Are roots, drinking the sky;
> And in the earth, the deep roots of a beech
> Seem silent summits.

When one sleeps at the same altitude as Shelley, and when he
dreams with every breath of air, the sea's great mountains and plains
constantly traverse the sleep of Earth and Ocean. In the turning
kaleidoscope of Day and Night, Earth and Ocean are rocked together
by an immense and immobile Sky. Both are asleep in the same joy.
Shelley's poetics is founded on the *rocking of space*. For Shelley, the
world is an immense cradle—a cosmic cradle—from which dreams
constantly take flight. Once again, as was noted so many times in my
studies on the material imagination of water, we can see a dreamer's
impressions *rising to a cosmic level*.

Some may accuse me of overstatement and inflated language instead of just giving my reasons. But unless we amplify and inflate,
something is missing in the psychology of dreams. Is a dream really a
dream if it does not change the boundaries of the world? Is a dream
that does not *enlarge* our world really a poet's dream? An aerial poet
enlarges the world beyond all limits. Louis Cazamian can say, in his

17. Materialized views of this kind are perhaps the way to explain
Schopenhauerian intuitions which claim colors to be combinations of light and
shade.

commentary on the "Eolian Harp," that Shelley's "whole being vibrates with the thousand sensory impulses that nature sends out in his direction and which perhaps produce on the universe's strings that 'ideal breath of air' that could be both the soul of every being and the God of Everything."[18]

Thus there is probably no poetry in any literature that is more boundless, more spacious, more expansive than Shelley's; to put it in more specific terms, Shelley's poetry is a space—a vertically dynamized space which expands and invigorates everyone and everything in the direction of height. No one can enter it without becoming a part of an upward movement, an ascension. No one can live in it without hearing the whispered invitation: "The day is come, and thou wilt fly with me." In Shelley's poetics, every object is always tempted to leave the Earth for the Sky. Images that formal imagination would find incomprehensible become clearer in their *direct* form once we have grasped the dynamic type that corresponds to them in the *direct* imagination of truly *elemental* impulses. For example, how else could passages like the following be interpreted:

> . . . . she would often climb
> The steepest ladder of the crudded rack
> Up to some beakèd cape of cloud sublime,
> And like Arion on the dolphin's back
> Ride singing through the shoreless air;—oft-time
> Following the serpent lightning's winding track,
> She ran upon the platforms of the wind,[19]

The sky has no shore because there are no obstacles in our path as we rise up. For an imagination dynamized in this way, all lines are furrows, every sign in the sky is a summons, and the desire to ascend is associated with verticality in every guise, even the most tenuous.

It can truthfully be said that the motion experienced in reading Shelley's poetry lays aerial images down along its path in the same way that the *élan vital*, according to Bergson, leaves behind living forms. Conversely, we must add a motion to every image created by the poet in order to understand its poetic action. Thus, the accumulation of clouds is not a *ladder* unless someone wants to climb it,

---

18. Louis Cazamian, *Etudes de psychologie littéraire* (Paris, 1913), 61.
19. Shelley, "The Witch of Atlas," lines 481-87, 383.

unless someone wants—from the depths of his soul—to go higher. The images become obscure or ineffectual if the reader refuses to participate in the particular poetic *élan* that produces them. On the other hand, a dynamically sensitive imagination will find them alive, that is, *dynamically clear*. For we can speak of dynamic clarity and of a dynamic distinctiveness. This dynamic clarity and distinctiveness correspond to natural and primary dynamic intuitions. In the hierarchy of dynamic imagination, every form is invested with a motion: no one can imagine a sphere without making it turn, an arrow without letting it fly, or a woman without making her smile. And it is when a poetic intuition stretches out to the universe that our inner life knows its greatest moments of joy. Everything leads us to the heights, clouds, light and sky, since we fly inwardly, since we have flight within us. Shelley understood:

> The vaporous exultation not to be confined!
> Ha! ha! the animation of delight
> Which wraps me, like an atmosphere of light,
> And bears me as a cloud is borne by its own wind.

We can see that the wind is in the cloud, that the cloud is the substance of the wind, that the cloud contains the principle of aerial mobility within its very substance. Mobility enriches a light substance. No one wishing to understand the primitive nature of material and dynamic imagination can ever meditate too long on images such as Shelley's where material and dynamic imagination are always interchanging their principles. Aerial beings all know quite well that their very substance flies easily and naturally, with no movement of wings. They "drink/With eager lips the wind of their own speed." Motion, more than substance, is what is immortal in us. Motion says: "I change, but I cannot die."

Is the image of a body in motion carried away by the "wind of its own speed" anything more than that Aristotelian antiperistasis that Piaget noted in children's minds? But the poet knows the secret for removing from it both everything that is childish and everything that smacks of philosophical theory. The poet, by giving himself body and soul to the *imagination*, has access to a primary psychic reality: to the *image*. He remains within the dynamics and the life of the image. That is why all rational or objective reductions lose their meaning.

As a person lives this image with Shelley, he becomes convinced that *images do not age*. There would be little point in writing about the *ages of the imagination*, whereas a book like Léon Brunschvicg's on *The Ages of Intelligence* gives a clear account of intellectual maturation. This is the equivalent of saying that the imagination is the principle of eternal youth. It makes the mind young again by giving it back its original dynamic images.

Nothing escapes this dynamizing imagination. Shelley says, for example, in "The Witch of Atlas":

> And sometimes to those streams of upper air
> Which whirl the earth in its diurnal round,
> She would ascend, and win the spirits there
> To let her join their chorus.[20]

For these spirits singing is acting; it is acting materially. They live in and on air. Through it all, life and movement are possible. A breath of air is what turns the Earth. An exquisite rotational movement is the dynamic imagination of this enormous globe of earth, as it is of every sphere.

This imaginary astronomy would make a rationalist smile. He would ask the poet what exactly is the "diurnal round of the Earth." Another rationalist might accuse Shelley's "vaporous" poetics of being nothing but a paraphrase of scientific laws on the expansion of gases.[21] To support such a contention, Whitehead reminds us of the enthusiasm of the modernist Shelley for the physical sciences. Classical literary criticism, eager to understand clearly, easily accepts that references to science have played a role. As a matter of fact, to believe that the doctrine of the "expansion of gas" played the smallest role in Shelley's aerial poetics is to forget the autonomous nature of this great poet's poetic reverie.

Paul de Reul's criticism, which is ordinarily so subtle and so capable of expressing shades of meaning, is no more pertinent than the suppositions of the philosopher-mathematician. He is disconcerted by "The Witch of Atlas," which makes a complex being out of "fire

---

20. Need I point out here that in Descartes' cosmogony, it is heavenly matter that makes the earth turn? This is another proof that the intuitions of a rational mind are not always so very different from a poet's visions.

21. Alfred North Whitehead, *Science and the Modern World*, (New York, 1960), 123.

and snow/. . . .With liquid love." A biologist could certainly take exception to that! But a real dreamer will immediately sense the dynamic force of this union. If fire brings forth life, if liquid love—an astonishing find—brings forth beloved matter, then snow gives whiteness, beauty, and the vision of the mountain peaks. Snow—and here it is an aerial snow, a snow of the peaks—gives the resultant being an unreal aspect which is, for a poet like Shelley, the peak of reality. Faced with these admirable lines:

> Yoked to it by an amphisbaenic snake—
> The likeness of those winged steeds,

De Reul is "tempted to rub his eyes." He says that such passages come straight out of psychoanalysis and adds: "Let us bring this indictment to an end, since it tends only to soothe a critic's conscience."[22] Is a critic then—how odd to admit it—a conscience to be soothed?

In passages that show more sensitivity to Shelley's work, de Reul had nevertheless written that Shelleyan verse is "an instrument lighter than air, the *wing* that allows and supports his flight." De Reul also says, and very rightly so, that for Shelley it is a question of "translating the soul's motion or a soul in motion." I will have occasion later to return to this synthesizing function of dynamic imagination, which sets the whole soul in motion. We will see that the shift from motion in the soul to the whole soul in motion is precisely the great lesson of oneiric flight. Oneiric flight gives an astonishing unity to dream experiences. It provides the dreamer with a homogenous world which allows him to verify the startling discoveries of his nocturnal life through what he sees during the day. It seems to me that there is no better way of characterizing Shelley's poetics than to say that it is an oneiric flight that moves upward toward pure light.

Imaginary music can easily accompany movement that is lived totally through the imagination. Great celestial motion produces divine harmony. No doubt when a philosophical astronomy, like Pythagorean astronomy, reflects on the agreement of numbers and the times of celestial revolutions, it must call upon all the metaphors concerned with harmony. But poetic contemplation, if it is sincere and profound, will hear these same harmonies more authentically. Because they are naturally active in the imagination, the philosopher

22. Paul de Reul, *De Wordsworth à Keats* (Paris, 1933), 213.

thinks he can find these harmonious relationships. Every true poet, while contemplating the starry sky, *hears* the regular revolution of the stars. He hears "aerial choruses" in the night, in "the gentle night that walks."

In order to hear things that belong to infinite space, we must reduce to silence all the noises on earth. We must also—do I even need to mention it?—forget all that we have learned from mythology and school books. Then we can understand that contemplation is essentially a creative power. We feel within ourselves the birth of a *will to contemplate* which almost immediately becomes a will to take part in the motion of what we are contemplating. Will and Representation are no longer two rival forces, as they are in Schopenhauer's philosophy. *Poetry is truly the pancalistic activity of the will.*[23] It expresses the will for beauty. All profound contemplation is necessarily and naturally a hymn. The function of that hymn is to *go beyond* reality and to project a world of sound beyond the silent world. Schopenhauer's theory of poetry is too dependent on the poetic theory that evokes natural beauty. As a matter of fact, a poem is not a translation of an immobile and silent beauty; it is a specific action.

These *direct* imaginary harmonies, which derive from the stimulation of the dynamic imagination, are found throughout the fourth act of "Prometheus Unbound." In a series of admirable passages, Shelley compares harmony, now to night, now to light. Here, for example, is the winter flute, a completely experienced image of that substantial clarity which unites the *clarity of winter air* and the *clarity of a shrill sound* so that the inspired soul accepts it readily:

> Listen too,
> How every pause is filled with under-notes,
> Clear, silver, icy, keen, awakening tones,
> Which pierce the sense, and live within the soul,
> As the sharp stars pierce winter's crystal air
> And gaze upon themselves within the sea.

23. To answer the objections that some have made over my use of the word "pancalism," let me point out that I borrowed it from Baldwin's terminology. I have used it to express the idea that pancalistic activity tends to transform any contemplation of the universe into an affirmation of universal beauty. Cf. James Mark Baldwin, "Pancalism: A Theory of Reality," in *Genetic Theory of Reality* (New York and London, 1915), ch. XV, 275 ff.

Listen to the rays of winter light. They flash from every direction. All space vibrates with the lively noises of the cold. There is no space without music since there is no expansion without space. Music is vibrating matter. Panthea rises "as from a bath of sparkling water:

> A bath of azure light, among dark rocks,
> Out of the stream of sound."

In the "Prometheus," this great bow stroke resounds through the skies:

> Hark! Spirits speak. The liquid responses
> Of their aëreal tongues yet sound.

While for a *terrestrial imagination* everything disperses and is lost when it leaves the earth, for an aerial imagination it clusters and grows richer as it rises. Shelley, the aerian, seems to have brought about a *correspondence* which can be compared to *Baudelairean correspondences*.

Baudelairean correspondences are based on a profound harmony among material substances. They bring into being one of the greatest *chemistries* of sensations, which is from many points of view more *coherent* than Rimbaud's alchemy. A Baudelairean correspondence is a powerful locus of the material imagination. At this locus, all "imaginary substances" commingle and fertilize one another's metaphors.

The *Shelleyan correspondence* is a harmonious relationship of all the dynamic images of phantasmal lightness. If the Baudelairean correspondence belongs to material imagination, the Shelleyan correspondence belongs to dynamic imagination. In Shelley's metapoetics, qualities are grouped according to their degree of ability to lighten one another. They become sublimated together and continue to help one another to reach ever greater heights of sublimation. André Chevrillon, in his *A Study of Nature in Shelley's Poetry* wrote:

> In England, Shelley is aptly called poet of poets. His Poetry is indeed the product of a double distillation. It is to others' poetry what their poems are to reality. . . . Volatile, unstable, ardent, imponderable, always on the verge of being sublimated. It is unembodied.

A few pages earlier, Chevrillon had stressed this aerial sublimation: "All (the) descriptions have one very important characteristic in common. As they develop, an object loses its individual details, one by one, as well as its substantiality, with each passing stanza, and is transformed into an indeterminate and luminous spirit." This evanescence of light is a kind of sublimation that is particularly discernible in Shelley's poetry.

The silence of the night increases the "depth" of the skies. Everything is in harmony in this silence and depth. Contradictions vanish, discordant voices fall silent. The visible harmony of signs in the sky quiets our earthly complaints and groans. Suddenly, Night is a hymn in a major key. Ariel's lyre sings out with romantic joy and happiness. Shelley is truly the happy poet of the air and the heights. Shelley's poetry *is the romanticism of flight.*

Such a romanticism full of air and flight gives wings to all earthly things. The mystery is transmitted from the substance to its atmosphere. Everything conspires to make the individual at one with the universe. In the days when I used to listen to the plums ripening, I saw the sun caress every piece of fruit, turn all their round surfaces to gold and put the finishing touches on all of nature's riches. The rippling of the green brook shook the bells of the columbine. A blue sound rose. The cluster of flowers released an endless flow of trills into the blue sky. I understood Shelley:

> And from her lips, as from a hyacinth full
> Of honey-dew, a liquid murmur drops,
> Killing the sense with passion; sweet as stops
> Of Planetary music heard in trance.

When a flower whispers like this, when the bells of the flowers sound at the tops of the umbels, the whole earth falls silent, and the whole sky speaks. The aerial universe is filled with a harmony of colors. The anemones with their many colors give color to the four winds of the sky. . . . Color mingled with voice and perfumes, as soon as flowers began to speak . . .

Now here is the problem that arises: in what sense must we say that a sound becomes aerial? When it is on the very edge of silence, soaring in a distant sky—soft and great. The paradox plays from the small to the large. It is the infinitely small sound, the *pause* in the flowers' harmony, that rocks the infinitely large universe of sound. We can really live in Shelleyan time in which "light is changed to love," to a whisper of love in which the lilies have such persuasive voices that the whole universe learns how to love. We hear the steps of a still wind. We hear the *rhythm of the continuum*:

> With motion like the spirit of that wind
> Whose soft step deepens slumber . . .

A very clear example of *correspondences* formed in the upper regions of the imaginary may be found in the work of the little-known philosopher, Louis-Claude de Saint-Martin, who wrote in *Man of Desire*:

> It is not at all as it is in the shadowy room of our home when sounds can be compared only to sounds; colors only to colors; and a substance only with its analogous substance. There everything was of one kind.
> Light gave sounds, melody gave birth to light, colors had motion because colors were vivid. Objects, too, were capable of sound, diaphanous and mobile enough to intermingle and cross all of space like a shot.

Anyone who follows the direction of Baudelairean images descends into a crypt of the senses where he discovers unity in the depths and the darkness of night. In the works of Louis-Claude de Saint-Martin, on the other hand, we are led toward the unity of light. More precisely, a synthesis of light, sound, and lightness determines a *vertical ascension*. Turning, as the sun does in the sky, would be merely following a visual image and missing the substantial meaning of divine insubstantiality. On the other hand, in *vertical ascension*, the "powers of the regions" uphold the soul "with their wings." With their living breath they chase away whatever remains of the stains that the soul has contracted during its sleep on earth. "Then with their fiery hands, the angels place on the soul a sign, testifying to its initiation, so that when it enters the next region, the way will be quickly opened to it, and it can receive a new degree of purification and a further reward."

This is the synthesis of purification and reward, both moral and physical, which has an effect upon the "lifeline"—which is the dynamic reverie of the air. What is transparent, light and filled with sound determines a kind of conditioned reflex of the imagination.

Such conditioned reflexes, which bring together qualities of imagina-tion, are what differentiate the various poetic temperaments. I will return to this topic later.

VII

Documents taken from a work as unusual as Shelley's might seem too exceptional, and we might be ill-prepared to understand the per-sistent impressions of oneiric flight in conscious reverie if we were to restrict our examination to poetry alone. It will be of interest, then, to consider very objective observers of the human mind from the point of view of dynamic imagination. In several of Balzac's works, we will find proofs of the psychologically real nature of "experiential psychological ascension." For example, the story entitled "The Exiles" seems to me very significant in this respect.[24] At first glance it appears that in certain passages the novelist uses ready-made images that could be accused of being mere verbal metaphors. But suddenly we encounter an episode that cannot be mistaken, for if we follow it carefully, we sense that Balzac's imagination continues sensations of nocturnal flight. If we then go back to the images which seemed arti-ficial at first, we are forced to confess that they are part of a real oneiric experience. We learn to dream the text which classical literary criticism tries only to understand and which in the end it neglects completely. Thus, when Balzac tells us that Dante, "Bible in hand, after spiritualizing matter and materializing the spirit . . . acknowledged the possibility of passing, through faith, from one sphere to another," we pay very little attention to this spiritualized matter or the materialized spirit. We *understand* so quickly that we forget to imagine. We lose the benefit of a material imagination that might allow us to experience the powerful reality of the mesomorphic state equidistant between mind and matter. The document may therefore appear to be barren verbiage. But if we are willing to *live* the words and understand that the Dante evoked by Balzac is speaking from a physical and material perspective, we will create that *mesomor-phic state* of imaginary physics. At that point, all of the metaphors will become coherent; all the metaphors of take-off, flight, ascension, and lightening will become positive psychological experiences.

24. Honoré de Balzac, "Les Proscrits," in *La Comédie Humaine*, ed. Marcel Bouteron, Bibliothèque de la Pléiade, vol. 10 (Paris, 1962).

Here, for example, we find the specific *tension* associated with take-off: "that painful tension through which we project our strength when we want to take flight, like birds ready to take off." Certainly we can disregard this dynamism and think only about *ideas*, believing that metaphors exist only to suggest ideas. But in so doing we abandon a whole series of psychological observations in the realm of *projective psychology*. To interpret this experience, which is not only the *élan* but the *will for élan*, psychology needs a very special, very important dynamic image, since it is an image that is intermediate between leap and flight, between discontinuity and continuity. The *tension* that Balzac must communicate is one that gives duration to an instant of decision. It is the awareness of a strength to act and to pursue an objective. It derives from the very essence of projective psychology. It is at the very heart of representation and will. This projection was first prompted by the dynamic imagination of flight. Why not accept it willingly? Moreover, there is in the same passage an explicit reference to oneiric flight: "I was in the night, but on the distant edge of day. I was flying, carried along by my guide, impelled by a power similar to the one which, in our dreams, snatches us away to spheres invisible to our bodily eyes."[25]

That flight takes place where night and day meet is the sign of a *complex* sublimation by which lightness ushers in light, and light ushers in lightness, as it does in Shelley's poetic "correspondences." This *complex sublimation* explains the simultaneously material and dynamic nature of the halo that surrounds the head of those who "ascend." In Balzac's story, the reader who "*is thinking*" will take this to be empty imagery. I want to be a reader who "imagines," therefore I will read the following lines in the powerful, physical sense of the words: "The halo that bound our brows made the shadows flee as we passed as if they were unsubstantial dust." Let us live the progression from the abstract to the concrete, since images must always give new life to words. We brush away the shadows from our forehead, we brush away from our forehead what obscures our gaze; we brush away cares like ashes, then like smoke, then like a far-away haze. This is how the halo seems to be a gradual and quiet physical conquest of

25. "Dante's living wings—these interior wings, are completely opposite to the mechanical, exterior wings of Leonardo and our own." Dmitry S. Merezhovsky, *Dante* (Paris, 1940), 449.

the mind that little by little becomes aware of its clarity. The struggle between a glimmer of light and shadow is engaged in the realm of the imaginary. It takes form, carried on from haze to haze, from fluid to fluid. The halo, in its nascent form, does not yet dart forth its rays of light. It confines itself to overcoming an "insubstantial dust." It is the material substance behind an auspicious motion. Victor-Emile Michelet writes in *Love and Magic*: "The astral body moves in its halo as a fish in water." Therefore, more abstractly, the halo provides a concrete form to show our success in overcoming every resistance to our rising. Resistance to rising is a resistance that *diminishes* progressively as we rise. It is diametrically opposed to the earth's resistance, which increases progressively as we dig deeper. This observation—do I even need to say it?—is truer and more uniform in the world of the imagination than in the real world where there are so many fortuitous circumstances.

A cosmic image, moreover, can contribute to enlarging the halo. For someone who is rising, the horizon expands and becomes clearer. For him, the horizon is an immense halo around the earth that is being contemplated by an elevated person. It matters very little whether the elevation is physical or moral. Anyone who sees in the distance has a clear view; his face lights up, his brow clears. The physics of the ideal is so coherent that it can accept all reciprocities.

But, if we are willing, as I propose, to materialize and dynamize literary images, there are no more metaphors in the traditional sense of the term. Every metaphor has within it a potential for reversibility. The two poles of a metaphor can play the role of the real and the ideal alternately. With these inversions, the most time-worn expressions, like the *flight of ideas*, can take on a bit of material substance, a bit of real motion. If in our imagination we make the effort required to set images in motion, then we can easily materialize, with its aerial matter, a text like the following. The great exile

> was traveling in space drawing impassioned souls with him on the wings of his words and making his listeners conscious of infinity by plunging them into the depths of the celestial ocean. So the doctor gave a logical explanation of hell in which suffering and darkness replaced light and spirit by means of other circles arranged in inverse order to the brilliant spheres that aspired to God. Torment and pleasure were both understandable. Terms of comparison ex-

isted in the transitions of human life, in life's different conditions of suffering and understanding.

The explanation he mentions is still, I think, more physical, or physiological, than "logical." Torment and pleasure are really components of a cosmology. They are the basic indicators of a dual cosmology in a terrestrial and aerial imagination. They touch upon our own experience. The dynamics of dream supplies a straightforward, though seemingly unimportant, meaning for our aspiration toward the heights. Why not compare Balzac's *unambiguous* passage to it? The celestial ocean would then be, in my opinion, the ocean of our nocturnal life. Our nocturnal life is an ocean because we float in it. In sleep we never live motionless on the earth. We fall from one sleep into a deeper sleep, or something in us wants to wake up: then it causes us to rise. We are forever rising or falling. Sleep has a vertical dynamic. It oscillates between sleeping more deeply and less deeply. Sleeping is rising and falling like a sensitive Cartesian diver in the waters of night.[26] Within us night and day develop vertically. They are atmospheres of unequal density, in which the dreamer goes up or down depending on the weight of his sins or the lightness of his pure state. Now we can understand how Dante tries, as Balzac says, "to tear out from deep within our understanding the true meaning of the word *fall* which exists in every language." What better way is there to say that the fall is a *primary literary image*? We talk about it before we think about it. It expresses a distant dream experience. It is truly "deep within" the dynamic imagination. Gravity is a very human psychic law. It is a part of us. It is a destiny that we must overcome, and those who have an aerial temperament foresee this victory in reverie. Dante explained, Balzac continues, "in a very lucid way the passion for rising that is shared by all men. It is an instinctive ambition, the constant revelation of our destiny." It is clear that this text is not referring to men's ambition to rise in society but embroiders on an *original image* that has its own immediate life in natural imagination. Even if they have a metaphorical significance, such passages do

26. Cf. Gérard de Nerval, who writes: "On that particular night I had a wonderful dream . . . I was in a tower, so deep on the earth side and so high on the sky side that my whole existence seemed to be spent going up and down." *Aurélia*, ed. Corti (Paris, 1927), 154.

not take on their true power unless we look upon them as lessons in a physics of morality, an ethics whose symbolic life already exists in the material elements. They are not metaphors, and still less allegories. They are revelatory intuitions. We can understand how Joachim Gasquet could write:

> Could motion be matter's prayer, the only language that God really speaks? Motion! Through it the love of creatures and the desire of things are expressed in their essential nature. Its perfection unifies everything and makes it come alive. It binds the earth to the clouds, and children to birds.

Thus, as Gasquet sees it, fundamental motion, because of its simplicity and perfection, is the vertical motion that likens "children to birds." Further on he adds: "In rarefied air, at the summit of the soul, does God not float like the dawn on snow as it grows whiter?"[27]

Some will no doubt object that Balzac's text upon which we have commented is, after all, a literary document. They will say that it represents only a literary evocation of the very traditional figure of Dante, and that, whatever I may say to the contrary, it may well be looked upon as an allegory. It appears, upon reading the drama of "The Exiles," that Balzac's "knowledge" of medieval philosophy and of Dante's cosmology is amazingly puerile. But that is just the point: the weaker the scholarship, the more important the imagination, and the more direct the images. The Dante imagined by Balzac represents only his own psychological experience, but it is a *positive* experience. It bears the mark of a very typical unconscious which grows out of a genuine oneiric world.

We will have confirmation of this in another of Balzac's works. *Séraphita*, in fact, is entirely given over to the themes of ascensional psychology. It seems that this account was written for the conscious enjoyment of unconscious ascension. Any reader who establishes a dynamic sympathy with this book will get a great deal of benefit from it. A personality as troubled as Strindberg's, at the time when, as he himself says, "the powers had condemned me for the time being to excremental hell," finds deliverance in *Séraphita*: "Séraphita became my gospel and led me to renew relations with the beyond, to such an extent that my life was now distasteful to me, and I was driven on by

27. Joachim Gasquet, *Narcisse* (Paris, 1931), 199, 214.

an irresistible nostalgia for heaven."[28] It is through Balzac that Strindberg was led to read Swedenborg. Given Strindberg's genuine feeling for drama, we cannot underestimate the psychic value of the possibilities for ascension that he found in *Séraphita*. Strindberg is torn between heaven and earth: "Orfila and Swedenborg, my friends, were protecting me, encouraging me, and punishing me." He is a chemist and a visionary. He is a being with two motions, a fact that produces a kind of *dynamic unhappiness* in him. The *dynamic unity* of *Séraphita* is, therefore, often of help to him. It is this dynamic unity that I am going to try to elucidate.

At a time when there was no way of determining the organic nature of our powers of orientation, Balzac wrote in *Séraphita*: "Only man has his feeling for verticality lodged in a special organ."[29] This feeling of verticality is dynamic in that it urges us always to attain *verticality*, to reach upward. Man is moved by a need to seem tall, to *lift his brow*. Here again, the metaphor should be grasped as close as possible to psychological reality: "Séraphîtüs was growing taller, lifting up his brow as though he wanted to take off." It appears that Séraphîtüs is indeed the tall, dynamized form of Séraphita. His brow thus becomes more masculine. Anyone who frees himself and is ready to "fly" has already tossed his hair back in the wind, in the wind created by his forward motion. Whole pages, like pages 509ff, are devoted to giving us in minute detail the psychology of the *heroic release* followed by *natural motion*, of flight that has become a reality. We will once again note, regarding the psychology of wings, that the imaginary wing comes *after* the flight. Anyone who flies feels that he has wings when he need no longer make an effort to fly. They appear at once, like a sign of victory, and then, as is demonstrated on page 473, we can see the psychology of gliding unfold. In reading this page, we recognize that the dynamic images that have been experienced dominate those derived from what has been merely seen. These visual images are, in essence, only dim memories. They are not what gives life to the creative word. The poetic novel *Séraphita*, like *Louis Lambert*, is a poem of will, a dynamic poem.

All the way through the work, certain material themes help to build up this ascensional imagery. For instance, in the panorama of

28. A. Strindberg, *Inferno, Alone and Other Writings* (Garden City, 1968), 164.
29. Balzac, *Séraphita*, 550.

Norway in winter, the characters' first appearance is hardly noticeable. The first *human* word the author uses is to designate an *arrow* crossing the distant sky. From that moment on, the flying arrow is the *inductive word*. It is a primary image that will produce secondary images. If we pursue this image as a system of analysis, the analysis will organize itself. On the other hand, if we fail to pay attention to this inductive image, whole passages will seem obscure, barren, and cold. They will be lifeless. We will not have joined the flow of their life.

An arrow is swift and straight. Because its image appropriately brings together these two qualities, it is a dynamic starting place. When this image of a simple arrow flying across a winter sky has had all the impact on the imagination that it is capable of producing, the writer will rationalize it as *ski* and *skier*. Then we can see that the skier crosses the horizon "like an arrow." *But the real object is mentioned after the imagined movement.* The writer describes the characters, outfitted with skis, only after participating in their motion by way of the dynamic imagination, which is that of a straight and swift arrow. This is a very clear case of the dynamic imagination's domination over the formal imagination. I always come back to the same conclusion: poetic forms are a deposit left by imaginary motion, just as matter in Bergsonian theory is a deposit left by the *élan vital*.

We are not concerned here, of course, with passing images and ephemeral observations alone. Not every movement automatically produces a series of images. The *arrow* that is the moving force in these passages from Balzac is an index of upward motion. Thus we can understand its role in a story which demands of its readers a deep participation in ascensional transformation. We take part in imaginary ascension because of a vital need, a vital conquest as it were, of the void. Our whole being is now involved in the dialectics of abyss and heights. The abyss is a monster, a tiger, jaws open, intent on its prey. It seems, Balzac tells us, "to grind up its prey in advance." Ascensional psychology, which is essentially an education in the art of ascending, must struggle against this polymorphic monster.

Then Séraphîtüs says to a still trembling Séraphita, as he makes her lift her head toward the sky: "You are looking without fear at even more immense spaces"; and he shows her "the blue halo that the clouds were forming, leaving a clear space above their heads":

At that height won't you perhaps tremble? The abysses are deep enough that you cannot even tell how deep they are; they now have the same uniform appearance that the sea has, the vagueness of clouds, and the color of the sky.

Let us for a moment experience dynamically this *dominance* over the chasm: we notice that the abyss loses its distinctive features because we move away from it. One who ascends sees the obliteration of the abyss' characteristics. For him, the abyss dissolves, becomes hazy, and grows more obscure. The animal images all lose their effect. The metaphor no longer has anything but a vague sense of animality. There is, however, a gain on the other side. Anyone who rises sees the heights becoming more clearly delineated and differentiated. The dynamic imagination is subject to an extremely powerful finalism. The human arrow lives not only its *élan*, but also its goal. It lives its sky. By becoming conscious of his power to ascend, a human being becomes conscious of his destiny as a whole. To be more exact, he knows that he is matter, a substance filled with hope. In these images, hope seems to become as precise as it can be. It is an upright destiny.

The imaginary ascent, then, is a synthesis of dynamic impressions and images. In a completely natural way, we see all the Shelleyan correspondences gathering in Séraphita's aerial wake. In the last chapter, entitled "Assumption," we read: "Light gave birth to song, and song to light; motion was a number endowed with speech; so everything was sound-filled, transparent, and mobile all at once."

The trilogy of sound, transparency, and mobility, according to the thesis that I am putting forth in this book, is the product of an inner impression of *growing lighter*. The exterior world cannot give it to us. It is a conquest made by one who was once weighed down and troubled, and who has become light, clear and vibrant through imaginary motion and through heeding the teachings of aerial imagination. It is possible, no doubt, to see nothing but ineffectual allegories in all this. But such an unfavorable judgment can come only from a reader who accepts unquestioningly the idea that formal images are the essential element in the life of the imagination. Given that the images derived from aerial forms are poor and insubstantial when compared to terrestrial forms, an *aerial imagination* can pass for being a *frivolous imagination*. All "positive" philosophers, all who portray reality, take delight in scorning it. That will not be the case for those willing to restore its dynamic import to the imagination. If sky images are in-substantial, their movement is free. And the feeling of freedom *projects* more marvelous images alone than all the memories of "things past." This feeling is at the very root of *projective psychology*, the one that will people the future. "Aerial freedom" speaks, illuminates, flies. Therefore it projects the trilogy of sound, transparency, and mobility.

Our examination of *Séraphita* intentionally omitted the ethical reality that underlies ascensional images. My purpose in the present work is, in fact, to discover the psychological conditions, in their purest possible state, of imaginative syntheses. A moralist working on the documents I have given here would have to acknowledge, I think, that in certain respects *height* is not only moralizing, but is in itself physically moral, so to speak. Height is more than a symbol. Anyone who seeks it, anyone who imagines it with all of his imaginative power, which is the driving force behind our psychic dynamism, recognizes that it is materially, dynamically and vitally moral.

VIII

Now that I have shown, through Shelley's and Balzac's images, the most diverse poetic images built on the inner experience of oneiric flight, and now that we understand the importance of Balzac's remark that the word *flight* is one "in which everything speaks to the senses,"[30] we will be able to undertake discovering indicators of imaginary flight in partial and momentary images that so often seem inconsequential and worn-out. If I am not mistaken in all this, studies of the dynamic imagination ought to contribute to setting in motion and revitalizing the inner image hidden in words. Forms become worn out faster than forces. Dynamic imagination must rediscover the hidden power in worn-out words. Within every word hides a verb. A sentence is an action, or better, a style of behavior and bearing. The dynamic imagination is actually a storehouse of these styles. Let us then experience anew the styles that poets suggest to us. For example, when Viviane, in Edgar Quinet's *Merlin the Magician* says, "I cannot run into a doe without being tempted to bound as she does," a reader who refuses sensitivity to texts will read this terribly banal expression without being moved by it. But how will such a reader understand landscapes that are essentially dynamic and which

30. Balzac, *Louis Lambert*, 356.

make *Merlin the Magician* such a powerful work from a psychological point of view? The "banal" image, however, keeps coming back with such insistence that it ought to make an impression on us. In the first volume, Quinet had already written: "Viviane is lighter than a goat, she is as light as a bird," and later: " 'There are times when I run faster than a deer,' Viviane said. 'I reach the mountain-top, where hope carries me, before he does. Come, let us climb to the mountain-top.' " If Viviane is lighter than the doe, the goat, and the deer, it is because she believes in the greater effectiveness of a kind of flight that partakes of these images, but which retains their essential dynamics. Viviane flies by *impulse* because she has sudden moments of lightness. She is an awakening force in Merlin's world. Viviane gives *moments* of flight to lifeless landscapes, and these moments of flight and awakening are so characteristic that they could serve as themes for an instantaneous representation; a metaphysician might express it this way: the world is the moment of my awakening, the representation of my morning. The reason that the dynamism of *Merlin the Magician* is so suggestive is that these *moments of flight* are moments of human flight. The bird's objective flight would be too external to our being, too foreign to our powers of dream. It would give too panoramic a vista, a world in repose caught by an unmoving vision. By evoking oneiric flight, Viviane is more faithful to the wonders of the dream than if she had described long reveries with images from waking life.

Geniuses that are less aerial and more terrestrial, such as Goethe's, will live the moment of the leap with less subtlety. In their verse, we will hear the heel strike the ground. Following the lead of their terrestrial intuition, the ground or the earth will give power to anyone who rebounds from it. Goethe will relive the myth of Antaeus, as most mythologists do, in the terrestrial sense. There will still be aerial traits, but they will be hardly noticeable. They will be subordinated dynamically. In the *Second Faust* we read:

Naked Genius unfledged, a faun exempt of faunic coarseness,
He will leap on solid ground, which like a springboard countervailing
Flings him upward high and higher, till by second, third rebounding
He has touched the lofty vault.
Anxiously his mother calls him: leap and spring as fancy takes thee
But forbear to fly, untrammeled flight is not vouchsafed to thee.
Thus the honest father warns him: in the earth inheres resilience

Which buoys thee up, if only thou adhere to it on tiptoe,
Like the son of earth, Antaeus, it will strengthen thee at once.

But Euphorion is not conscious of this enrichment. He is more dynamic than material, more aerial than terrestrial. Euphorion is only the euphoria of bounding:

> Now let me leap
> Skyward and higher,
> Now let me skip,
> Buoyant desire
> Takes me already
> Into its grip.

How much better we can understand these passages when we know the ecstasy of oneiric flight and when we have lived dynamically the image of wings on the heels!

When Euphorion crashes to the ground, his fall does not eliminate the triumph of the leaper. It seems that in the fall Euphorion is divided and that the two elements that were united in his nature separate and return to their respective places: "the corporeal vanishes at once: the aureole rises like a meteor to the sky; robe, cloak, and lyre are left behind." We can recognize, moreover, how lifeless these formal images of aureole and lyre are. It is as though the poet were satisfied with finding allegorical meanings for these images, thus recognizing implicitly that he no longer felt their power as the dynamic, vertical imagination.

The very rhythm of the foot striking the ground, moreover, must have been the basis for musical rhythms. André Schaeffner sees in primitive dancing the assembling of myths about the close relationship between earth and vegetation. One of the original purposes of the dance "is for the earth, the mother, to be trampled underfoot and for the leaps to be higher since it is to their height that the vegetation will grow: springtime symbols and rites of fecundity are involved here —the *Rites of Spring* will be filled with such ritual tramplings of the earth—giving this crushing and these bounds a meaning which was perhaps the original one." A human being, in his youth, in his taking off, in his fecundity, wants to rise up from the earth. The leap is a basic form of joy.

IX

To conclude this chapter and to bring together the ideas expressed in it, I will give a very simple, clear example of the continuity of reverie that likens the desire to grow with the desire to fly. In this way everyone will understand that in human imagination flight is a transcendence of mere size. I will borrow my example from Keats:

> I stood tiptoe upon a little hill,
>
> .   .   .   .
>
> I gazed awhile, and felt as light and free
> As though the fanning wings of Mercury
> Had played upon my heels: I was lighthearted,
> And many pleasures to my vision started;
> So I straightway began to pluck a posey
> Of luxuries bright, milky, soft, and rosy.

This is a bouquet of heavenly flowers. One must rise up in order to pick them. "As light and free"—these two expressions are so traditionally united that we forget to look for the characteristic regularity of their union. Only the dynamic imagination can help us understand this synonymy. Both impressions derive from the same tropism of aerial imagination. We see, therefore, that it is the tropism, the excessive tropism of oneiric flight, that draws all aerial dreamers.

2

The Poetics of Wings

> The wings invisible are those that fly the farthest.
> Every virgin can be a messenger. . .
> GABRIELE D'ANNUNZIO, *The Dead City*

I

UNLIKE CONCEPTUALIZATION, reverie does not create a composite picture consisting of many similar objects by using Galton's method of assembling portraits of a whole family on the same photographic plate. Reverie does not suddenly take on a sympathetic feeling for a flying or swimming bird by seeing a great variety of birds in the sky or on the water. The motion of flight produces an immediate and overwhelming abstraction, a dynamic image that is perfect, complete, and total. The reason for such speed and such perfection is that the image is dynamically beautiful. The abstraction of beauty defies all philosophers' polemics. These polemics are generally useless in all those cases in which the mind's activity is creative, whether in the rational abstractions of mathematics or in aesthetic activities, which so rapidly abstract the lines of essential beauty. If more attention were given to the imagination, many false psychological problems would readily be cleared up. The kind of abstraction that material and dynamic imagination bring about is so alive that, despite a multiplicity of forms and movements, it lets us live in our chosen matter simply by following a given motion wholeheartedly. But for those very reasons, abstraction eludes discursive scrutiny. It appears that participation in the idea of the beautiful determines an *orientation* of images that in no way resembles the tentative orientation arrived at by the formation of concepts.

Nevertheless, it is an *abstraction* that led us to this uneventful flight, one we learned in our unvarying nocturnal experience, one with no formal images, totally condensed in the joyful impression of lightness. Since this *flight-in-itself*, this *abstract flight*, serves as an axis around which the colorful and varied images of our diurnal existence cluster, it presents us with an interesting problem: How can an image be embellished when, through an amazing abstraction, its primary beauty is immediately apparent?

Excessive adornment by the many and diverse types of beauty is not the answer, for the contemplation of beauty can be too prolific. When a person filled with amazement is experiencing this wonder, he makes an abstraction of the rest of the universe in order to concentrate on one characteristic of fire, or on one motion that sings.

We must beware of generalities, however, and pose the problem in the delimiting area of the poetics of flight. I would posit that the reason birds trigger the flights of our imagination is not their brilliant colors. What is primordially beautiful about birds is their flight. Flight is a primordial beauty for the dynamic imagination. The beauty of the bird's plumage cannot be seen until it has landed on earth, that is, until it is no longer a bird in our reveries. We can affirm, then, that there is an imaginary dialectic that separates flight and color, motion and adornment. We cannot have everything. No bird can be both a lark and a peacock. The peacock is eminently *terrestrial*. It is a treasure house filled with the beauty of the mineral world. To press my paradox to its limits, I will have to show that, in the realm of the imagination, *flight must create its own color*. We observe, then, that the imaginary bird, the bird that flies in our dreams and in genuine poems, cannot be one of *gaudy* colors.[1] It is most often blue or black; it flies upward or downward.

Multiple colors flicker. They are the colorations of fluttering movements. They are not found in the powerful reveries that contain fundamental dreams. The butterfly appears in entertaining reveries or in poems that look to nature for picturesque examples. In the real world of dreams, where flight is a unified and unvarying motion, the butterfly is a ridiculous accident—it does not fly, it flutters. Its too beautiful and too large wings prevent its flying.

Basing my argument, then, on the oneiric valorization that I emphasized in the last chapter, I will now show that only the bird, of all the creatures that fly, continues and realizes the image which, from the human point of view, can be said to be a primary image.

1. The kingfisher, with its fiery brilliance, is the exception. Has he retained all of the river's reflections?

This is the one that we experience in the deep sleep of our happy youth. The visible world is created in order to portray the beauty found in sleep.

II

I am going to begin by giving an example of a case in which the valorization of the bird image is overdone, in which the ideal and the real, dream and reality, are bound together with little subtlety or skill. Then it will be easier to appreciate poetic images which properly link images of motion and form. I am thus applying a critical principle that I have often mentioned. If you make a poetic image a little too *specific*, you will make it laughable. If you remove some of this specificity from an insignificant or ridiculous image, you will give rise to a poetic emotion. That is why, when reading Toussenel, people often have the impression of being on the boundary line between enthusiasm and absurdity. From page to page, the reader goes from the dream of a poet to the account of a hunter. This very strange mixture does not prevent Toussenel from being a great connoisseur of birds. In their preface to Delamain's book on the songs of birds, the brothers Tharaud give him his due.

From the very first pages in Toussenel's book, which is entitled *The World of Birds*, we are certain that the central interest in this natural history of birds is the natural history of human reverie. In fact, Toussenel invokes nocturnal experience at the outset: "When you were twenty, you sometimes felt your body in sleep leave the ground as it grew lighter and float in space, protected from the laws of gravity by unseen powers." Toussenel at once valorizes the nocturnal memory by virtue of the infinite smoothness of oneiric flight: "It was," he says, "a revelation from God and a foretaste that He gave you of the joys that pleasant aromas give our lives." This is a life that awaits us in the future, at a time when we will have returned to our purely aerial state, according to the true Fourierist harmony of the beyond. Flight becomes at once a memory of our dreams and a desire for the reward that God will grant us. Therefore, "we envy the bird's lot in life, and we attribute wings to what we love, because we instinctively feel that, in the domain of bliss, our bodies will be blessed with the ability to go through space as the bird goes through the air." We see that a 'pteropsychology' creates an ideal, a transcendence that gives reality to what we have already experienced in dream. Man, according to this ideal, will become a super-bird which, far from our world, will fly through the infinite space between worlds, transported by "aromatic" forces into his true environment, into an aerial land.

> The wing, an essential attribute of flight, is the ideal cachet of perfection in almost all realms. Our soul, escaping from the corporeal envelope that holds us down in this lower life here on earth, is incarnate in a glorious body, lighter and faster than any bird.

Can we compare Plato and Toussenel without being irreverent? The same transcendence by means of wings plays a part in the *Phaedrus*: "The natural function of the wing is to soar upwards and carry that which is heavy to the place where dwells the race of the gods. More than any other thing that pertains to the body, it partakes of the nature of the divine." With its *aerial materialism*, this participation gives a most concrete meaning to the abstract doctrine of Platonic participation. As soon as a feeling *rises* in the human heart, the imagination evokes the heavens and birds. Thus Toussenel, in a lovely phrase, cries out: "I have never loved without giving *her* wings."[2]

It is not hard to realize that the qualities attributed to the bird in Toussenel's pteropsychology were certainly not perceived visually: "The bird," he says, "lively, graceful, and light, prefers to reflect images of love, youth, sweetness, and purity." These last qualities are, in fact, *primary psychic realities*. We attribute so many *moral* qualities to the bird that we see crossing the sky during the day because we experience through our imagination a joyful flight, one which gives the impression of youth. It is also because oneiric flight is often—contrary to what is taught by classic psychoanalysis—*pure voluptuousness*. Here we have the opportunity to meditate on a very clear example of a symbol, or, more exactly, a symbolic force that exists before images. Even in our unconscious, all the various impressions of lightness, liveliness, youth, purity, and pleasantness had interchanged their symbolic values. Later, the wing merely gave a name to the symbol, and, last of all, the bird embodied the symbol.

2. When Elizabeth hears the nightingale sing, she knows that the bird "constantly needs to fly away and love beyond his wings." Cf. Francis Jammes, *La légende de l'aile ou Marie-Elisabeth* (Uzès, 1938), 77. The wing is the origin of innumerable metaphors of expansion.

The way that Toussenel thought he could relive the creative act shows very clearly that aerial matter and free motion are themes that tend to produce bird images. We might say that, in the realm of the creative imagination, the bird's body is made out of the air that surrounds it and that its life is made up of the motion that transports it. Imagination, which is both material and dynamic, is in no way *selective*. It does not *designate*; it *lives* abstract values. Toussenel's imagination makes an immediate connection between the *purity of air* and the *motion of wings*. "The bird, created to live in the purest and most rarified element, is necessarily the final, most independent, and most glorious of all the forms of creation."

Along the same lines, Marceline Desbordes-Valmore writes in her novel, *Violette*:

> Birds! whose flight is so high, what were you before being those free songs scattered above our heads? A thought—held slave, perhaps; some word from God confined by violence in a soul that finally broke so that you might get wings and so that it might get back its own.[3]

The objection will no doubt be raised that such statements refer only to futile, useless reveries. But I always answer that these *reveries are natural*. They take on life *naturally* in a soul given to dreaming, that is, in one that, during the day, continues its nocturnal experiences. Unfortunately, Toussenel is not a poet. There was certainly continuity between his nocturnal dream and his daytime reveries, but he did not know the continuity that links reverie to a poem. For him the bird's *eternal youth* was only a confused impression, whereas it is an astonishing valorization. He did not follow along with the beautiful fictional bird that *makes us forget time* and snatches us away from the linear travels of the earth to take us, as Jean Lescure puts it, on a *motionless voyage*, where the clock no longer strikes, *where age no longer weighs us down*. But we must give Toussenel credit in that he, a man who hunted and stuffed animals, did recognize that birds in dreams do not die. No bird *in flight* ever dies in a natural dream. Birds that are caressed are quite a different matter. They are doomed to die quickly, as psychoanalysts are well aware. In a dynamic dream, no bird struck by death ever falls vertically out of the sky, because oneiric flight never ends in a vertical fall. Oneiric flight *is a happy*

3. Marceline Desbordes-Valmore, *Violette* (Brussels, 1839), II:203.

phenomenon of sleep, not a tragic one. We only fly in our sleep when we are happy. How true, then, is this remark by Pierre Emmanuel:

> . . . no more distress
> with a bird. No more dark flights . . .

The bird is an uplifting force that wakes all of nature. In the Comtesse de Noailles' *Domination*, we may read these lines, which could be entitled "the bird brings verticality to spring":

> Spring came back. All over the earth it was emerging, small, light, green, and straight. In the woods could be heard the never-ending cry of a bird, the cry of spring, keen and clear. It was as though the bird had a new little leaf of delicious turpentine tree in its irritated throat. It never stopped crying out, as if it wanted to give strength to the flowers buried in the ground. This cry said to the hyacinth, the jonquil, and the tulip: "One more push; one more heave; try harder to pierce the hard earth. Reach up; soon you will have air and sky; come, I am your bird. . . ."

Even more soothing is this other remark: "The very sight of you living sets the mind at rest; souls rising upward; people transported to the summit; wings! birds! nobility of the air."

Victor Hugo's work is the source of a great number of images in which the bird is a soul.

> I love. O winds, chase winter away,
> The plains are filled with sweet scents,
> The bird, in Aser woods, seems
> A soul in the green boughs
>
> . . . .
> As if I soared in the air which calls me back,
> And as if I had a soul
> Made of birds' wings.

Jean Tardieu expresses this oneiric identification of the bird image and the inner potential for flight even better, perhaps, in these beautiful lines:

> An amazing dream surrounds me:
> I am walking along releasing birds,
> everything that I touch is within me
> And I have lost all limitations.[4]

4. Jean Tardieu, *Le témoin invisible* (Paris, 1943), 32.

III

If we put Toussenel's oneiric perspective on a sound footing, as I propose to do, we will not be surprised that, in his works, a purely imaginary ornithology continues where real ornithology leaves off. For Toussenel, God did not stop at creating warm and living birds that play in the blue and in the clouds. He also created "for the faithful, aerial types of Genies, Angels, and Sylphs." And, since only the superior can explain the inferior, Toussenel more or less consciously deduces the bird from the sylph. One might say—and herein lies the supremacy of the imagination!—that there are birds in Nature precisely because there are sylphs in imaginary air. In fact, since it is the *purity of the air* that is truly creative, this purity must create the sylph before the dove, the purer thing before the more material.

This filiation, which comes from spirit down to corporeal beings, is a great truth in the psychology of the imagination. Psychologists do not pay attention to it, because they confuse the methods proper to the imagination with those pertaining to conceptualization, as if an image were merely a vague, blurred concept. They contaminate the fundamental image of flight with the concept of bird. They do not realize that in the realm of the imagination, flight effaces the bird for a dreamer, and that the realism of flight causes the reality of the bird to take second place. They therefore take *phantoms of the air* to be mere digressions, without ever wondering why the imagination seeks phantoms in an invisible element. Everything, moreover, seems to prove them right—even stories! We must admit that in stories sylphs are far less numerous than other elementary spirits. But in my opinion, this scarcity merely shows that aerial imagination is rarer than that of water, fire, and earth. This is no reason to consider them less well established. Aerial imagination, because of an intrinsic fatality, must recreate aerial spirits.

Further, we can find very specific examples in which it is possible to see aerial imagination working along the lines of a filiation from sylph to bird. I will cite a case that I found particularly instructive, because it appears in an environment of reflective, albeit humorous, thought. A Carthusian monk who calls himself Vigneul de Marville, at a gathering in the home of Rohault, a Cartesian professor of physics, expresses the curious idea that *elemental spirits*—who roam about the universe and live in elemental substances—*dwell* in the bodies of birds, fish, or mammals, to live as their essences dictate. They are the ones who act on *animal spirits* and who make animal machines move. "A sylph who is a dreamer finds a place inside an owl, a brown owl, or a screech owl. On the other hand, a sylph who is of a merry disposition and who likes to sing little songs, slips into a nightingale, a warbler, or a canary."[5] Thoughts that are fabricated, entertaining, and dream-like join forces here. The importance of their inversions, their interplay, is underestimated. That is how imagination and scorn leave their marks on the life of the mind. This lighthearted overview adds some sensitivity to Descartes' rigid theory of animals as machines and makes the vague belief that spirits inhabit the elements more concrete. On both sides, Marville makes light of the dualism of those two feuding brothers: dream and theory.

In solitude, far from the nonsense found in scientific salons, reasonable people dream in the same way. Gassendi, Jules Duhem reminds us, asserts the important effects of a subtle fluid in the flight of birds. A bird flies because it participates in light air. In his chapter on "Electricity" Duhem cites a bird named "Stellino," which, it is imagined, is "drawn by the planet Mercury and rises to the loftiest regions of the air in order to worship it." To get a proper understanding of this text, we must recognize that this attraction contains a material-spiritual ambivalence. "Stellino" is really the *sublimation of a bird*. It is a bird that is pure enough to worship the purest regions of our atmosphere and to rise up by the sheer force of its light substance.

The air's purity, however, is so active in the dreams of aerial imaginations that we can recognize the dream in incredible inversions of material images. A bird's inner warmth has, of course, struck many observers. So they attribute the ability of birds to fly to a pure and elemental fire. They say that birds left the earth in order to live in the purity of sun-drenched air. But here is the inversion that the imagination of an eighteenth-century philosopher has no hesitation in formulating: "The effect of the powerful fire that animates them is salutary in the place where they live, because it absorbs the bad air. From this it follows that the kite, a prodigious aerial acrobat, is looked upon in the Orient as a purifier of the atmosphere." What

5. Cited by P. V. Delaporte, *Du Merveilleux dans la littérature française sous le règne de Louis XIV* (Paris, 1891), 124.

better proof could we have that the notion of *purity* is what creates images? Such inverted values allow us to have a better understanding of the problems of sublimation. Here we can see the *material imagination of purity* taking direct action.

How can psychologists who do not dream make decisions about the psychic realities of the life of the imagination? They are afraid of spending their time studying madness, and they want to know how images are formed! They want to study real images, and they are unconcerned with the living images that *assert themselves* at night behind our closed eyes! As for me, I am inclined to believe that flight is a warm wind before being a wing. I do not reject the teachings of a dreamer who believes that a sylph will teach him what a bird is. In dynamic imagination, the first flying creature in a dream is the dreamer himself. If someone or something accompanies him in flight, it is a sylph, a cloud, a shadow; it is a veil, an aerial form, enveloped and enveloping, happy to be undefined and to live at the edge of the visible and the invisible. To see birds of flesh and feathers fly, the dreamer must climb back up toward day and assume once more his human, clear, logical thoughts. But if the clarity is too great, the spirits of sleep will disappear. It is for poetry to find them again, as though they were reminiscences of a beyond. A person who does not forget can make no mistake on this point: the dream, like Toussenel's God, creates the *soaring spirit* before creating the bird.

IV

If purity, light, and the sky's splendor summon up pure and winged creatures; if, through an inversion that is only possible in the realm of values, the purity of a creature gives purity to the world in which it lives, we can easily understand that the imaginary wing takes on the colors of the sky and that the sky is a world of wings. We will murmur like the sleeping Boaz, with the soul's voice:

> There angels flew, but darkly, of course,
> For at times there was seen, going by in the night,
> Something blue, that might be a wing.

Every dynamic azure, every furtive azure is a wing. The blue bird is a product of an aerial motion. As Maeterlinck said, "It changes color when put in a cage."

If, in our reveries, soft light and joyful motion really produce blue motion, a blue wing, a blue bird; then conversely something somber and heavy will cluster around images of night birds. This is why many imaginations consider the bat a sign of an ill-fated flight, one that lacks sound, color, or upward movement—the antithesis of the sonorous, transparent, and light flight of Shelley's trilogy. Forced to beat its wings, the bat does not experience the dynamic restfulness of gliding. "In it," says Jules Michelet, "we see that nature is searching for a wing, but till now has found only a hideous membrane that nonetheless functions as a wing."

I am a bird; see my wings.

"But the wing doesn't make the bird." In Victor Hugo's cosmology of wings, his poem "God," the bat is cursed and personifies atheism. It is at the bottom of the scale, below the owl, the crow, the vulture, and the eagle. But we have looked at the problem of symbolic flying creatures only incidentally, and to deal with them, we will have to examine in detail the problem of the animalizing imagination, that is, the dynamic imagination that specializes in animal motions. Here we need only stress the vertical line along which dynamic imagination valorizes living creatures. Toussenel's intuition is very instructive on this point.

In *The Animals*, Toussenel writes: "The bat has helped more than anything else to entrench the more or less fabulous myths of the hippogryph, the griffon, the dragon, and the chimera into the minds of credulous mortals."[6]

We should note carefully in passing that Toussenel's Fourieristic optimism allows him both to assert that God created the sylph and to accuse anxious people of credulity when they talk about the hippogryph and the chimera. Such a contradiction does not affect an imagination as surely oriented toward height as Toussenel's. For a well-dynamized aerial imagination, everything that *rises* becomes awakened to and involved in being. Conversely, everything that falls is dispersed into empty darkness and becomes a part of the void. *Valorization determines the nature of being.* This is one of the great principles of the Imaginary.

6. Buffon took pleasure in defining the bat as "a monster-being," whose "movement through the air is less a flight than it is an uncertain fluttering, which it seems to accomplish only awkwardly and with great effort."

V

Now that we have seen at great length the priority of dynamic imagination over formal imagination, we are better able to understand the almost total impossibility of adapting a bird's wing to a human body. The impossibility does not lie in a conflict between forms. The problem stems from the absolute divergence between the condition of human flight (oneiric flight) and the clear representation of flight derived from attributes belonging to real creatures flying through the air. There is, in the imagination of flight, a separation between dynamic and formal images.

We can better appreciate the difficulty of representing human flight by looking at the many ways that formal imagination has used to suggest the movement of flight. Mlle J. Villette has published a memorable book on *The Angel in Western Art* in which there is a great deal of documentation.

As Villette says, "Asking a sculptor to create the illusion of immateriality is like making a bet, the limitations imposed by his work stand in his way to such a large extent." It is immediately apparent that *human wings* are a hindrance. Whether the artist makes them large or small, trailing or uplifted, ruffled or smooth, they remain motionless; the imagination cannot make the connection. The image, the winged statue, is static.

In the last analysis, indirect procedures provide the best solution —within the limits of the possible—to the problem of representing human flight. Wings will still be used like allegorical signs of flight, to satisfy tradition and logic. But we will look elsewhere for dynamic suggestions, since suggestion is often more effective than depiction. We should note, for example, that artistic genius reveals a kind of foreknowledge in that it draws our attention to a movement that dynamizes the heel. Villette notes that with certain of Michelangelo's angels, "a slight movement of their upraised foot seems to be enough to direct their flight."

Villette also notes that many artists took their inspiration from swimming to solve the problem of depicting angels in flight. "The body is leaning or placed almost horizontally on the clouds. The upper half of their body erect, their arms outstretched and their legs lifted, the angels cross the firmament in the same way as swimmers breast the waves. The long parallel streaks in which they appear strengthen this illusion." Water images dominate to such an extent in this example that the image of the water's wake is superimposed on the aerial imagination. On page 80, Villette reproduces one of Benozzo Gozzoli's frescoes which illustrates this very well. The painter's trick—replacing flying by swimming—seems especially interesting, since we have already seen that for certain kinds of imagination there is a continuity from swimming to flying—but there is no continuity from flying to swimming. The wing is essentially aerial. We swim in the air, but we do not fly in the water. The imagination can continue its water dreams in the air, but it cannot then experience an inverse transcendence. We may conclude, then, that artists unconsciously follow the regular filiation of dynamic imagination and that they use swimming in dreams to suggest flight to their audience.

Sometimes the sculptor will create, not the illusion of flight, but a kind of invitation to sympathetic flight by forcing the eye to *move* from one form to the next. That is why, according to Villette, the artist gives "elongated proportions to the form and accentuates their effect by arranging simple draperies with clearly vertical lines. The eyes follow these ascending lines and forget the weight of the material." In other words, dynamic imagination is awakened to its normal dream and moved to rise up under the impulse of a static, but *elongated* form.

We can never spend too much time meditating on the expression *an elongated form*, which is an image in which formal and material imagination intersect. Words become so timeworn that, in this case, the dynamic characteristics virtually disappear. To give the image its true power, and therefore its full meaning, we would have to graft onto it, its converse. We would reawaken it and give it renewed life, no doubt, by coming to the realization that an *elongated form* is a *formal élan*. In the *formal élan*, dynamic imagination would regain its role as a creator of forms. It is to be noted that any *elongated form* reaches out toward the heights, toward light. The *elongated form* is a *formal élan* that unfolds in pure, luminous air. We could not conceive of an elongated form going downward, suggesting a fall. That would be—in the realm of the imagination—aerodynamically absurd.

VI

To help us live at the intersection of formal and dynamic imagination, the work of William Blake, a poet and engraver, is particularly useful. This work—powerfully oneiric—is also enlivened by such great *poetic eloquence* that it provides a rich example of *life as expressed in words* to which I will return in my conclusion. Some of Blake's poems could be called *absolute poems*, that is, poems that do not translate ideas, but that tie together, in the words themselves, imaginary mat-ter and ghostly forms, the movement of words and of bodies, "thought and motion" or better, speaking and moving. For example, the flight of ideas is not a worn-out image or a weakened allegory in Blake's work. Here the old expression is very fresh, having the same psychological enthusiasm that gives life to the *Prophetic Books* in which verbal images prophesy. There is no underlying prophetic thought. For Balzac, the flight of thought was certainly a real motion, but it remained general and dependent on a uniform aerial imagina-tion. For Blake the *flight of ideas* takes on the pluralism of all birds' real flights. Blake's psychology is truly an ornipsychology.

The "Visions of the Daughters of Albion," is filled with eagles, nightingales, larks, falcons, pigeons, swans, tempests, sighings, winds. . . . In ten pages the reader can count fifteen things that fly and more than twenty-five flights. Actual flights form the very basis of cosmic motions that run through the text. Wonderful images teach us that for the *imagination of flying*, it is flight itself that sweeps the universe along with it, mobilizing the wind, and sharing its dynamism with the air. Thus Blake writes in "Visions of the Daughters of Albion": "The sea fowl takes the wintry blast. for a cov'ring to her limbs." How can we fail to feel dynamically that the bird takes its own *wake* as a wrap? And is it not this wrap waving in the wind that produces the wintry blast? Mythological beings breathe the storm. The tempest is in their mouths. For Blake the whole body creates the storm. The sea bird is a creature intimately bound to the storm. It is the dynamic eye of the storm.

For Blake, flight is freedom in the world. Therefore, the dynamism of air is insulted by the sight of a bird held prisoner. In "Auguries," we read this moving couplet:

A Robin Red breast in a Cage
Puts all Heaven in a Rage.

Thus the bird personified free air. We should not forget that the German language acknowledges the bird's true nature in a maxim on freedom. It does not say, elliptically, "free as the air," but rather "free as a bird in the air," "frei wie der Vogel in der Luft."

How, therefore, can we fail to feel dynamically the *wandering thought* in this passage:

> Where goest thou O thought? to what remote land is thy flight?
> If thou returnest to the present moment of affliction
> Wilt thou bring comforts on thy wings. and dews and honey and balm;
> Or poison from the desart wilds, from the eyes of the envier.

How can we resist declaiming such a passage when just a few lines earlier we read the question, "Tell me what is a thought? & of what substance is it made?" To understand Blake's imagination we must answer the question this way: Thought is made up of the being that its motion creates. Blake's thought is aquiline *matter*. For example, is the thought of an eagle's powerful flight not cruel in itself? By itself, it creates the voracious eagle. For anyone who can move quickly from one idea to the next, the power of the wing beat devours the lamb.

Other wings bring *honey*: "Arise you little glancing wings, and sing your infant joy!/ Arise and drink your bliss, for every thing that lives is holy!" And this time the wings are singing.

Reading Blake *dynamically*, the reader quickly becomes conscious of the fact that he is the hero in a battle between earth and air. More precisely, he is the protagonist in an *uprooting*, he is the being who raises his head up out of matter, the strange being that unites two dynamics: coming out of the ground and taking off into the sky. In "Tiriel," Blake writes: "And when the drone has reachd his crawling length." This *elongation* of the snake wakens all the *reptile* elements in our dynamic imagination. The dynamics of *crawling* is apparent in many of Blake's passages which become clear when they are read dynamically, not merely with what energy happens to be available, but with all possible motions. In this regard, moreover, the crawling movement in Blake could be compared with the undulating, smooth movement of the *caterpillar* in V. Rozanov's "Apocalypse."[7] Then we will be able to distinguish clearly between the movement in living protoplasm and the movement that is conscious of its well-knit articulations. William Blake is a poet of *vertebral dynamics*. He uses all of its images; its history is a part of him; he knows all of its regressions. In the realm of the imagination, as in paleontology, birds

---

7. V. Rozanov, "L'Apocalypse de notre temps," trans. V. Pozner and B. de Schloezer, in *Commerce* (Summer 1929), 206.

develop from reptiles. Flying in many birds is an extension of a snake's crawling. In his oneiric flight, man triumphs over the crawling body. Conversely, when we find contortions in our dreams, the spinal column sometimes remembers having been a snake.[8] Blake writes:

> 6. In a horrible dreamful slumber;
> Like the linked infernal chain;
> A vast Spine writh'd in torment
> Upon the winds; shooting pain'd
> Ribs, like a bending cavern
> And bones of solidness, froze
> Over all his nerves of joy.
> And a first Age passed over,
> And a state of dismal woe.

We will examine the nightmare of this terrestrial imagination a little more closely to better understand the aerial dream in flight. We will see then that the aerial images are late conquests, that the aerial organism represents the difficult process of breaking free.

First we must understand that the consciousness of anything that crawls is centered on its *loins*.

> 5. All day the worm lay on her bosom
> All night within her womb
> The worm lay till it grew to a serpent
> With dolorous hissings & poisons
> Round Enitharmons loins folding . . .

To have such pain from this torsion requires vertebrae. The pain will create twisting, the twisting will create the vertebrae. The worm is too soft to suffer; it will become a snake. The snake is covered with *loins*.

> 6. Coild within Enitharmons womb
> The serpent grew casting its scales,
> With sharp pangs the hissings began
> To change to a grating cry,
> Many sorrows and dismal throes
> Many forms of fish, bird & beast,

8. "The spinal column has its reveries." Victor Hugo, *L'Homme qui rit* (Paris, 1912), 75.

> Brought forth an Infant form
> Where was a worm before.

Thus, forms are born out of tortured protoplasm. They are *forms* of pain. Genesis is born out of Gehenna. What is upright rises out of what is twisted. For Blake, everything terrestrial is subject to the dynamics of torsion. Torsion is an initial image. Watch him look at a brain:

> 8. So twisted the cords, & so knotted
> The meshes: twisted like to the human brain . . .

From this twisted universe, from this contorted thought, misunderstood because its original tortured nature was not recognized, comes an *aerial principle* reflected in Blake's *Emanation*: an emanation that remains painful, but nevertheless becomes free and straight without ever losing the primordial pain of achieving the upright posture.

> My Spectre around me night & day
> Like a Wild beast guards my way
> My Emanation far within
> Weeps incessantly for my Sin
>
> . . . .
> Poor pale pitiable form
> That I follow in a Storm
> Iron tears & groans of lead
> Bind around my akeing head.

Aerial phenomena are always stirring in Blake's imagination. They are "energetic." It is expressive energy. This is what Jean Lescure articulates so well in his excellent article in *Messages 1939*. He writes that Blake "embodied this very creative energy that kept urging him to pull something out of his painful and useless confusion and to formulate it as life and action."

> Awake! awake O sleeper of the land of shadows,
> wake! expand!

This *tension* is preparatory to attaining uprightness, which is, in the end, the ultimate dynamic lesson that Blake's poetics teaches us.

I want to come back now to a less tension-filled, more specifically aerial poetry. I have merely tried to show the sufferings of someone held prisoner by the earth, but acted upon by imaginary forces that seek to leave the earth. Throughout Blake's poetry, we can see a new Prometheus at work stretching his chains. This Prometheus is filled with vital energy. His motto might be *"Energy is only life, and is from Body. Energy is eternal Delight."* This energy demands that it be imagined. Its *reality* is by nature *imaginary.* Imagined energy passes from a potential to an active state. It tries to create both formal and material images, to give substance to forms and to bring matter to life. For Blake, dynamic imagination is an inquiry into energy. To understand his work the reader must learn to become totally alert physically and to add another key ingredient, a breath of inspired anger. He will then succeed in giving its true meaning to what might be called *harsh inspiration*, a term that may well characterize Blake's own inspiration. This painful breath is truly the prophetic voice that speaks in the books of Urizen, Los, and Ahania. In "A Descriptive Catalogue of Pictures, Poetical and Historical Inventions," painted by William Blake, he writes,

> A Spirit and a Vision are not, as the modern philosophy supposes, a cloudy vapour or a nothing: they are organized and minutely articulated beyond all that the mortal and perishing nature can produce. He who does not imagine in stronger and better lineaments, and in stronger and better light than his perishing mortal eye can see does not imagine at all.

To imagine, then, is to heighten the tone of reality. It appears that Blake's phantoms necessarily have a deep gutteral voice, more "carefully articulated" than the voices in poems where no one "imagines at all." If we listen to the *Prophetic Books* as though they were poetry written by a painful breath, they will seem to be litanies to energy, like *interjections that think.* Beneath the works, we must become more acutely aware of an imagination that lives or a life that imagines. William Blake is a rare example of that *absolute imagination* which controls matter, forces, forms, life, thought, and which can give legitimacy to a philosophy that explains, as I am trying to do, the real by the imaginary.

VII

I have devoted this chapter to a preliminary check list of the very varied poetic themes furnished by the aesthetics of wings or, more precisely, by the energy that produces lightness and joy. I am pursuing a general goal: to work with as much precision as possible on the difficult problem of the relationship between form and force, each experienced through the imagination. I do not consider myself qualified to go into an exhaustive examination here of all the images that might cluster around a single example. It would be interesting, however, to examine the different poetic images furnished by a particular bird. A fauna of literary images would contribute to a general doctrine of pancalism, just as the fauna of mythological images—as established by de Gubernatis—was used in mythology. But this is too great a task for me. Moreover, by dwelling too long a time on examples, I would lose sight of the philosophical task that I had contemplated, which requires coming back constantly to the *general* laws of the imaginary and to a thoughtful consideration of its basic elements.

Nevertheless, I should like to close this chapter by setting forth one very specific example that will validate, I believe, my general thesis: the supremacy of dynamic over formal imagination. The image that I have in mind is the lark—a very common image in various European literatures.

To begin on a polemical note, I will point out that the lark is an outstanding example of a *pure literary image*. It is nothing but a *literary image*. It is the source of many metaphors which are so immediate that people believe, when they write about the lark, that they are describing reality. But in literature, the reality of the lark is a particularly pure and clear case of *metaphor's realism*.

The lark, lost in the heights and the sunshine, does not even exist for the painter's eye. It is too small to be on the same scale as the landscape. The same color as the furrowed fields, it cannot add a single flower to the autumn earth. So the lark—which plays such a large role in literary landscapes—can have no place in those created by painters.

If the lark is evoked by a poet, it appears in some ways to be as important as the forest or the stream, despite the question of size.

In *Memoirs of a Good-for-Nothing*, Joseph von Eichendorff gives the lark its place among the most important elements of the landscape:

> My guide in life is God alone,
> Who stream and bark and sea and land

And earth and Heaven alike doth own:
My life and fate lie in His hand.[9]

But can the author himself give us a real description of it? Can he really interest us in its *form*, in its *color*? Michelet tried to do so in passages that have touched the popular mind. But this description of the bird "so poorly dressed, but so rich in heart and in song," quickly becomes a moralistic character study. We must call it "Michelet's lark." The lark "is now and will always remain a person," as Michelet himself has characterized a bird described by Toussenel. Pressing the issue, Toussenel provides more of a political commentary than a character study: "The lark wears a gray coat, the drab work clothes worn for field work, the most noble and useful, but least paid and most unappreciated of all work. . . ." The lark will always be "the field-worker's companion." It is a daughter of the furrows and fields. As Petrus Borel puts it: we sow for it.[10] But moral and political symbolism lead us away from the natural or cosmic symbolism which, as we will see, is associated with the lark.

The examples of Michelet and Toussenel, however, are symptomatic of a problem: to *describe the lark* is to *abandon* the task of description. It is to find a beauty that cannot be described. An "image hunter" with a sharp eye, like Jules Renard, who plays with great skill and tireless energy on the kaleidoscope of forms, finds himself suddenly caught short of the picturesque when he comes to the phenomenon of the lark.

> I have never seen a lark and I waste my time getting up before dawn to try. The lark is not a bird of the earth . . .
> But listen, as I have listened,
> Do you hear somewhere up there pieces of crystal being broken in a golden cup?
> Who can tell me where the lark sings?
> ·
> The lark lives in the sky, and it is the only sky bird whose song reaches us.[11]

9. Joseph Freiherr von Eichendorff, *Memoirs of a Good-for-Nothing*, trans. Ronald Taylor (London, 1961), 15.
10. Cf. Petrus Borel, *Madame Putiphar* (Paris, 1877), 184.
11. Maurice Blanchard, through the clash and interplay of images extracted from their dense matrix, describes the lark's surrealistic nature in a few lines: "Strident larks splattered against the mirror and since then, they are pieces of fruit that sing the *Alleluia*. Their transparent throats have become black specks lost in the ivory of the

Poets evoke the lark while refusing to describe it. Its color? This is how Adolphe Retté paints it: "Now listen: it is not the lark that is singing . . . it is a bird the color of infinity." I would also like to add: the color of ascension. The lark is a burst of Shelleyan sublimation: it is light and invisible. It is a *tearing itself away* from the earth that meets with immediate success. Its cry has nothing Blakean in it. It is not deliverance; it is freedom from the outset. There is a transcendent tonality in every note of its song. We can understand Jean-Paul's axiom about the lark: "You sing, therefore you fly." The intensity of the lark's song seems to grow in proportion as the bird rises. Tristan Tzara gives to the lark a destiny "after" its final act: "Some of the lark's swooping movements, involving as they do a follow-up to its final act, are always advisable."

Why does a *song's verticality* have such a powerful effect on the human soul? How can we get such great joy and hope from it? Perhaps it is because this song is at once lively and mysterious. Before it is more than a few feet from the ground, in the light of the sun, the lark *makes moats of dust*. Its image vibrates as do its trills; we see it disappear into the light. To give form to this dazzling invisibility, could we not bring to poetics the great syntheses of scientific thought? Then we would say: *In poetic space, the lark is an invisible corpuscle that is accompanied by a wave of joy.* This wave of joy is what a poet like Eichendorff receives from the dawn:

> At last a few long rays of pale, red light spread across the sky, quite faintly, as when one breathes on a mirror, and the sound of the first lark came from high above the silent valley. At this welcome from the dawn a weight was lifted from my heart, and my fear left me.

And the philosopher, throwing caution to the winds, would propose a wave theory to explain the lark. He would let it be known that it is by means of *vibration* that we come to know the lark; it can be described dynamically by an exercise of the dynamic imagination. It cannot be described formally by referring to the perception of visual images. A *dynamic description* of the lark depicts an awakening world

---

vertebrae. A glazier's cry gives them back their crystal plumage." "Le surréalisme encore et toujours," in *Cahiers de Poésies* (August 1943), 9. Thus the lark has the transparency, hardness and sound of crystal. Here the hardness of matter characterizes the lark's supermaterialistic nature.

that at one stage is singing. But you will be wasting your time if you try to capture this world at its point of origin when its existence is already expanding. You will be wasting your time if you try to analyze it when it is a pure synthesis of being and becoming—of flight and song. The world that animates the lark is the most undifferentiated of universes. It is the world of the plains, and of the plains in October when the rising sun is completely dissolved in endless mist. Such a world is unostentatiously rich in depth, height, and volume. The invisible lark sings for just such a formless world. "Its gay, light, effortless song seems to be the joy of an invisible spirit that would like to console the earth."

The startling invisibility of the lark has never been sung better—as a wave of joy—than by Shelley in "To a Skylark." Shelley understood that it was a cosmic joy, an "unbodied joy," a joy that is always so new in its revelation that it seems a new race has made it their messenger:

> Like an unbodied joy whose race is just begun.

Like a cloud of fire, it gives wing to the blue depths. For the Shelleyan lark, song is soaring and soaring is song. It is a piercing arrow that flies through silvery space. The lark defies all metaphors of form and color. The poet "hidden/In the light of thought," does not know the harmonies that the lark flings "to every crossroad of the sky":

> What thou art we know not;

and Shelley writes:

> Teach us, Sprite or Bird,
>   What sweet thoughts are thine:
> I have never heard
>   Praise of love or wine
> That panted forth a flood of rapture so divine.

The lark does not express the joy of the universe, it embodies it; it *projects* it. Listening to the lark, the imagination becomes dynamic through and through; no *languor* can survive, nor can any trace of boredom. Is this shadow, which Shelley calls a "shadow of annoyance" or nostalgia, not a *nostalgic ennui* which still lies dormant in an Old French word that has passed into a foreign language? Who has not felt this "annoyance" in the solitude of a plain lighted by the sun on a cold morning? A single song of the lark is enough to banish this nostalgic *ennui.*The cosmic quality of the lark stands out in this stanza:

> What objects are the fountains
> Of thy happy strain?
> What fields, or waves, or mountains?
> What shapes of sky or plain?
> What love of thine own kind? what ignorance of pain?

The lark also seems to me to be the very model of the *joyous romanticism* that is the essence of Shelley's poetics, the ideal of vibrant air that cannot be surpassed.[12]

> Teach me half the gladness
> That thy brain must know,
> Such harmonious madness
> From my lips would flow
> The world should listen then—as I am listening now.

Now we can understand the first lines of the poem: "Hail to thee, blithe Spirit!/Bird thou never wert." The real creature teaches us nothing; the lark is "pure image," pure spiritual image, that can find life only in aerial imagination as a focus of metaphors of air and ascension. We see that speaking of a "pure lark" makes sense in the same way that "pure poetry" does. *Pure poetry* refuses all descriptive tasks, all tasks assigned to a space inhabited by beautiful things. Its pure objects must transcend the laws of representation. A pure *poetic object* must, therefore, absorb both the subject and the object in their entirety. Shelley's pure lark, with its "unbodied joy," is a sum of the subject's joy and that of the world. People have made jokes about the toothache that belonged to no one. No poetic soul would make fun of that "unbodied joy" that reflects the happiness of a *universe in expansion*, a universe that grows as it sings.[13] "The lark," says Michelet, ". . . carries the earth's joys to heaven."

By embodying hope in song, the lark creates it. For Leonardo da

12. "The lark is in flight as though everything in life were going well." George Meredith, cited by Lucien Wolff in *George Meredith, poète et romancier* (Paris, 1924), 83.

13. Victor Poucel also writes: "The lark, up above, is no longer anything but jubilation in the azure sky. I hear it in the morning as I cross the fields and it seems to

Vinci, the lark is both prophet and healer. "They say that if a lark is carried in to a sick person, it will look away if he is to die. . . . But if he is to get well, the bird will look fixedly at him, and by its gaze, the sickness is relieved."

I have such great confidence in the indicative power of the *pure lark* as a pure literary image that it seems to me that an aerial landscape unquestionably becomes a dynamic whole when it falls under the sign of the skylark.

Here, by way of example, is a passage from d'Annunzio in which the lark appears at first to be only a metaphor, but the passage seems to get its aerial and ascensional sign from the metaphor itself.

The whole evening sky rings with a marvelous choir of larks.
. . . .
It was a canticle of wings, a hymn of feathers and quills, so broad that even the Seraphim could not equal them. It was the vesper symphony of all of winged springtime.

(The symphony) rose, rose in an unbroken stream (*as the lark rises and sings*), and, little by little, under the sylvan psalm, there was aroused a music made of screeches and tones, converted into melodious notes by virtue of distance and poetry. . .

And the bells rang, just as they do on the blue mountains.[14]

In the quiet of an evening, the lark "converts" all the dissonance arising from a bustling countryside into a sonorous unity, a musical world, a rising anthem. An aerial imagination will immediately feel that it is the *rising* that determines the harmony. Nor will it have any trouble experiencing the unity that is at once aesthetic and moral, the continuity between esthetic and moral emotion found in this passage:

The psalm was endless. Everything seemed to rise up, and rise again and still rise in the delight of this song. The rhythm of the Resurrection lifted the earth. I no longer felt my knees, and I was no longer

---

me that I am the one who is happy." *Mystique de la terre. Plaidoyer pour le corps*, preface by Paul Claudel (Paris, 1937), 78.

Paul Fort in *Ballades françaises inédites* writes: "The ding, dong, and silence": "far up in the sky we hear a lark sing, and within our breasts hearts beating madly."

14. Gabriele d'Annunzio, *Contemplazione della morte* (Milan, 1912), 129-30.

occupying my narrow place with my person; rather I was a multiple ascending force, a substance renewed to feed future divinity.

The same multi-faceted intoxication can be found in d'Annunzio's *The Dead City*:

All the fields are covered with little wild flowers that are dying; and the song of the larks fills the sky! It is marvelous! I never heard such impetuous singing. Thousands of larks, a countless multitude. . . . They flew up from everywhere, darting toward the sky with the speed of arrows; they seemed mad, vanishing without reappearing, as if consumed by their own song or devoured by the sun. . . . One fell suddenly at the feet of my horse like a stone, and lay there lifeless, struck down by intoxication from having sung with too much joy.

All poets unconsciously obey this *unity of song* which is achieved in a literary landscape by the lark's song. Lucien Wolff, in his excellent book *George Meredith, Poet and Novelist* writes: "The lark's song is no longer the individual fervor of a bird, but rather the expression of all pleasures, of all the joys of both the animal and the human world." And he quotes these lines from Meredith's "The Rising Lark": The song of the lark:

He is the hills, the human line;
The meadows green, the fallows brown,
The dreams of labour in the town;
He sings the sap, the quickened veins;
The wedding song of sun and rains
He is, the dance of children, thanks
Of sowers, shout of primrose banks,
And eye of violets.

It seems that at the lark's call, the woods, the waters, human beings, the flocks—and the ground itself with its meadows and its hillsides—become aerial and participate in aerial life. From it they get a kind of *unity of song*. The *pure lark*, then, can certainly be considered the sign of sublimation par excellence. "The lark," says Wolff in another place, "moves what is purest within us."

The same purity is to be found in its tapered ending, in the disappearance, and the silence that rests on the farthest point of the sky.

Suddenly, we no longer hear it. The vertical world falls as silent as an arrow that no one will ever shoot again.

> The sky lark died
> Not knowing how to fall.[15]

15. Jules Supervielle, "Le Matin du Monde," in *Gravitations* (Paris, 1966), 110.

3

The Imaginary Fall

> We lack wings, but we always have
> enough strength to fall.
> PAUL CLAUDEL, *Positions et propositions*

I

IF WE WERE to make a balance sheet of metaphors of falling and rising, we could not help but be struck by the fact that those pertaining to the fall are much more numerous. Even before any reference to morality, metaphors of the fall are fixed, it would appear, by an undeniable psychological reality. These metaphors all produce a psychic impression that leaves indelible traces in our unconscious: the fear of falling is a *primitive fear.* We find it as one component in fears of many different kinds. It is what constitutes the dynamic element of the fear of the dark. One who flees feels his legs giving way. Blackness and fall, the fall into blackness prepares facile dramas for the *unconscious imagination.* Henry Wallon has shown that agoraphobia is actually just a variation on the fear of falling. It is not a fear of meeting other people, but rather a fear of being unprotected. At the slightest regression, we tremble with this infantile fear. Our dreams themselves know vertiginous falls into bottomless pits. This is why Jack London has stressed the drama of the oneiric fall to the point of making it a "racial memory." For him, this dream

> dated back to our remote ancestors who lived in trees. With them, being tree-dwellers, the liability of falling was an ever present menace. . . . It will be noted . . . that in this falling dream which is so familiar to you and me and all of us, we never strike bottom. . . . You and I are descended from those that did not strike bottom (in these terrible falls they *clutched branches*); that is why you and I, in our dreams, never strike bottom.

On the basis of this, Jack London develops a theory of a dual human personality: an oneiric personality and a rational one, which makes a decided distinction between our daily and our nocturnal life.

> It must be another distinct personality that falls when we are asleep, and that has had experience of such falling—that has, in short, a memory of past-day race experiences, just as our wake-a-day personality has a memory of our wake-a-day experience.

"The commonest race memory we have is the dream of falling through space." The extent of these hypotheses allows us to understand the many reasons that *metaphors of the fall* intrude upon the most diverse psyches.

It would seem, then, that a *psychology of verticality* should devote a long study to the feelings and metaphors of the fall. Still, I am going to write only a short chapter on it simply to show more precisely what I believe to be the truly *positive* experience of verticality, which is, in my opinion, the dynamized verticality of the heights. In fact, despite the frequency of our impressions of falling and the reality that these have for us, I believe that the true axis of *vertical imagination* is directed upward. To put it another way, we *imagine* the upward élan, and we *know* the downward plunge. The fact is that we have great difficulty in imagining what we know. On this point, Blake writes: "Natural Objects always did & now do Weaken deaden & obliterate Imagination in Me . . ."[1] The higher, then, takes precedence over the lower. The *unreal* commands the *realism of imagination*. Since this thesis needs constant justification, let me give the grounds for my choice of method.

Although images of the fall are numerous, they are not nearly as rich in dynamic impressions as might first be thought. The "pure" fall is rare. Images of the fall are, for the most part, enriched by the addition of other things. The poet adds to them circumstances that are completely external. In that case, he does not really set our dynamic imagination in motion. For example, it means nothing to our dynamic imagination to say, as Milton does in his *Paradise Lost*, that Lucifer, cast out of heaven, fell *for nine days*. This nine-day fall does not make us feel the wind rushing by as he falls, and the immensity of the space covered in no way increases our terror. If we had been told that the devil fell for a century, the abyss would not have seemed any

---

1. Cited by Herbert Read, "Le poète graphique," in *Messages* (1939).

deeper to us. How much more active the impressions are when the poet can communicate the *differential of a living fall*; that is, the change in the very substance of the one who is falling and who, as he falls, becomes *more* weighted down, heavier, and guiltier. This living fall is the one whose cause and responsibility we carry within us, in the complex psychology of the fallen creature. The union of cause and responsibility will increase its tonality. If it is given a moral tone, the fall is no longer on the order of an accident, but rather of substance. The whole image must be enriched with metaphors to give life to the imagination. The imagination, the first principle of an idealist philosophy, requires that the subject, the whole subject, be a part of every one of the images. For someone to imagine a world, he must hold himself respnsible, morally responsible, for that world. Every doctrine of imaginary causality is a doctrine of responsibility.[2] Every contemplative person always trembles a little when he reflects on his elemental powers.

Symbolism, then, requires greater powers of association than those supplied by visual images. In Milton's work, Lucifer is no doubt the symbol of a moral fall, but when Milton shows us the Fallen Angel as an *object* overthrown and cast out of heaven, he extinguishes the light of the symbol. Quantitative vertigo is often the antithesis of qualitative vertigo. If we wish to imagine vertigo, we must deal with it according to the philosophy of the moment; it must be captured in its total differential when our whole being is losing its strength. It is an overwhelming becoming. If we are to have images of it, the *psychology* of fallen angels must be aroused within us. The fall must contain *all meanings* at once; it must be simultaneously metaphor and reality.

II

But the *dynamic poverty* of the images of falling is not the only reason for choosing height as the positive direction of dynamic imagination. A more important reason guides me. I believe that in doing so, I am being faithful to the essence of dynamic imagination.

When the dynamic imagination concentrates on calling up images of motion and is not limited to a cinematographic description of

2. Otto Rank has demonstrated at great length the relationships between the notion of causality and guilt. Cf. "Creation and Guilt," chapter XXI in *Will Therapy and Truth and Reality* (New York, 1950), 270ff.

exterior phenomena, it imagines *heights*. Dynamic imagination really creates only images of impulse, *élan*, and soaring; in short, images in which the *motion produced takes its direction from the force* that is imagined actively. Imaginary forces always have positive work to do. dynamic imagination is not suited to images of resistance. In order to really imagine, it is always necessary to be active and aggressive. No doubt real movement, perceived by sight, contaminates the dynamic image. But in its origin, the image *seeks* movement, or to put it more precisely, dynamic imagination is very specifically the *dream* of will; it is the *will that dreams*. This will, dreaming of its success, cannot deny its own nature. Above all, it cannot be denied in its original dreams. Therefore, the naive life of the dynamic imagination is a recounting of conquests over weight. No dynamic metaphor is directed downward; no imaginary flower blooms from beneath. This is no facile optimism. We must not conclude from this that the imaginary flowers that live in a terrestrial dream are not beautiful. But the flowers themselves that open up in the night of the soul, in the warmly terrestrial heart of a subterranean man, are nevertheless flowers that rise upward. *Rising* is the real meaning of the production of images. It is the positive act of the dynamic imagination.

It therefore seems to me impossible to feel the imagination at work unless we have *first* sensitized the vertical axis in its rising. A living hell is not one that we dig, but a hell that is burning, one that rises up, one that contains the tropism of flames and screams, a hell in which suffering is always increasing. Pain that only ached more would lose its *infernal differential*. If we examine the principle of the dynamic imagination of growth—and if, consequently, we consider the growth of its geometrical and abstract aspects—we will recognize that growing is always *lifting*. Some people, in their imaginary life, lift with a great deal of difficulty—they are the terrestrials. Others lift effortlessly—they are the aerials. With the imaginary elements of earth and air, almost all *dreams of the will to grow* can be described. In the realm of the image, everything grows.

III

Thus we will study the imagination of the fall as a kind of sickness of the imagination of rising, as an *inexpiable nostalgia* for heights.

I will begin by giving an example of this nostalgic meaning attached to the dynamic imagination of the chasm. A striking expression of it is found in this passage by Thomas de Quincy, cited by Arvède Barine:

> Every night it seemed to me that I went down—literally, not metaphorically—into chasms and abysses where there was no light, beyond all known depth, with no hope of ever being able to get back up again. When I woke I did not have the impression *of rising back up.*[3]

Here we find that, in contrast to Milton's image, the fall is not described in terms of time; it is more deeply stamped by its despair, by its substantial and enduring nature. Something in us takes away the hope of ever "getting back up again," which leaves with us forever the consciousness of having fallen. The fallen creature "sinks deeper" into his guilt.

We should take careful note of the essentially dynamic nature of the chasm in the work of Thomas de Quincy. The abyss is not *seen*; the darkness of the abyss is not the cause of our terror. Sight plays no part at all in the image. The chasm is *deduced* from the fall. The image is *deduced* from the motion. Thomas de Quincy gives life to his text with direct and dynamic images. I fall, therefore a chasm opens up beneath my feet. I am falling endlessly, and therefore the chasm is bottomless. My *fall creates the abyss*; in no way is the abyss the cause of my fall. I will see light again, but it will not matter; nor will it matter that I will be returning to the living. My nocturnal fall left an indelible mark on my life. I can never have a feeling of having risen again because the fall is from now on a psychological axis engraved upon my very being: the fall is the destiny of my dreams. The dream, which normally makes people happy while they are in their aerial home, takes me far away from the light. The most unhappy is he whose reverie is weighted down! Unhappy is he whose dream suffers the abyss.

Edgar Allan Poe also knew that the reality of imaginary fall is one that we must seek in the suffering substance of our own being. The problem of the creator of imaginary abysses is to communicate this

3. Arvède Barine, *Les Névrosés* (Paris, 1898), 100.

suffering directly. We must find the means of inducing this imaginary fall in the soul of the reader *before unrolling the film of objective images.* The writer must arouse, then demonstrate. The apparatus of discursive terror can operate only secondarily, when the writer has touched the soul of his reader with a basic fear that moves him in the depths of his being. The secret of Poe's genius is that he based his work on the supremacy of the dynamic imagination. For example, from the very first page of "The Pit and the Pendulum," in which terrifying circumstances are to become excessive, the imaginary fall is created in its true, substantial tonality. "The blackness of darkness supervened; all sensations appeared swallowed up in a mad rushing descent as of the soul into Hades. Then silence, and stillness, and night were the universe. I had swooned. . . ."[4] And Poe describes the swooning as though the fall were somehow within our own being, an ontological fall in which first an awareness of physical and then of moral being disappears. If we can live, through dynamic imagination, at the very edge of the two worlds—that is, if we are truly and uniquely an imagining being, the first form of the psyche—we can evoke, Poe tells us, "these impressions eloquent in memories of the gulf beyond. And that gulf is—what? How at least shall we distinguish its shadows from those of the tomb?" Further on, alas, the story becomes mechanics bonded onto terror; it loses the majesty of deep terror, the tone of black melody that made its beginning so poignant. But the themes of the "black overture" are skillfully taken up again, so that the story as a whole will retain one of the most powerful of unities: *the unity of the chasm.*

This *unity of the chasm* is all-powerful; it easily encompasses moral values. In *Marginalia*, Poe indicates that when we faint, we get a feeling for what the annihilation of our being after death will be like. "And the danger of the annihilation might be indicated nightly by slumber, and occasionally, with more distinctness, by a swoon." Failing and fainting: the great synonymy of ethics and imagination.

The storyteller feels, moreover, that he cannot give the impression of this essential fall, at the very limits of death and the abyss, unless he tries to make associations with the effort to *rise up again,* to "regather some token of the state of seeming nothingness into which

4. Poe, "The Pit and the Pendulum," in *The Complete Tales and Poems of Edgar Allan Poe* (New York, 1938), 246-247.

my soul had lapsed; there have been moments when I have dreamed of success." It is these *efforts* to rise up again, these efforts to become conscious of the vertigo, that give a kind of undulating effect to the fall, that make the imaginary fall an example of that undulating psychology in which the contradictions between the real and the imaginary constantly change places, reinforce each other, and inter-act with each other as opposites. Then vertigo becomes stronger in this dialectics wavering between life and death; it reaches the point of that *infinite fall*, an unforgettable dynamic experience that so deeply affected Poe's soul.

> These shadows of memory tell, indistinctly, of tall figures that lifted and bore me in silence down—down—still down—till a hideous diz-ziness oppressed me at the mere idea of the interminableness of the descent. . . . Then comes a sense of sudden motionlessness throughout all things; as if those who bore me (a ghastly train!) had outrun, in their descent, the limits of the limitless, and paused from the wearisomeness of their toil . . . and then all is *madness*—the madness of a memory which busies itself among forbidden things.

As we can see, this account—in which can be found a mixture of reason that "breaks down," flesh that "faints," and imagination that "falls"—very effectively creates the link between image and metaphor that is so characteristic of the "literary image." With the "literary image" of the fall, we see how a *commentary* begins to be superimposed on the *storyline*, because the function of literary imagination is to *comment* on its images. The commentary projects the mind in all directions; it evokes a very long past and brings into focus a poly-valent mass of dreams and fears. By virtue of this fact, what is really imaged in the story is reduced to a minimum: the "ghastly train" is given no form; no effort is made to give them a body, or even con-sistency. The poet knows very well that the motion can be imagined *directly*; his dynamic imagination has total confidence that the reader can imagine vertigo dynamically with his "*eyes closed.*"

Without a dynamic knowledge of the imaginary swoon, of the ontological fall, of the wavering temptation of weakness; without an effort to be reborn or to rise up again, we really cannot live in the imaginary world where material elements come to dream within us and where the matter of things symbolizes with "the gossamer web of some dream."

He who has never swooned, is not he who finds strange palaces and wildly familiar faces in coals that glow; is not he who beholds floating in mid-air the sad visions that the many may not view; is not he who ponders over the perfume of some novel flower; is not he whose brain grows bewildered with the meaning of some musical cadence which has never before arrested his attention.

This sensibility, refined as our being weakens, is entirely dependent upon the material imagination. A mutation is needed so that our being is less terrestrial and more aerial, more capable of changing form, further removed from well-defined forms. This sensibility, increased by the diminution of being within us, is subjected, as if by a direct induction, to the physical influence of words. If words fail to evoke visual images, they lose some of their power. But words are the insinuation and fusion of images; they are not an even exchange for rigid concepts. They are a fluid that moves our fluidic nature, a breath that arouses within us an aerial matter when we have "reduced" our terrestrial matter. Thus, for Poe, who has known the state in which we fly through the air in our dreams, or in which we struggle against the *spirit of the fall* that seeks to darken us, the power of words is very close to being a material power governed by material imagination. "And while I thus spoke, did there not cross your mind some thought of the *physical power of words?* Is not every word an impulse on the air?" Nothing in all this suggests the occult. It refers to a simpler and more direct reverie. It seems then that meditation on dynamized poems, which is what Poe's stories are—stories that are often a splendid framework of *pure literary images*—serves to make us a part of a system of dynamic language and mobilizes us within a system of expressive movements. Language, according to this view of things, can claim to be an *association of motions* as it can be an *association of ideas*. The imaginary fall, spoken of within its proper dynamic, works dynamically on our imagination; then it causes formal imagination to accept fantastic visual images that no real experience could awaken. The images are born directly from the whispering, insinuating voice. *Nature as it is expressed in words* is a prelude to *natura naturans*. If we give the Word, creator of poetry, its rightful place, if we realize that poetry creates a psyche which then creates images, we will then add two terms to the traditional plan: nature as it is expressed awakens *natura naturans*, which in turn produces *natura naturata*, which is heard in nature that expresses itself. Yes, as so many poets have said, for anyone who listens, nature speaks. Everything in the universe speaks, but man, the great speaker, uttered the first words. Therefore, in the group of movements that we are studying, the more the spoken soul falls, the more fantastic are the sights that are manifest in its fall. In a general way, a soul must be *mobilized* if it is to receive the visions of any *invitation to travel*; it must move toward the depths in order to find the images of the black chasm, images to which normal, rational sight is particularly unsuited. From this point of view, it is very instructive for a psychology of the imagination to compare a story like "A Descent into the Maelström" to the account that appears to have been its source. We will have a good way of measuring the distance that separates an *imagined* account from an *imaginary* one. We will also understand the *autonomy of the imagination*, a thesis that, alas, has not yet found its philosopher.

To make this comparison, I have at my disposal, unfortunately, only the French version of the story in question. It is included in the nineteenth volume of *Imaginary voyages: Dreams, Visions, and Cabalistic Novels*. The account was published following *The Subterranean Voyage of Nicholas Klimm*, a book that Poe cites among those that he read with Roderick Usher in the unsettling evenings at the house of Usher. The second account in the collection, the one which interests us, is entitled *An Account of a Voyage from the Arctic Pole to the Antarctic Pole through the Center of the Earth*. Its author is unknown. The work, according to the editor, was printed for the first time in 1723.[5]

The geographical precision of the two tales, "A Descent into the Maelström" and "Voyage to the Center of the Earth" allows no room for doubt about the connection that I am postulating. This eighteenth-century author writes: "We were then at a latitude of 68 degrees, seventeen minutes" and does not give the longitude. Poe writes: " 'We are now,' he continued, in that particularizing manner which distinguished him—'we are now close upon the Norwegian coast—in the sixty-eighth degree of latitude . . .' " Despite his love for

5. In the same year an anonymous book came out in Rouen entitled *Principales merveilles de la nature* in which is found a detailed description of a Norwegian chasm, "the sea's navel." All the waters of the seas pass through this chasm. "This is done," the author says, "in the same way that the artery in a human body distributes blood to all of the veins." Le Chevalier de Mailly, *Principales merveilles de la nature* (Rouen, 1723), 49. The author, like Poe, refers back to Kircher.

minutia in maritime matters, Poe did not mention the seventeen minutes.

The same starting point, the same geographical focus, the same care to evoke popular legends at the outset in order to place their own account within a tradition, the whole group of similar ideas expressed early in the work only underscore the differences between the two imaginations. The story by the eighteenth-century author takes the fantastic in things as a pretext for evoking the fantastic in the social life of men. He quickly turns an imaginary country into a utopian society. When the story is well under way, at the very moment that it might have become as dramatic as a dream, the narrator inserts a dreamless sleep. He will wake from this sleep to depict the mores of subterranean men, in the same way that the author of *Persian Letters* depicts Parisian mores.

Conversely, Poe's imagination becomes increasingly *oneiric* before he has even finished the first page. In other words, Poe takes the real and imperceptibly changes it to the imaginary, as if the very function of perception in extraordinary things were to release dreams. If we pursue for a moment this gradual process by which everything becomes oneiric, we will see that it confirms my thesis on the necessity of engaging images in a fundamental imaginary movement.

Since the stories in question deal with a journey into the depths, and since they evoke a reverie of the fall, the feelings of vertigo must be the starting point. From the very beginning of the tale, before the terrifying story, before revealing the *objective* causes of the terror, the writer makes every effort to suggest vertigo in his two interlocutors, the speaker and the listener. *This common feeling of vertigo is the first attempt at objectivity.* By the second page of the tale, the vertigo is so intense that the narrator can write: "I struggled in vain to divest myself of the idea that the very foundations of the mountain were in danger from the fury of the winds." The vertigo has passed from co-enesthesis to ideas. The idea of extreme mobility provides a commentary on the co-enesthetic feeling of vertigo. Nothing is fixed, not even the mountain.

Poe's method, which often consists of comparing what is real to a dream, is extremely clear in this case. When he describes the ship carried by the waves into the whirlpool of the Maelström, he can find no better way to do it than to compare the descent to a fall occurring in a nightmare:

. . . a gigantic sea happened to take us right under the counter, and bore us with it as it rose—up—up—as if into the sky. I would not have believed that any wave could rise so high. And then down we came with a sweep, a slide, and a plunge that made me feel sick and dizzy, as if I was falling from some lofty mountain-top in a dream.

Readers do not begin to read this tale with a lively sympathy—or with nervous antipathy, for there are some who are more revolted by than attracted to Poe's stories—until the moment they experience, with the narrator, the *nausea of descent*, that is, until the moment when the unconscious is drawn into an experience of elemental life. It must be admitted, therefore, that the terror does not derive from the *object*, the *scenes* suggested by the narrator. Rather, the terror comes to life and is constantly renewed in the *subject*, the reader's soul. The narrator has not faced his reader with a frightening situation; he has put him in a *frightening situation*. He has stirred his reader's dynamic imagination. The writer directly *induces* the nightmare of the fall into the reader's soul. He discovers a kind of primal nausea that depends on a reverie deeply engraven in our inmost nature. The *primordiality of the dream* can be recognized in many of Poe's tales. The dream is not a product of waking life. It is the fundamental subjective state. A metaphysician can see a *kind of Copernican revolution of the imagination* at work here. In fact, images can no longer be understood by their objective *traits*, but by their *subjective meaning*. This revolution amounts to placing:

> dream before reality,
> nightmare before event
> horror before the monster,
> nausea before the fall;

in short, the subject's imagination is vigorous enough to impose its visions, its terrors, its unhappiness. If dream is a reminiscence, it is a reminiscence about a state that comes before life, the state of a life that is *dead*, a kind of mourning that comes before happiness. We could go one step further and put the image not only before the thought, before the account of it, but even before all *emotion*. A kind of *nobility of soul* is associated with terror in poems. This nobility of a tormented soul reveals such a primordial nature that it guarantees the primacy of the imagination forever. It is the imagination that thinks and the imagination that suffers. It is the imagination that acts. This is what is released directly into poems. The idea of symbol is too intellectual. The notion of poetic experience is too "experimental." Thought and random experience are no longer enough to reach the primordiality of the imaginary. Hugo von Hofmannsthal writes, "You will not find intellectual or even emotional terms by which the soul of such urges as these can be discharged; in this context the image releases it." The dynamic image is a primary reality.

On a theme as limited as the fall, Poe knows how to enrich the fundamental dream with only a few objective images and to make the fall *endure*. To understand Poe's imagination, we must experience this *assimilation* of external images by the movement of the *inner fall*, and we must remember that this fall is already on the order of fainting and death. Reading can then be so filled with emotion that, with the book closed, the reader still has the feeling that "he has not risen back up again."

Since Poe's reverie is characterized by weight, it weighs down all the objects on which it dwells. Even breaths of air take on weight and slow down as they stir draperies and velvet hangings. In the course of the tales, and in many poems, all *veils* imperceptibly become heavier.[6] Nothing flies. No one who knows dreams could mistake the signs: the *draped wall* in Poe's poetics is *the dream wall slowly coming to life, the soft wall with the "soft and nearly imperceptible waving" of the draperies.* The seventh room—the last one—of Prospero's palace in "The Masque of the Red Death" is "closely shrouded in black velvet tapestries that hung all over the ceiling and down the walls, falling in heavy folds upon a carpet of the same material and hue." In "Ligeia" the

> lofty walls, gigantic in height—even unproportionably so—were hung from summit to foot, in vast folds, with a heavy and massive-looking tapestry—tapestry of a material which was found alike as a carpet on the floor, as a covering for the ottomans and the ebony bed, as a canopy for the bed and as the gorgeous volutes of the curtains which partially shaded the window.

Further on, the hangings will tremble, shifting their long folds,

6. Cf. Poe, "The Raven," 943.

without their permanent weight being in the least disturbed. In any of the rooms where Poe places dramatic events, the action of this *enveloping heaviness* will be felt. All the objects are always *a little heavier* than objective knowledge or static contemplation would dictate. A little of the *will to fall*—a disorder of the will that prevents ascent—is communicated to them through the poet's particular dynamic imagination:

> And, over each quivering form,
> The curtain, a funeral pall,
> Comes down with the rush of a storm.

Death, in a horrible caress, places her heavy shroud upon all things.

As Poe's heavy reverie weighs things down, it also weighs down the *elements.* In my book, *Water and Dreams,* I studied the water peculiar to Poe's poetics, a heavy, slow water. The tranquil air in his poems and tales is also endowed with the same slowness and heaviness. The dynamic sensation of the "weakening of the soul" occurs in a *weighted atmosphere.* Very few poets can give *life* to this banal image. Any reader who is willing to go back and reread "The Fall of the House of Usher" *as a poem,* slowly and intensely as prose poems ought to be read—as a poem in which the rhythm is *in the thought*—will feel its strange power. This story must be reread dynamically, with the dynamics of slow movement, with half-closed eyes, giving less emphasis to the image-filled part, which is only an arpeggio of visions above the dynamic melody of heaviness. Then, little by little, the reader will feel the *weight of evening's shadow.* He will understand that the *weight of evening's shadow* is a *pure literary image* that is animated by a triple pleonasm. This weight of aerial matter that grows darker will give us a better feeling for the weight of "clouds (that) hung oppressively low." Once we have been sensitized to this old image of "heavy clouds," of the heavy, overcast sky, we will feel the action of that "paradoxical law of all sentiments having terror as a basis," a law that Poe evokes without explanation, but that seems to me to be the synthesis of anguish and fall, the substantial union—the union in our substance—of what oppresses us and what grounds us. Then the air around us, the air which ought to give us freedom, is our prison, a narrow prison in which the atmosphere is *heavy*. Terror returns us to the earth.

> I had so worked upon my imagination as really to believe that about the whole mansion and domain there hung an atmosphere peculiar to themselves and their immediate vicinity—an atmosphere which had no affinity with the air of heaven, but which had reeked up from the decayed trees, and the gray wall, and the silent tarn—a pestilent and mystic vapor, dull, sluggish, faintly discernible, and leaden-hued.

I continue to raise the same question: Is it sight that provides us with these images? In the tissue of adjectives in this narrative, should we attribute life and primary power to this "faintly discernible," "leaden-hued" vapor that surrounds the house of Usher? Doesn't sight contradict itself by using two adjectives that associate what is transparent with lead? On the contrary, everything becomes consistent if we *dynamize* the images and trust in that psychic power which is our imagination. The adjectives in this text that convey the power of the imaginary and have the power to create images are *ponderous* adjectives, which live *vertically*. It is heaviness, sloth, and the weight of the mysterious which burden the unhappy dreamer's soul. Sight loses its acuteness, no longer distinguishes clean formal lines, and becomes accustomed to nebulous reverie—*heavily nebulous*. It concurs with the strongly substantialized correspondence in which someone actually breathes "an atmosphere of sorrow." When Poe tells us: "An air of stern, deep, and irredeemable gloom hung over and pervaded all," the reader must enter into a substantial sympathy with Poe and feel the melancholy air enter *as a substance* within himself. For Poe fills these worn-out images in such richness that they regain their complete and original vigor. There are those who can make the rarest images trite. They always have concepts into which they fit their images. Others, true poets, restore life to the tritest of images: listen! in the shallowest idea, they make life ring out. At this point, poets who use platitudes will rise up and say: we speak *strongly, vigorously,* and *vividly*, too. They all use elaborate images and sonorous alliterations in their works. But this wealth of imagery is strange and all the sounds clash. There is no life or true movement—poetic *constancy*, the

very matter of beauty—in these decorative elements. Only material
and dynamic imagination can produce true poems.

The fidelity of Poe's poetics to its "substantial motion" is so great
that it appears in the shortest tales. For this reason, the reader will
have the same feeling of universal weight when rereading the three
pages of "Shadow" or the twenty pages of "Ligeia":

> A dead weight hung upon us. It hung upon our limbs—upon the
> household furniture—upon the goblets from which we drank; and
> all things were depressed, and borne down thereby—all things save
> only the flames of the seven iron lamps which illumined our revel.
> Uprearing themselves in tall slender lines of light, they thus re-
> mained burning all pallid and motionless.

Who does not sense that these slender, vertical, still flames have no
life?—they do not make anything rise up toward the sky. They are
simply a referential axis to give verticality its ideal line. Around
them, everything falls, everything is drooping; reverie lighted by pale
flames is a *heaviness* belonging to someone who is dying, someone
who thinks and imagines within the dynamics of death.

Need I stress the fact that, for some imaginations, a tapered flame is
one that is pulled at each end by the earth and by the air? It is
lengthened dynamically. *The imagination perceives it as actively
elongated.* It is, then, a complex image of takeoff and uprooting. We
can get some idea of this dynamic image from a passage by Cyrano:
"Thus as soon as a plant, animal, or man dies, their souls rise up,
without dimming (to become part of the body of lights), just as when
you see the flame of a candle leap upward, despite the soot that clings
to its feet."

For an imagination that has been duly sensitized, the slightest sign,
the slightest indicator points to a destiny. Putting "the Pentagram
upside down," as Victor-Emile Michelet puts it in *Love and Magic*, is
pledging your soul to the lower world. Michelet expresses it this way:
"In the temples of Siva [whom the writer associates with the devil],
the flames from the candlesticks are crossed by horizontal metal
plates that are designed to keep the flame from rising as it should,
that is, toward heaven."

To become light or to remain heavy—within this dilemma, some
imaginations can epitomize all the dramas of human destiny. The

simplest, poorest images—from the moment that they are aligned on the vertical axis—participate both in the air and the earth. They are essential, natural symbols always recognized by the material and dynamic imaginations.

IV

Since we now know that imaginary fall is a psychic reality that governs what it portrays and gives direction to all of its images, we are ready to appreciate a not uncommon poetic theme: *the fall upward*. Sometimes it will appear as the intense desire to go skyward in an accelerating motion. It can be heard ringing out like the cry of an impatient soul. In accordance with my method, I will take my examples from only one poet. In "The Psalm of the King of Beauty," O. V. de L. Milosz cries out: "I would like to fall asleep on this throne of time! To fall from the depths to the heights in the divine abyss."

There are, however, cases in which this desire to be *hurled* upward produces images in which the sky truly seems to be an *inverted abyss*. We remember that Séraphîtüs showed the timid soul abysses of blue sky, abysses that were more attractive for a truly aerial soul than the chasms in the earth were for a terrestrial soul. The terrestrial soul always wants to protect himself from the abyss. The fall into the sky is unambiguous. What moves faster is then happiness.

Only a few rare individuals have had pleasant experiences with vertigo. In such cases, a kind of unconditioned ascent and an awareness of a heretofore unknown sense of lightness begin. The transmutation of all dynamic values determines a transmutation of all images. Later we will see passages in which Nietzsche shows us that *depth is found in the heights*. Such images cannot come from sight alone; they are projections of dynamic imagination. For a soul in which the good is more pronounced and in which the assurances of good build confidence, *height* takes on such a richness that it can draw all the metaphors of depth to it. The elevated soul is *profoundly* good. Suddenly the adverb gives perspective to the adjective. It adds an historical qualification to the quality itself. How rich words are when they are read passionately!

In his poems, Milosz often associates images of ascent and the fall. They sum up the poet's Manicheism. Here is the dialogue between the man and the chorus in "Lemuel's Confession":

Chorus. Is is true? You remember? An immobile arch
　　　In space

　　　. . . . .
　　　The golden peaks of meditation.

　　　. . . . .
　　　And then the return—try to remember—
　　　The fall—the first Straight Line.
Man.　Carried by a cloud of voices, I don't know where;
　　　Suspended from on high, in the desired Nothingness,
　　　Inaccessible to motionless, harsh, silent flight
　　　Of the black, empty, terrible spaces.
　　　And I fell
　　　And forgot, then, suddenly, I remembered.
Chorus (much whispering).
　　　From life to life. What a road!

How can a reader experience such poems without participating in the First Straight Line, that Line that tells us of both Good and Evil, the fall and the golden summits of meditation? Great poets like Milosz support Albert Béguin's view: "Beginning down here on earth . . . the soul belongs to two worlds, one a world of heaviness, the other of light." And he adds: "But it would be false to believe that the one is nothingness and the other reality." The relationship between light and heaviness corresponds to a kind of dual realism of the imaginary that governs all of psychic life. Ricarda Ruch reminds us that "Schelling saw in light and heaviness the primordial duality of nature."

V

In the works of great dreamers of verticality, there can be found even more exceptional images in which the being appears to unfold in the direction of two destinies at once: height and depth. We will see an example of this astonishing image in the work of Novalis, a genius of dreams: "If the universe is in some way a precipitate of human nature, the world of the gods is its sublimation."[7] Then Novalis adds this profound thought: "The two are made *uno actu*." Sublimation and crystallization are accomplished in a *a single act*. There is no

7. Novalis, *Journal intime suivi de Hymnes de la nuit et de Maximes inédites*, trans. G. Clarette (Paris, 1927), 98.

sublimation without a deposit, and conversely, there is no crystallization without a light vapor emanating from matter, without a spirit
running along above the earth.[8]

But because this intuition is too close to alchemical images, it
falsifies the very thinking of Novalis, the great *psychologist* of alchemy.
In alchemical images, the dynamic imagination is too often inhibited
by material imagination. The results—salts and essences—with their
material dreams cause us to forget the long dynamic dreams of
distillation. We think of forms more than functions, and, just as in
our *dream stories*, we contaminate them with thought. In order to
remember *oneiric functions* rather than *oneiric objects*, we must be
extremely faithful to our dreams. In the preceding document, then,
we must give due emphasis to the expression *uno actu*. It is *uno actu*; it
is in the *act itself*, lived as a unified whole, that dynamic imagination
must be able to experience the double human destiny of depth and
height; the dialectics of the sumptuous and the radiant. (Who would
mistake the different vertical orientations of the sumptuous and the
radiant? Who, even one ignorant in matters of dynamic imagination,
could put sumptuousness in the air and splendor in the mine?)

Dynamic imagination unites the two poles. It allows us to understand that something within us rises up when some action penetrates
deeper—and that, conversely, something penetrates deeper when
something else rises. We are the link between nature and the gods or
—to stay closer to pure imagination—we are the strongest links
between earth and air. We are two kinds of matter in one act. Such
an expression, which seems to me to characterize Novalis' oneiric experience, is comprehensible only if we acknowledge the imagination's
superiority over every other spiritual function. We then settle into a
philosophy of the imagination for which the imagination is being itself,
the being that produces its own images and its own thoughts. Dynamic imagination, then, takes precedence over material imagination. Imagined motion, when it slows down, creates terrestrial being.

8. We can compare Novalis' thought to this passage from Milosz: "Bathed in the
ecstasy of ascension, dazzled by the solar egg, toppled into the madness of the black
eternity next to it, my limbs bound in the shades' algae, I myself am still in the same
place, since I am in the very place, the only one that is stable." "Le Cantique de la
Connaissance" in "La Confession de Lemuel," *Poesies II* (Paris, 1960), 149. The
alchemical tone of this canticle shows rather clearly that he is dreaming the separation of height and depth *uno actu*.

As it speeds up, it creates the aerial counterpart. Since, however, an essentially dynamic being must always remain within the immanence of its movement, it cannot conceive a motion that stops entirely nor one that accelerates beyond all limits; the earth and the air are, for a dynamized being, indissolubly linked.

With this in mind, we can understand how Novalis could sometimes describe heaviness as the bond that must "prevent the flight toward heaven." For him, the world is a beauty born of the waters, in accordance with the concepts of "Neptunism" so often meditated upon by the poets of his century. It is a castle that is "old and wonderful; it has fallen from the depths of deep oceans, and stands up, unshakable so far; to prevent a flight toward heaven, an invisible bond imprisons the subjects of this kingdom inside it."

The *subjects of this kingdom* are minerals, such as they are dreamed by material imagination. Thus, due to the invisible bond, the sky's colors are kept on earth in crystal. You can dream "aerially" of the blue of the sapphire as if the stone were a concentrate of the sky's azure; you can dream "aerially" of the topaz's fire as though it were in sympathy with the setting sun. You can also dream "terrestrially" the sky's blue by imagining that you are condensing it in the hollow of your hand—in its solidified form of sapphire. Terrestrial and aerial imagination come together in crystals and precious stones. At least they are both always potentially present waiting for the exalted soul, or the contemplative soul, to give them imaginary dynamism. We will return to this problem when, in another work, I will be able to study *the contemplation of crystals.* In the concluding paragraphs of this chapter, which bring together elements of a dynamics of the imagination, I wanted to make the reader feel the dual possibility of dreaming while *falling* and dreaming while *rising.* In the same crystal, two directions of the vertical dream are then born: dreams of depth and dreams of exaltation—earth and air. Great is the soul that can preserve these dreams, like every imaginary object, in their true verticality as well as in their potential verticality, *uno actu.*

Sometimes a slight disequilibrium, a slight disharmony, disrupts the reality of our imaginary being. We evaporate or we condense—we dream or we think. If only we could always imagine!

4

The Works of Robert Desoille

If you had really opened your eyes and
seen this one phrase: "he rose . . ."

DANTE

I

FOR MORE THAN twenty years, Robert Desoille has been working on a
psychology of the waking dream, or more precisely, a method of
directed reverie that could be considered preparatory to *Ascensional
Psychology*. Basically, Desoille's method is less a means of research
than it is a medical-psychiatric technique. By way of ascensional
reverie, it aims at finding a way out for blocked psyches, and at providing a satisfying outcome for confused and ineffectual feelings. His
method has been used in a number of clinics in Switzerland. It is, I
believe, likely to become one of the most effective procedures in this
Psychagogy of which Charles Baudouin is one of the principal movers.
The Geneva journal *Action and Thought* has published a number of
Desoille's studies. They have also been treated in a book, *Exploration
of Subconscious Affectiveness by a Method of Waking Dream: Sublimation
and Psychological Gains*.[1] I should like to bring out the important
points in this book while taking every opportunity to bring Desoille's
observations to bear on my own theories of the metaphysics of the
imagination.

The essential part of Desoille's method consists of clearly determining the ways in which a dreamer ascends in his dreams. It gathers
unmistakable images that will activate "unconscious" images and
strengthen the axis of a *sublimation* which, little by little, becomes
conscious of itself. Persons trained by Desoille's method gradually
discover the verticality of aerial imagination. They realize that it is a
life line. For my part, I believe that *imaginary lines* are the real life
lines, the ones most difficult to break. Imagination and Will are two

1. (Paris, 1945).

aspects of a single profound force. Anyone who can imagine can will. To the imagination that informs our will is coupled a will to imagine, a will to live what is imagined. By suggesting images in the right order, consistent behavioral patterns can be accurately determined. If subjects accept Desoille's sequences of images, they can acquire the habit of reaching a clear, untroubled, active sublimation. The *waking dream*, when managed in this way, allows the subject to use oneiric forces—disordered and sometimes neurotic—to create a conscious state in which he is finally able to control his actions and feelings in a rational way—because his images become coherent. I would not be unfaithful to Desoille's thought if I said that there is in his method a transformation from oneiric energy to moral energy, in the same way that a diffused heat can become motion. Moralists like to talk about discovery in morality, as though moral life were the work of the mind! Instead they should talk about the primordial power of the *moral imagination*. It is this imagination that should provide us with the sequence of beautiful images for the dynamic schema that we call heroism. As far as ethics is concerned, example is causality. But examples furnished by nature go deeper than those provided by man. The exemplary cause can become a substantial cause when a human being imagines that he is in tune with the world's forces. Anyone who tries to raise his life to the same level as his imagination will feel a sense of nobility welling up within him as he dreams of something rising, or as he experiences the aerial element in its *ascension*. It is obvious that I will have no trouble analyzing Desoille's theories along the lines of my metaphysics of aerial imagination.

II

For the person blocked by an unconscious complex, Desoille's method not only brings the means for "unblocking" as does classical psychoanalysis, it also offers a way of starting the process. While classical psychoanalysis concerns itself only with unblocking the complexes "by resurrecting emotions from the past," without ever giving direction to feelings that had already proved to be worn-out and inappropriate, Desoille's psychoanalysis encourages maximum sublimation by preparing the paths of ascent for sublimation. He does this by "having the subject experience new feelings," which are the very models of affective ethics. Classical psychoanalysis analyzes difficulties in the early development of the personality. It reduces that which, in the past, crystallized around a frustrated desire. Desoille's psychoanalysis—which might be more aptly termed psycho-synthesis—puts its major efforts into determining what conditions of synthesis are necessary for developing a *new* personality. These new affective elements that are added to a personality—and newness is, in my opinion, the function best suited to the imagination—will often correct a poorly integrated past. Naturally, Desoille realizes that he, psychiatrist and educator, should *clear away* everything that might hinder the psyche's future. In this respect the psychoanalyst's work is still useful.[2] But it is advisable to suggest future forms *as soon as possible* to someone who has just been released from the weight of a heavy past. It happens often that Desoille—since he hesitates to ask the subject to reveal any *painful* secrets—begins directly by suggesting ascensional images, future images. Without this early or even immediate suggestion of a potentially unlimited future, a person suffering for so long from his faults and mistakes might be overcome once again by his suffering and continue to live in his troubled state. Before his psychoanalytic cure, his soul was *heavy.* No one becomes *light* in a day. While pleasure may be natural and easy, happiness must be learned; one must become conscious of all of the values that lightness and happiness have in common.

This excellent method of treatment is described in very simple steps in the course of Desoille's book, with exercises that, intellectually, seem very easy. This is no doubt why philosophers have disregarded it. But what is easy to conceive is not necessarily easy in the realm of action, and even less so in the realm of the imagination. Anyone who wishes may avoid imagining. It is not a question here of imagining just anything. On the contrary, the dramatic change toward euphoria must come to grips with the *unity of the imagination*, which is a difficult task. To attain this unity of the imagination and this dynamic blueprint for happiness, we must come back to one of the great principles of material imagination. This is not a sufficient condition for happiness, but it is a necessary one. No one can be happy with a *divided imagination*. Sublimation—a positive effort of the

2. In a book soon to be published, Desoille gives case histories that include a complete account of waking dreams directed by patients with virtually no psychoanalysis simply by re-establishing the function of sublimation.

imagination—cannot be an occasional, rare, scintillating state. An element of calm must surround all the passions, on principle, even those associated with power.

III

Let us follow Desoille's method in all its apparent simplicity. Get rid of your cares. That would no doubt be the first piece of advice that a psychiatrist would give an anxious subject. But Desoille will not use this abstract formula. Instead, he will replace this very simple abstraction with a very simple image: sweep away your cares. But don't limit yourself to words. Feel the gestures; visualize the images; pursue the life of the image. To do this, we must give the imagination "control over the broom." Become *homo faber*, which is what this poor sweeper is when faced with a very monotonous task! Little by little you will come to participate in his dreams, in his rhythmic reverie. What do you have to sweep away? Cares or scruples? You will not take quite the same sweep of the broom in the two instances. You will sense the dialectics of scrupulosity and resolution come into play. But what slows down your soul—perhaps simply the roses of a faded love? Then work slowly and realize that the dream is over. How well your dying melancholy dies! How well your past passes! Soon your task will be over and you will be able to breathe again, with a collected soul, at peace, a little enlightened, unburdened, and free![3]

This very small, image-filled psychoanalysis delegates to images the task of the terrible psychoanalyst. Let "everyone sweep his area" and we will no longer need *indiscreet* help. Anonymous images are here given the responsibility of curing our personal images. Images cure images; reverie cures memory.

But perhaps it would be useful to have one more example. Desoille also uses the "ragpicker's way" successfully. It is more analytical than the "sweeper's way." It is good for getting rid of cares that are somewhat more conscious than the thousand vague or poorly for-

---

3. Nietzsche, the master of imagery in ethics, writes:

> I'd like to help as best I can:
> I wield a sponge, as you recall,
> As critic and as waterman.

"Fool in Despair" in *The Gay Science*, trans. Walter Kaufmann (New York, 1974), 365.

mulated problems that can be merely "swept away." Desoille counsels the subject who is bothered by a specific concern to put it with all the others in the ragpicker's bag, in the sack that he carries *behind his back*. This is in keeping with the very expressive and effective gesture of the hand that throws everything it scorns behind the back.

Some will object that this *gesture* is only vain pretense, that the person frees himself only on a deeper and more personal level. But they forget that we are dealing with psyches that cannot decide to make up their minds and who do not listen to rational rebukes. We can have an effect on them only if we begin with imaged behavior. We give them gestures of freedom precisely because we have confidence in the collective nature of a psychology of behavior that is formulated according to elemental images.

The alternative, of course, must be considered: the simulated, pretended, or imagined gesture. If the subject, strong in his resistance to psychoanalysis, stops at *simulating* the gestures suggested, then Desoille's method will do him no good. Through simulation, the subject adopts an intellectual state of mind, ready to criticize or argue. This will not happen if the subject really imagines, with his entire soul, if he imagines sincerely—which is a pleonasm, for what would imagination be without sincerity? The imagination shows forth as a direct, immediate, unitary activity. It is the faculty that allows the psychic being its greatest unity and, above all, the one in which the principle of unity really abides. Specifically, the imagination dominates emotional life. For my part, I believe that emotional life is really hungry for images. An emotion is awakened by a group of emotive images. These images are normative and seek to provide the foundation of moral life. It is always a good thing to offer "images" to an impoverished heart.

Desoille's method, which has been practiced for twenty years, confirms the power of "imaged behavior." We ourselves could supply many examples of the ethical nature of certain very simple, very common physical actions. We could show that tools, which are not solidified objects but well-coordinated gestures, evoke specific reveries that are almost always salutary and energetic—reveries of work. To them are attached "words," closely knit words, poems about energy: a theory of the *homo faber* can be heard in poetry—joyful, always joyful, poetry. To create from them a theory of intelligence and utility is to look at only one side of things. Work is a source of vague reveries as well as a source of knowledge. The tool—the good old tool—is a "dynamic image." It can be used in the realm of the imagination and in the realm of real power. In work, as in leisure, is developed the epic of dreams.

IV

Suggesting images of freedom rather than advice to the free imagination of the subject once again corresponds to a principle that I must stress: Desoille avoids *hypnotic suggestion*. By doing so, he remains faithful to the basic principle of his method. Basically, what is needed is to cause an autonomous sublimation that is a real training of the imagination. Hypnotism, then, must be discarded since it is usually accompanied by amnesia and therefore cannot be *educational*. This is another striking difference between classical psychoanalysis and Desoille's psychosynthesis. Desoille's method is essentially a rational sublimation, conscious and *active*. In putting the subject's soul at rest, Desoille no doubt requires a passive attitude on the subject's part so that he will not reject the very simple initial image that will be suggested to him. But Desoille emphasizes the fact that this passive attention has nothing in common with the state of *hypnotic credulity*, "a state incompatible with the preservation of a healthy mind."

When the spirit has thus been somewhat prepared for freedom, when it has been unburdened of *terrestrial* cares, then its training in imaginary ascension can begin.

Desoille then suggests to his patient that he imagine himself walking up a *gently sloping path*, an unbroken path, with no abysses, no vertigo. Perhaps he could be helped gently here by the rhythm of his gait, feeling the dialectics of the past and future that Crevel pointed out so well in *My Body and I*: "One of my feet is called past, the other future." But I hesitate to add this note, because I have not yet linked the ideas of rhythm and ascent well enough. It does seem, however, that the dream diminishes the jolt we get from imaginary steps. The subject sometimes has no trouble establishing a *gently* rhythmic pace. He actualizes the marvel that every aerial dreamer will recognize, a rhythm incorporated into a continuous movement. It seems that joyous breathing is part of an ascensional destiny.

But whatever the benefits of this potential assimilation of ascensional and rhythmic walking, aspiration toward the heights takes on its true imaginary value only when we leave the earth. Robert Desoille has a whole series of images to suggest to the conscious dreamer, depending on his psychic state. The mountaintops, trees, pictures, and birds are all *inductive images*.[4] By offering them to the subject in the right order, at the right time, and in the right place, Desoille induces a regular movement that curves upward into flight, and then levels off with the body stretched out at full length. Little by little an aerial destiny replaces terrestrial life in the subject's imagination. Then the subject gets the benefit of an imaginary aerial life. The heavy cares are forgotten, or better, replaced by a kind of hopeful state, a kind of ability to "sublimate" everyday life.

Sometimes the directing psychologist realizes that the subject's dynamic imagination will not go beyond the point at which certain images intersect. This is because the images suggested have deviated from the line of images that the subject was living. If this happens, Desoille asks the subject to imagine himself rotating on his own axis. In this *dynamic solitude*, which is an imaginary rotation, the person has an opportunity to rediscover his aerial freedom. He can then continue his imaginary ascent by himself.[5]

Let us add that after every session of imaginary flight—and after every hour of flight—Desoille, who fully understands the psychic realities pertaining to weight, suggests a carefully managed descent that is to bring the dreamer back to earth, without any disturbance, vertigo, trauma, or fall. When he lands, he should be on a level just a bit higher than the one from which he took off, so that, contrary to what Thomas de Quincy noted, for a long time the dreamer retains the impression that he has not "come down" completely, and he will be able to continue to live his ordinary life in the heights of his aerial flight.

A few weeks later there is another session. Little by little the subject is led into a kind of reverie that allows him to experience the psychic well-being of an aerial personality. Desoille's cures will not

---

4. An aerial psyche will find inductive images of flight proliferating. As the poet said: "I knew that there was a wing hidden in the heart of things." Guy Lavaud, *Poétique du ciel* (Paris, 1930).

5. A pirouette is a breaking away from others, a rupture. —In the waltz, the couple is isolated from the others. In Descartes' time, the weather vane was called a "pirouette."

surprise those who know the salutary properties of oneiric flight that they have experienced during sleep.

V

With a view to simplifying our explanation, I have left out one characteristic of the *directed ascensional dream* upon which I would like to focus now.

As a matter of fact, Desoille's method takes into account an *ascension in color*, in the same way that we speak of *hearing in color*. It seems that an azure, or sometimes a golden color, appears on the heights to which we ascend in dreams. Often without any suggestion, the dreamer, as he is living this imaginary ascent, will reach a luminous place where he perceives light in a substantial form. Luminous air and aerial light, in a reversal from substantive to adjective, are joined in one matter. The dreamer has the impression of bathing in a light that carries him. He actualizes the synthesis of lightness and clarity. He is conscious of being freed both from the weight and the darkness of his flesh. In certain dreams, there is a possibility of classifying ascents as being ascents into either azure or golden air. More precisely, there should be a distinction between ascents in gold and blue and those in blue and gold, according to the dream's color of transformation. In all cases the color is volumetric; happiness pervades the whole being.

We should note that the imagination of forms and colors cannot give this impression of volumetric happiness. It can be attained only by joining to forms and colors the kinesthetic sensations which are entirely dependent on material and dynamic imagination.

Of course, if the supervised dreamer does not discover this by himself, then the *guide* can suggest an azure light or a golden light, the light of the dawn or of the heights. Light, then, is an inductive image in the same way as the bird or the hill.

We discover the source of this *imaginary* light—the light that is born within us—in the meditation that frees us from our daily troubles. In place of the *enlightened spirit*, an *enlightening soul* is born. Metaphors collectively yield spiritual realities. Living fully in the realm of images, we can understand passages like those of Jacob Boehme:

> Therefore consider from whence the tincture proceedeth herein the noble life springeth up, that thus becometh sweet from harshness,

bitterness, and fire, and you shall certainly find no other cause of it than the light: But whence cometh the light, that it can shine in a dark body? If you say it cometh from the light of the sun, then what shineth in the night, and enlighteneth your senses and understanding so, that though your eyes be shut, you perceive and know what you do?

This *body* of light does not come from an exterior body. It is born in the very center of our dreaming imagination. This is why there is an *emerging* light, an early morning light where blue, pink, and gold mingle. Nothing garish. Nothing vivid. Here is a beautiful synthesis, round and diaphanous, pale alabaster lighted by the sun! There, within the dreaming soul, we may find the primary meaning of Boehmean ideas: we truly feel light *originating*. At the very least, we will find in it the *origin* of Boehmean idealism. To understand him, we must always consider the subjective origin of metaphors before the objective word.

> And now if we meditate and consider of the original of the four elements, we shall clearly find, see, and feel the original . . . For the original is as well known in man, as in the deep of this world; although it seemeth wonderful to the unenlightened man, that any should (be able to) speak of the original of the air, fire, water, and earth . . . .

As general a word, as abstract a concept as light will take on, through the passionate adherence of the imagination, a concrete, personal meaning, a *subjective origin*.

This universal light engulfs and blurs objects little by little; it makes contours lose their sharp lines. It obliterates the picturesque in favor of the radiant. At the same time, it rids dreams of all those "psychological what-nots" that the poet mentions.[6] Thus it gives a feeling of serene unity to the contemplative person. It is in this light, in these heights, with this consciousness of an aerial being, that the *physics of serenity* exists. It is this serenity which seems to me to characterize Desoille's work.[7] The *elevation* of the soul goes hand in hand with its serenity. There is a dynamic connection between light and height. By contrast, the same poetic connection can be felt by

6. Jules Laforgue, *Lettres à un ami 1880-1886* (Paris, 1941), 152.
7. This physiognomic construction of serenity could be compared to Heinrich Stilling's remarks in *Heimweh* (Warburg, 1800), 507.

meditating upon the inverse dynamic image: "The abyss is troubled darkness."

VI

In the last chapters of his book, Desoille examines telepathic phenomena and mind reading with the greatest care. If two minds could live an imaginary ascent together, they might be sensitive enough to exchange images and ideas. It seems that by placing oneself on the axis of the aerial imagination and by accepting the *linear* filiation of images that produces ascensional motion, a double reason for communion becomes possible: mind reading takes place in a state of calm, and it is done along the path to ecstasy gradually moving toward sublimation. This mind reading, Desoille says,

> is not the result of a will that reaches out, but of a personal representation of thought in the form of a visual image (most frequently), which must be very well formed, on which the transmitter can focus his attention *with no distraction*, all the while experiencing, if possible, a certain affective state.

If the *imagination* is really the power that forms human thoughts, we can easily understand that the transmission of thoughts can only take place between two imaginations that are already *in accord*. Ascensional imagination induces one of the simplest, most orderly, and most durable kinds of harmony. It is very understandable, then, that it fosters "mind reading." To provide proof of this mind reading, Desoille has applied the only suitable approach, given our state of uncertainty with regard to such phenomena: he studied the probability of two different minds settling on the same thought. From his numerous experiments he has learned that probability increases considerably if the two minds are willing to *prepare themselves* for mind reading through training in imaginary ascent (in particular, see Desoilles' comparative tables). Since the thoughts that are guessed have no relationship with ascensional images—they may be merely the choice of one out of eight cards—Desoille was led to believe that inducing imaginary motion is true reality.

Before Desoille, Caslant suggested a similar method designed to foster experiments in telepathy and clairvoyance. In many passages of his book, *A Method of Developing Supra-Normal Faculties*, there is evidence of a thorough knowledge of the imagination's role. It is a real art to maintain the unity of the image and to revive it by making slight adjustments whenever it seems to be stagnating. It is not difficult to foresee that a consciousness so attuned to images will also be sensitive to impressions and experiences that everyday life causes us to neglect.

Since I have done none of these experiments myself, I want to limit myself to these brief comments on this part of Desoille's and Caslant's theories. These experiments go beyond the scope of my subject, which is an inquiry into dreams and poetry.

It is in this last sense that I would like to expand Desoille's method a little. It seems to me that the ascensional dream should make us more sensitive to aerial poetry. I never fail to be amazed at the scorn that is heaped on expansive poetry, or on poetry that is too dreamlike, or a little vague and evasive, and that loses sight of the earth. I think that readers could benefit more from mystical poetry. To do so, they should begin by listing all of its different kinds. Thus Jean Pommier, in a profound work, was able to describe the mysticism of both Baudelaire and Proust. In a psychology as social and worldly as Proust's, Pommier found elements of such unique *spiritual tension* that we can speak of it as a *mysticism of tension.*

But it is also possible to conceive of certain poetic states of mind that reveal a *mysticism of relaxation*. To characterize the ethereal state attained through certain imaginary ascents, I would risk speaking of a *tension of relaxation*, of a kind of relaxation that is attained by vigilant attention to keeping ourselves safe from all that might make us lose that blissful *aerial state*.

VII

A great poet will reveal the grandeur, and therefore the eminent reality of this *aerial state*, this *aerial relaxation*, and this *aerial dynamism*. Let us reread the last five pages of O. V. de L. Milosz's *Letter to Storge*:

> On the fourteenth of December, 1914, around 11 p.m., in the midst of a perfect state of wakefulness, my prayers said, my daily Bible verse contemplated upon, I suddenly felt, without the slightest astonishment, a most unexpected change taking place throughout my whole body. I suddenly noticed that I had the ability—until that

day I did not know I had it—to rise freely into the air. A moment later I found myself on top of a great mountain which was enveloped in indescribably fine, soft, bluish mists. I was spared at that time the difficulty of rising under my own power, for the mountain, pulling its roots up out of the ground, transported me quickly toward unimaginable heights, toward silent misty regions streaked by lightning . . .

Thus, this dynamic imagination is so powerful that it is translated into a *cosmos of elevation*; a world is created by rising. Milosz meditated, in the realm of the imagination, on the physics of relativity. His work illustrates a kind of *general imagination* in the way that one speaks of *general relativity*. For him, there is an *image* whenever there is a transformation in one who is *imagining*. On the level of the experienced image, the relativity between subject and object is complete. Trying to distinguish between them would amount to failing to understand the unity of the imagination; it would be forfeiting the benefits of experienced poetry. When the feeling of elevation reaches its peak, the universe is as peaceful as the mountaintops.

Then a perfect, absolute immobility strikes the sun and the clouds, providing me with an indescribable sensation of extraordinary accomplishment, an uninterrupted, absolute calm, a complete halt to every mental process, and a superhuman actualization of the ultimate Rhythm.

The same imaginary relativity forms an inseparable union between the solar corona and the dreamer's halo. Rising into the clouds, toward the world of luminous repose, Milosz had the impression of a brow that conquered its light and attained the "absolute place of Affirmation." "Above the top of the head, a little toward the back, there then appeared a light like a torch reflected in stagnant water or an old mirror." These dawning gleams soon mingle with the dawn in the sky. There will be in this light a complete relativity between the dreamer and the universe.

Listen, my child, I will never tire of saying it; the whole universe courses through your body, lighting, with its wonderful halo, the head of the omnipresent.

VIII

To conclude, I should like to stress the role played by *induced sublimation* in Desoille's research. Desoille practices psychoanalysis *after* having induced conscious sublimation. Far from considering sublimation to be an illusion that covers or compensates a denied instinct or a deluded passion, he shows that this sublimation is the normal, happy, desirable way to a new life. The personality that he analyzes will, for the most part, be one that is already enlightened by induced sublimation. The second psychoanalysis has as its goal to strengthen the dreamer's consciousness of this sublimation. "It has always seemed to me," he says, "that there is in fact a sure advantage to waiting, whenever it is possible, for the subject's images to be sufficiently sublimated before beginning depth analysis." Isn't it only when the sublimation begins to tug a little at whatever is keeping it in our unconscious that we can hope to break the thread that stops us on the way to reaching an unequivocally liberating sublimation?

> Later, after the subject has produced a sufficiently sublimated image, then we can have him call up the dream or the image that he set aside at first, by asking him to superimpose it upon, or rather to integrate it with, the image associated with his present affective state.

Desoille's method, then, is an integrating of sublimation into normal psychic life. This integration is facilitated by images of aerial imagination. Shelleyan correspondences have a deep psychological meaning in this context. The soul feels at home in them. An initial calm is replaced by a conscious calm, *the calm of the heights*, the calm from which one sees from "on high" the turmoil down below. Then a pride is born in our sense of morality, in our sublimation, and in our life's story. That is when a subject can allow his memories to rise up spontaneously. Memories have a better chance at this stage of being more meaningful, of revealing their causality, since the conscious dreamer is, in a certain sense, at a high point in his life. His past life can be judged from a new point of view, one that we might almost say is absolute: the person can judge himself. The subject often realizes that he has just acquired new knowledge, has just become psychologically lucid.

But psychologists want *understanding*, when they really should be *imagining*. They need to experience the power of the imagination, the supreme power of completed sublimation, willed and adumbrated throughout all of its "correspondences." In the intellectual life, instead of *living* the imagining being, do we not instead suppress its sublimations? People make fun of naive, sparkling images. To make an image sparkle is, for some, to cover it with tinsel. Therefore, when Desoille suggests that a conscious dreamer replace the image of an earthen pot with a crystal or alabaster vase, some—without having done a single experiment—will refuse to believe in the direct benefit that can be derived from this sublimation.

Still, these *improved images* correspond well to positive spiritual activity, since they frequently appear in poems. What damage we would do to a psyche like Shelley's—how we would stunt his growth—if we denied him crystal and alabaster! To induce an image that is so alive in a poet's soul into a soul that is inert—is this not a way of reviving a repressed sublimation and vitalizing hitherto unknown poetic powers that are seeking expression?

If we could organize these very disparate poetic forces, then instead of a kind of telepathy that seeks expression in the riddles of thought, perhaps we could see the work of a telepoetry that would be the divination of images. To set this telepoetry in motion, we must first restore to the imagination its dominant place in a philosophy of repose. In other words, we must put to rest active, utilitarian, descriptive. We must understand that repose is a *state of dream* which Makhali Phal very rightly designates as a basic condition of the psyche.[8] A classification according to material and dynamic imagination would allow dream states to be more uniformly categorized. If we start from the dream states that are defined by water, earth, air, or fire, we might hope to arrive at a *telepoetry* more dependable than poems of multiple authorship built on a formative image. The imagination would be, as it were, animated in its *production* of images. An imaginative *super-ego* would develop along the lines of certain images. Instead of feeling that a *super-ego* is at work forcing us to compose, we would find one that invites us to do so. But the problem of a poem of multiple authorship has never attracted the attention that it deserves. The excellent article by Gabriel Audisio and Camille

8. Makhali Phal, *Narayana ou celui qui se meut sur les eaux* (Paris, 1942), passim.

Schuwe has not been discussed; the surrealists' efforts in this area are scarcely better known.[9] The same problem arises, moreover, between the poet and his reader. The reading of a poem should be a telepoetic activity. Hugo von Hofmannsthal has mentioned the "positive productivity" that should connect the reader to the literary work.

> When positive productivity awakens mysteriously, on a day that is not like other days, with a wind and sun that are not like the wind and sun to which we are accustomed, the role forces the actor to act; he does not do it of his own free will, he obeys a command: "Today you will read me and I shall live through you."

This command can already be felt in a *productive image*. The reader will feel that he has to *play* with this felicitous image and to *experience* it through the same kind of *active imagination* that gave it life. Such images are the schemata of inductive and induced life. The writer of imaginative genius thus becomes a *positive* super-ego for the reader. The *super-ego* of aesthetic imagination, if it is taken on while experiencing the poems, is a guiding force of which utilitarian and rationalistic education is all too prone to deprive us. But alas! the poetic super-ego is influenced by literary criticism. That is why it seems to be an oppressor. Isn't it obvious that literary criticism has made an almost unconditional treaty with "realism," and that it takes umbrage at the slightest attempt at idealization? Far from supporting sublimation, the critic—the Terror of Tarbes—thwarts it, as Jean Paulhan has so well demonstrated. Beyond the suppression of the ideal, a suppression that is thought to be based on a reality—but which is only a reality of repression, which is also considered to be founded on reason, which is only a systematizing of repression—it is absolutely essential to rediscover the *positive* poetic super-ego which summons a soul to its poetic destiny, to its aerial destiny—that which is shared by real poets: the Rilkes, the Poes, the Baudelaires, the Shelleys, and the Nietzsches.

9. Gabriel Audisio and Camille Schuwer, *La Revue Nouvelle* (March, 1931), 34.

5

Nietzsche and the Ascensional Psyche

> . . . The place where we are now,
> Malchut, is the milieu of Height.
> O. V. DE L. MILOSZ
> *Psaume du roi de beauté*

I

TO APPROACH A THINKER like Nietzsche through a study of the imagination might seem to indicate a failure of understanding the profound meaning of his doctrine. In fact, the Nietzschean transmutation of ethical values involves the whole being. There is a very precise correlation between it and a transformation of vital energy. To study such a transmutation by way of a reflection on the *dynamism of the imaginary* is to mistake the echo for the voice, the copy for the original. However, an in-depth examination of expression in Nietzsche's poetics has little by little convinced me that the images that give such distinctive energy to Nietzsche's style have their own destiny. I have even recognized that certain images evolved, untouched, at an amazing speed. I have found examples, I believe—but perhaps I am overly confident about my theory on the primordial power of the dynamic imagination—where it is this rapidity of the image that induces thought.

Thus, by limiting myself almost exclusively to a study of his *Poetry* and the lyrical *Thus Spoke Zarathustra*, I believe that I have been able to prove that, in the case of Nietzsche, the poet partly explains the thinker, and that Nietzsche is the prototype of the *vertical poet*, the *poet of the summits*, the *ascensional poet*. More precisely—for a genius is always in a class by himself—I will show that Nietzsche represents a special type, one of the clearest, of dynamic imagination. Especially by comparing him to Shelley, we shall see that flights toward the summits can offer very different destinies. Two poets like Shelley and Nietzsche, both keeping rigorously to an aerial dynamic, represent —as I will demonstrate—two opposing types.

First let me justify the aerial stamp that I attribute to Nietzsche's imagination. To do this, before going on to demonstrate my thesis, which will cast light on the amazing life and power of aerial images in Nietzsche's poetry, let me begin by showing that earth, water, and fire are secondary in Nietzsche's poetics.

II

Nietzsche is not a poet of *earth*. Humus, loam, cleared and ploughed fields do not provide him with images. The metal, minerals, and gems that a "terrestrial" loves for his *inner* riches do not provide him with *personal reveries*. Stone and rock often appear in his works, but only as a symbol of hardness. They retain nothing of that slow life, the slowest of all lives—life defined by its slowness—which the revery of a *lapidary* attributes to them. Rock does not live for him like a horrible gum that has emerged from the Earth's bowel.

Soft earth disgusts him. How he scorns things that are "spongy, cavernous, compressed." Some will object that in this example I am taking as *things* that which in psychological reality corresponds to *ideas*; they will think this a good opportunity to prove right from the beginning how inane it is to study metaphors out of context. And still, the adjective *spongy* is so revealing an image of the depths of the imagination that it alone is enough to allow a diagnosis of material imaginations. It is one of the most reliable touchstones; only an impassioned lover of the earth, only a terrestrial who is also somewhat under the influence of water, can avoid the *automatically pejorative* nature of metaphorical *sponginess*.

Moreover, Nietzsche is not a poet "of matter." He is a poet of action, and I intend to consider him as an illustration of dynamic rather than material imagination. Earth, in its mass and depths, will provide him primarily with themes of action. This is why many references to a *subterranean life* can be found in Nietzsche's work. But this subterranean life is subterranean *action*. It is not a dream-like exploration, or a wondrous voyage, as it is in Novalis' imagination. It is an active life, uniquely active; it is a life of great courage and lengthy preparation. It is the symbol of an aggressive and vigilant patience. Even in subterranean work, Nietzsche knows where he is going. He would not submit to the passivity of an initiation; he works directly against the earth. In many dreams, the anxious dreamer wanders around labyrinths. Innumerable examples of such a trial by labyrinth can be found in Stilling's *Heimweh.* It will have its place among the *four tests of elemental initiation.* It is a good example of the four initiations (by fire, water, earth, and wind) that I want to add to the various *tetravalences of material imagination* which I have already discussed in my previous studies.[1] But for Nietzsche there is no initiation; he is always primarily the *initiator,* the absolute initiator, the one whom no one has ever initiated. Underground, his labyrinth is straight. It is a hidden power that makes its own way, that creates its own path. There is nothing winding or blind about this path. The mole is an animal that Nietzsche scorns doubly. Even when he works underground, Nietzsche knows "the formula of [his] my happiness: a Yes, a No, a straight line, a *goal.*"[2]

* * *

Nietzsche is not a *water* poet. There are, of course, water images. No poet can do without liquid metaphors. But, with Nietzsche, these metaphors are ephemeral. They do not determine *material reveries.* Dynamically, it is the same with water which too easily becomes servile. It cannot be a true obstacle or a true adversary for a Nietzschean fighter. The *Xerxes complex,* which is scarcely noticeable in a poet as cosmic as Nietzsche, is quickly overcome.

> O ye waves,
> Wondrous waves, are ye wroth with me?
> Do ye raise me your crests in wrath?
> With my rudder I smite
> Your folly full square.[3]

How curt and unemotional we find "this blow with the rudder" dealt to baser passions, to uncontrolled emotions, to the vain spray! A simple smack of the ruler on mischievous or disobedient hands sets the schoolboy back on the right path. In the same way the master of

---

1. Heinrich Stilling, *Heimweh* (Warburg, 1800), passim.
2. Nietzsche, *Twilight of the Idols,* in *The Portable Nietzsche,* trans. and ed. Walter Kaufmann (New York, 1954), 473.
3. *Fragments of Dionysus-Dithyrambs,* #75, trans. Paul V. Cohn in *The Complete Works of Friedrich Nietzsche,* ed. Dr. Oscar Levy (New York, 1964), XVII:202

himself and of the world, sure of his destiny, immediately says to the mischievous and turbulent waves:

> This bark ye yourself
> To immortal life will carry along

that is, in the sky, but not with the soft inflection of dreamers who are cradled and who never notice when they have left the water for the air. Here, order and motion *take off* like arrows.

On those rare days when we can relax, there will appear great images of cosmic maternity. These images will be the intermediaries of the dynamic images that I will need to characterize. Water then will be a quiet movement, a beneficial milk to feed the universe. Nietzsche will call the "cows of the sky" to get from them the nourishing milk that will give the Earth new life. Thus in the poem "On the Poverty of the Richest," a need for gentleness, darkness, and water enters in.

> Ten years passed by—
> Not a drop reached me,
> No damp wind, no dew of love
> —A *rainless* land. . .
> . . . .
> Once I bade the clouds
> Depart from my mountains—
>
> . . . .
> Today I entice them to come:
> Make darkness around me with your udders!
> —I want to milk you,
> You cows of the heights!
> Milk-warm wisdom, sweet dew of love,
> I flow over the land.

This relaxation, this feminine reward—after ten years of cold and pure solitude—serves as an antithesis to the drama of tension. It is not the primary *dynamic reverie*. When we have seen more clearly that Nietzsche's cosmos is a *cosmos of the heights*, then we will also understand that this soothing water is the Sky. In Nietzsche, as in early Mythology, Poseidon is a sky god. There are very few "springs" in the Nietzschean universe.

Water's substance never gets beyond this ability to relax. Specifically, it never represents a temptation to death and dissolution. How clearly Nietzsche has refused the *Cosmos of melancholy!* the cosmos that is blurred by clouds and rain! "—the evil routine of drifting clouds, of moist melancholy, of overcast skies, of stolen suns, of howling autumn winds—"

the evil routine of our own howling and cries of distress. . . .[4]

How can we fail to recognize what has been evoked and stigmatized here? It is our irascible melancholy, with its moist lower lip stuck out, as it passively scorns, without making any effort to struggle against it, the whole world of things that have lost their will to resist. Nietzsche has written against European melancholy: "for near them the air was equally good, bright, and oriental; never was I farther away from cloudy, moist, melancholy old Europe."

In many passages we will notice a scorn for *stagnant waters*. To a *swamp creature*, for example, Nietzsche says: "Does not putrid, spumy swamp-blood flow through your own veins. . . ?"

It is possible, no doubt, to see in all this only clichés without wondering why these ideas need to be given this concrete form, or why these particular forms were chosen. In other words, we can refuse to experience material imagination in the curious uniformity of our images. In so doing, we miss the tonality of the adjectives. Let me demonstrate. There are, in Old Europe, regions that are cloudless, dry, and filled with joy. Conversely, clouds pass over the Oriental desert, but the thinker meditating on an anti-European wisdom, an Oriental wisdom, or more precisely, the wisdom of the new Orient, knows with the material imagination's energetic partiality that these *desert clouds*, since they exist in a clear and favored air, *are not cloudy*. In the same way, the water that falls on Nietzschean summits is not *aquatic*; the milk taken from the sky cows is not *lactic*, it is not *milky*; these cows are Bacchic. Here we have a very apt example for elucidating my general theses. What I would like to show, in general, is that we must determine the exact weight of every adjective if we wish to understand the metaphoric life of language. We must also guard against thinking that the imagination of an adjective describing

4. "Among Daughters of the Wilderness," *Thus Spoke Zarathustra*, in *The Portable Nietzsche*, 416.

appearance automatically carries with it the imagination of the substantive. To go from an *impression of humidity* to *imaginary water*, we need the help of *material imagination*. There are hundreds of examples proving that the Nietzschean imagination is not attracted in a substantial way to water adjectives. It is not impregnated with a nourishing milk. It scorns everyone "whose soul is made of whey."

The point of view of both dynamic and material imagination also allows us to deny the imagination of water any prerogatives. To see this, we need only meditate on the objections that Nietzsche made to Wagnerian music. He reproaches Wagnerian music because "he overthrew the physiological presupposition of . . . music." Instead of *walking* and *dancing*—Nietzschean ways of doing—we are invited to swim, to soar . . . with Wagner's "infinite melody":

> One walks into the sea, gradually loses one's secure footing, and finally surrenders oneself to the elements without reservation: one must *swim*. In older music, what one had to do in the dainty, or solemn, or fiery back and forth, quicker and slower, was something quite different, namely, to *dance*.

The *walker*, the man who seeks to ascend, also says: my foot "demands of music first of all those delights which are found in *good* walking, striding, dancing." None of that is found in the joy provided by water, in the mystique of fluid imagination. Nietzsche's material imagination is reserved for giving *substance* to adjectives of air and cold.

On this particular point, we also arrive at a polemical conclusion that I would like to formulate in passing. I will put the *burden of proof* on those who object that I give too much importance to material and dynamic imagination and ask them why, when he wants to compare two *kinds of music*, a philosopher would end up comparing *swimming* and *walking*—the total abandonment in the infinity of the sea to a dancer's pirouette. I have no difficulty with this: what determines it is the dialectic of what flows and what springs forth, the dialectic of *infinite* water and a lively, playful breathing. For Nietzsche, music that gives us aerial life—a special aerial life made up of clear morning air—is incomparably superior to music that accepts metaphors of the floods and waves of the infinite sea.

* * *

It is a more delicate task to show that Nietzsche is not a *fire poet*. For a poet with genius calls on metaphors belonging to all of the elements. Metaphors of fire, moreover, are the natural flowers of language. Gentleness and violence in words find a fire that expresses them. All impassioned eloquence is an inflamed eloquence. A little *fire* is always required for the metaphors of other elements to be lively and clear. Multi-colored poetry is a flame that takes on the colors of the earth's minerals. It would be easy, therefore, to bring together many documents on *Nietzschean fire*. But if we look a little more closely, we will see that this *fire* is not really substantial, that it is not the *substance* that impregnates and tonalizes Nietzsche's material imagination.

In fact, in Nietzsche's images, fire is less a substance than a force. It has a role to play in a very specialized *dynamic imagination* which I have undertaken to define carefully.

One of the best proofs of the essentially dynamic nature of Nietzschean fire is that it is, for the most part, *instantaneous*. Nietzsche's fire is a *flash of lightning*. *It is, therefore, a projection of Anger*, of a divine and joyous anger. Anger, a pure act! Resentment is a *matter* that builds up. Anger is an *act* that can be differentiated. Resentment is foreign to what is Nietzschean. On the contrary, how can an act be decisive if it is not incisive, that is, enlivened by a little anger, the anger of a pointing finger. In cases where this energy is faced with a terrible task, Nietzschean anger is so sudden that what is Nietzschean is not threatening. The being from whom the lightning will spring forth can quietly hide his thoughts:

> He who with lightning-flash would touch
> Must long remain in a cloud!

Lightning and light are ready arms, *cold steel*:

> A lightning-flash became my wisdom:
> With sword of adamant it clove me every darkness!

Instead of a Shelleyan light that bathes and penetrates a pure soul with its gentle substance, Nietzschean light is an arrow, a sword. It inflicts a cold wound.

From another point of view, when fire can be possessed, like a matter, with simple pleasure, then it is *a poor man's benefice*, an object of scorn to the superman. "Turn out your light, will-o'-the-wisp!" That is what "the great, eternal Amazon, never feminine or soft as a dove," says to anyone touched by inner warmth.

Even intuitions that might be considered *digestible* tend, in Nietzsche's writings, to give *energy* rather than *substance*:

> They are cold, these men of learning!
> Would that a lightning-flash might strike their food,
> And their mouths could learn to eat fire!

This alimentary lightning is, for Nietzsche, a nerve-soothing food. It does not correspond to a fire nourished while food is being slowly and pleasantly digested. In the great duality of imaginary digestion and respiration, we must search for Nietzsche's poetic valorizations in his poetry of joyful and vital breath.

A quatrain entitled "Ice" is part of a chapter in "Joke, Cunning, and Revenge: Prelude in German Rhymes" to *The Gay Science*:

> Yes, at times I do make ice,
> For it helps us to digest.
> If you had much to digest,
> You would surely love my ice!

With this in mind we can understand the invective against the gods of fire: "I do not pray . . . to the potbellied fire idol."

> Even a little chattering of the teeth rather than adoring idols
> —thus my nature dictates. And I have a special grudge against all
> fire idols that are in heat, steaming and musty.

But the nature of *Nietzschean fire*, which is both dynamic and transitory, will no doubt come out even more clearly if we recognize this strange paradox: *Nietzschean fire desires coldness*. This is an *imaginary* value that is to be transmuted into a greater value. The *imaginary*, too—the imaginary above all—gets life from the transmutation of values. In "The Beacon" we read these revealing lines:

> This flame with gray-white belly
> —into cold distances it shoots out its desire,
> it stretches its neck into ever purer heights—
> a snake reared up in impatience . . .

Fire is a cold-blooded animal. Fire is neither the snake's red tongue nor its steel head. Coldness and height are the homeland of fire.

For Nietzsche, even honey, which for so many dreamers is a buried fire, a warm and balsamic substance, is icy: "Bring me honey, ice-cold honey from the golden comb." In the same way, Zarathustra asks in "The Honey Sacrifice" for "yellow, white, good, ice-fresh, golden comb honey." Again in "The Voluntary Beggar": "You will also find new honey in my cave, ice-fresh golden-comb honey: eat that!" For the material imagination, golden honey, the golden head of grain and golden bread are all bits of sun, of fire's matter. In Nietzsche's work, honey is a *cold fire*, a delicate union that will surprise only logicians, who are unaware of the syntheses of dreams.

The same synthesis of warmth and coldness is discernible in the images of the *cold sun*, of a brilliant, cold sun. In the beautiful "Night Song" in *Zarathustra*, we read: "The suns fly like a storm in their orbits: that is their motion. They follow their inexorable will: that is their coldness." To see here only the translation into images of a calm arrogance, or a pride that nothing can turn from its path, is to fail to understand the strange will not to participate in blessings given with a prodigal hand. The sun gives its warmth *coldly*. For dynamic imagination, the way that something is given, the energy involved in giving, is *worth* more than what is given.

A fire so violently drawn toward its opposite has more dynamic characteristics than it does substantial wealth. With Nietzsche, as soon as there is *fire*, there is *tension* and *action*; fire, here, is not the well-being that comes from warmth, as it is in Novalis. Fire is just a *flash upward*. Fire is the ardent will to rejoin the pure, cold air of the heights. It is a factor in the transmutation of imaginary values in favor of those belonging to the imagination of air and cold. We will better understand these dialectics of imaginary elements when we have demonstrated that *cold* is one of the dominant qualities of *Nietzschean air*. Let us, then, move to the positive part of this demonstration and prove that *air* is the true substance for Nietzsche's material imagination.

III

Nietzsche describes himself as an *aerial being*:

> Storm clouds—why should you be a concern
> for us, the free, the aerial, the joyous spirits?

For Nietzsche, in fact, air is the very substance of our freedom, the substance of superhuman joy. Air is a kind of matter that has been mastered, just as Nietzschean joy is human joy that has been mastered. *Terrestrial* joy is richness and weight—*aquatic* joy is softness and repose—*igneous* joy is love and desire—*aerial* joy is freedom.

Nietzschean air, then, is a strange substance: it is substance with no substantial qualities. It can thus characterize being as equal to a philosophy of absolute becoming. In the realm of the imagination, air frees us from substantial, inner, digestive reveries. It frees us from our attachment to matter. Thus it is the matter of our freedom. For Nietzsche, air brings *nothing*. It gives *nothing*. It is the immense glory of a Nothing. But is not *giving nothing* the greatest of gifts? The great giver with the empty hands takes away our desire to hold out our hand. He gets us used to receiving nothing so that we can take everything. "Is it not up to the giver," says Nietzsche, "to thank the one who is willing to take?" Later we will see in more detail how the *material* imagination of air gives way, in Nietzsche's work, to a *dynamic* imagination of air. But we must understand right away that air is the homeland of the *predator*. Air is that *infinite substance* that is crossed in a flash with a sense of offensive and triumphant freedom like a bolt of lightning, an eagle, an arrow, or an imperious, sovereign glance. In air, we bring our victim out into broad daylight. We do not hide.

Before developing these aspects of dynamism, though, let me demonstrate the particular material characteristics of *Nietzschean air*. What are, usually, for most material imaginations, the most strongly *substantivized* qualities of air? They are *odors*. For some material imaginations, the primary function of air is to provide a *medium* for odors. An odor has, in the air, an infinity. For someone like Shelley, the air is an immense flower, the floral essence of the whole earth. The purity of air is often dreamed of as if it were filled with the fragrance of balsam and incense. Its warmth is dreamed as if it were a resinous pollen, or a warm, sugared honey. Nietzsche dreams only of the tonicity of air: its coldness and its emptiness.

For a true Nietzschean, the nose must give the happy *certitude* of an odorless air. The nose must bear witness to the immense joy, the blessed awareness, of experiencing nothing. It is the guarantee of the total absence of odors. The *sense of smell*, in which Nietzsche took such pride, is not a power allowing for *attraction*. It is given to the superman so that he can *withdraw* at the slightest suggestion of impurity. A Nietzschean cannot take pleasure in any odor. Baudelaire, the Countess of Noailles—both terrestrials, which, of course, is another sign of power—dream and meditate on fragrances. Perfumes then have infinite resonances. They bind memories to desires, an enormous past to an immense and unformulated future. In Nietzsche, we read:

> Drinking this most beautiful air,
> My nostrils distended like cups,
> Without future, without reminiscences . . .[5]

Pure air is awareness of the free moment, the moment that opens up a future. Nothing more. Odors are perceptible bonds. There is a continuity in their very bodies. There are no discontinuous odors. Pure air, on the contrary, is an impression of youth and newness: "but with his nostrils he drew in the air slowly and questioningly, as one tastes the new foreign air in a new country." I would venture to say: a new void and a new freedom, for there is nothing exotic, heady, or intoxicating in this new air. The atmosphere is made of pure, dry, cold, and empty air.

> I sit here, sniffing the best air,
> Verily, paradise air,
> Bright, light air, golden-striped,
> As good air as ever
> Fell down from the moon— . . . [6]

The Nietzschean imagination abandons odors in proportion to its detachment from the past. Everyone who clings to the past dreams of indestructible odors. Foreseeing is the opposite of feeling. In a somewhat brutal but very striking dialectic, Rudolf Kassner has set forth this antithetical nature of sight and smell:

> When we take away, cut off, or strike down the part of the past that projects into the future, . . . our entire imagination, which is based on time or is wrapped up in it, becomes memory. That is, it is cast off to be shifted into memory. Everything that we see, then, is

5. Ibid., 419.
6. Ibid.

necessarily transformed into an odor, since there is no future
... but as soon as we once again fit the memory that we have just
cut off into time, the odor will become sight.

If air symbolizes a moment of repose and relaxation, it also makes
us aware of future action, an action that frees us from an amassed
will. Thus, in the simple joy of breathing pure air, we find a promise
of power:

> the air fills with promises
> I feel the breath of unknown lips pass over me
> —the great freshness is coming.

What better way of expressing that these unknown lips are not
promises of intoxication than by this sudden freshness?

With this freshness—this great freshness to come—a Nietzschean
value is introduced which, in this perceptible form, designates a
profound reality. It is one type of those *direct and real* metaphors that
constitute the immediate and elementary axioms of a doctrine of the
imagination. Basically for Nietzsche, this *freshness* is the true *tonic*
quality of air, the one that makes breathing a joy, the one that
dynamizes motionless air—a true dynamization in depth, which is the
very life of dynamic imagination. This *freshness* must not be taken for
a mediocre or a nondescript quality. It corresponds to one of the
greatest principles of Nietzschean cosmology: *cold*, the cold of the
heights and glaciers and uncontrollable winds.

Let us follow the path that leads to the hyperborean regions:

> Beyond the north, the ice and today
> Beyond death,
> to one side:
> *our* life, *our* happiness
> Neither over land,
> nor over water,
> will you find the path
> that leads to hyperborean realms.

Neither by land nor water, but in the air, the journey to the highest
and coldest of solitary places.

It is at the *mouth* of the cave—the strange cave that is at the *summit*
of the mountain, which, I believe, takes away its terrestrial, cavern-

ous nature—that Zarathustra will give his lessons on the tonicity of cold.

> You alone make the air around you strong and clear. Have I ever found such good air anywhere on earth as here in your cave? Many countries have I seen; my nose has learned to test and estimate many kinds of air: but in your cave my nostrils are tasting their greatest pleasure.

As early as "Das Wort" we hear the call of the "cold nature of the mountains, barely warmed by the Autumn sun and devoid of love."

It is in this mountain climate that we can truly gain access to this curious birth. From out of the cold, life rises, a cold life:

> . . . Then the moon and the stars rise
> and the wind and the frost.

Thanks to the cold, air acquires *offensive qualities*; it takes on that "joyous malice" that awakens the will to power, a will to react coldly, in the ultimate freedom of coldness, with a cold will.

Attacked by a *brisk* air, man attains "a higher body" (*ein höheren Leib*). This does not, of course, refer to the *astral body* of the magi and the mystics, but very specifically to a living body that *knows how* to grow by breathing in tonic air, a body that *knows how* to choose the air of the heights, an air that is refined, brisk, and subtle (*dünn und rein*).

In this cold air of the heights, we will find another Nietzschean value: silence. Is this winter sky with its silence—this winter sky, which "often tacitly hides even its sun"—is it not the opposite of the Shelleyan sky, which is so musical that it might be called music transformed into substance? Is it from the winter sky, Nietzsche wonders, that he learned "the long bright silence"? When we read in "The Return Home," "Oh, how this silence draws deep breaths of clean air!" how can we refuse to acknowledge the substantial synthesis of air, cold, and silence? Through air and cold, it is the silence that is breathed, it is the silence that is an *integral* part of our very being. And this integration of silence is very different from the integration of silence in Rilke's ever-painful poetry. It has, in Nietzsche, a brusqueness that breaks initial anxieties. Anyone who refuses to accept the suggestions of material imagination and fails to understand that for an active material imagination *silent air* is silence achieved in a primary element, diminishes the *tonality* of the images and transposes the experiences of concrete imagination into the abstract. How, then, could he receive the salutary organic influence to be derived from a reading of Nietzsche? Nietzsche has warned his readers in his Preface to *Ecce Homo*:

> Those who can breathe the air of my writings know that it is an air of the heights, a *strong* air. One must be made for it. Otherwise there is no small danger that one may catch cold in it. The ice is near, the solitude tremendous—but how calmly all things lie in the night! How freely one breathes! How much one feels *beneath* oneself!

Cold, silence, height—three roots for a single substance. To cut one of the roots would be to destroy Nietzschean life. For example, a cold silence needs to be on the heights; lacking this third root, silence becomes withdrawn, unfriendly, terrestrial. It is a silence that does not *breathe*, that does not enter the lungs like the air of the heights. In the same way, a howling wind for Nietzsche is just a beast to be tamed, one that must be *silenced*. The cold wind of the heights is a *dynamic being*; it neither howls nor whispers; it keeps silent. Finally, a warm air, which might claim to teach us silence, might lack the necessary briskness. Silence needs the biting quality of cold. It is clear that the triple connection is upset when any one of the attributes is removed. But these negative proofs are artificial; anyone who is willing to live in Nietzschean air will have innumerable positive proofs of the *correspondences* that I am pointing out. This correspondence will point up, by contrast, the triple correspondence between gentleness, music, and light by which the Shelleyan imagination breathes. As I have said several times, the different types of material imagination, however much they may be a determining factor, never mask the individual character of a genius. Shelley and Nietzsche are two geniuses who have adored opposite gods in the same aerial land.

IV

Having given so much time in this book to the *dream of flight*—aerial sleep—I will now take a closer look at a passage from Nietzsche that clearly demonstrates a *winged oneirism*. This hymn to nocturnal peace and to the lightness of aerial sleep will serve as an introduction to an examination of the lively early morning hours and invigorating awakenings of Nietzsche's vertical life.

How could we fail, in fact, to suppose from the first paragraph of "The Three Evil Things" that a *dream of flight* underlies it? "In my dream, in my last morning-dream, I stood today on a promontory—beyond the world; I held a pair of scales, and *weighed* the world." A reader who, because he has been corrupted by intellectualism puts abstract thought before metaphor, one who believes that writing is the search for images to illustrate thought, will certainly object that this *weighing* of the world—and he will probably express it as this ponderous evaluation of the world—is only a metaphor for expressing a value, for evaluating an *ethical world*. How interesting it would be, though, to study this shift from the ethical to the physical world. Every philosopher of ethics must at least consider the problem of *verbal expression* of ethical facts. A thesis like mine, concerning the imagination as a fundamental psychic value, poses the same problem in reverse. It asks how images of elevation prepare the dynamics of ethical life. In my view, Nietzsche's poetry plays this role of precursor; it prepares the way for his ethics. Rather than delve too deeply into polemics, I should like to remain in the realm of a study of the imaginary and ask my opponents a polemical question on the psychological plane: Why, in a dream that comes in the morning, should we picture ourselves on top of a promontory? Why, instead of describing the panorama of a world that we command in this way, should we *weigh* it? Should we not find it amazing that a dreamer should become involved so easily in a *weigher's dream*? But let us read a little further: "weighed by a good weigher, attainable by *strong pinions* . . . thus did my dream find the world." Without using the principles of ascensional psychology, who can explain how the dream that *weighs* the world is suddenly one whose strong wings will overcome *weight*? The *weigher* of the world suddenly and immediately has winged lightness.

How could we fail to see that the real filiation of images goes in the opposite direction: it is because the dreamer has winged lightness that he can *weigh* the world. Flying, he asks all the creatures of the earth: Why are you not flying? What is this weight that prevents your flying with me? Who is making you remain motionless on the earth? Step on my scale and I will tell you if you can be my companion and disciple. I will tell you not your weight, but your aerial future. The *weigher* is the master of lightness. A *heavy* weigher is a contradiction in terms for Nietzsche. To *evaluate* superhuman powers, it is necessary to be aerial, light, and capable of ascending. *Fly* first, then there will be time to come to know the earth! Then we can accept less obvious metaphors, whose effect has more continuity. They are the ones that really stir the thinker's imagination. As soon as we give dynamic imagination its rightful place as primordial, then these lines from Nietzsche are perfectly clear: "My dream, a bold sailor, half-ship, half-hurricane, silent as the butterfly, impatient as the falcon: how had it the patience and leisure today for world-weighing!" Surely the dynamic engram of all of these images is the *dream of flight*, the weightless life of aerial sleep. It is the joyous consciousness of winged lightness.

In the chapter entitled "On the Spirit of Gravity," Nietzsche says, "He who will one day teach men to fly will have moved all boundary stones; the boundary stones themselves will fly up into the air before him, and he will rebaptize the earth—'the light one.'" George Meredith also says: "Barriers are for those who cannot fly."

For the *material imagination*, flight is not a technique to be discovered, it is a matter to be transmuted; it is the fundamental basis for a transmutation of all values. Our *terrestrial* being must become *aerial*. Then it will make the whole earth *light*. Our own earth, within us, will be "the light one."

The text that follows is enriched with great thoughts; it teaches man to love himself, to become truly alive through his love for himself. Given the wealth of Nietzschean thoughts and the simplicity of my remarks, a facile criticism will be possible: I will be told once again, that I have stopped being a philosopher to become a mere collector of literary images. But I will defend myself by repeating my thesis: the literary image has its own life; it *moves as an autonomous phenomenon above profound thought.* It is this autonomy that I have set out to establish. Nietzsche is a striking example, because he gives evidence of a double life: that of a great poet and of a great thinker. Nietzschean images have that dual coherence which animates—individually—poetry and thought. These Nietzschean images are proofs of the material and dynamic coherence that is given by a well-defined material and dynamic imagination.

But *verticality* requires a long apprenticeship: "he who would learn to fly one day must first learn to stand and walk and run and climb and dance: one cannot fly into flying." For some, the *dream of flight* is a Platonic reminiscence of a former sleep and a former lightness. It will be rediscovered only in patient, infinite dreams. We must go on, then, collecting the most diverse pieces of evidence of ascensional psychology in Nietzsche's work.

V

We will discover first that in Nietzsche's philosophy there are numerous examples of a psychoanalysis of heaviness that has the same appearance as a psychoanalysis carried out according to Desoille's methods. For example, let us take this poem:

> Throw thy pain in the depths,
> Man, forget! Man, forget!
> Divine is the art of forgetting!
> Wouldst fly?
> Wouldst feel at home in the heights?
> Throw thy heaviest load in the sea!
> Here is the sea, hurl *thyself* in the sea!
> Divine is the art of forgetting!

There is no question here, as would be the case for a sea-oriented psyche, of plunging into the sea in order to be regenerated by the waters. It is a question of casting away all our *weight*, our regrets, our remorse, our resentment, everything in us that looks back to the past —we must throw *our whole heavy being* into the sea so that it can disappear forever. In this way we will annihilate our weighty *double*, that part of us which is *earth*, that which is our *hidden inner past*. Then our aerial *double* will shine forth. Then we will rise up again, *free* as the air, out of the dungeon of our own secrets. Suddenly, we will be honest with ourselves.

Need I repeat that such a poem can be read in two different ways: first as though it were an abstract text, like a text on ethics whose author feels obliged to use concrete images to make himself clear— and then, following my present method, as a direct, concrete poem that was initially formed by the material and dynamic imagination and that creates new ethical values by virtue of enthusiasm for a new poetry? Whichever choice the reader makes, he must still recognize that the *aestheticization of ethics* is not something superficial. It is not a metaphor that can be removed without risk. A thesis like mine considers this aestheticization to be a profound and urgent need. It is the imagination in this case that raises being to a higher level. The most efficacious imagination, *ethical imagination*, is inseparable from the renewal of fundamental images.

It seems to me that Nietzsche, by underscoring the word *thyself*, was trying to attain the metaphor's *absolute*, to cast aside all the minor metaphors that a less accomplished poet might have accumulated, and to invoke the metaphor's absurdity in order to live its absolute reality: cast yourself *entirely* into the depths in order to be able to rise up *entirely* toward the summits, accomplishing *uno actu* liberation and the conquest of the superhuman being. Beyond that contradiction in terms—high and low—the imagination at this point works on an analysis of symbols that are perfectly matched: cast *yourself* into the sea, not to find death in oblivion, but to consign to death everything within you that could not forget, this whole creature of flesh and earth, all those ashes of knowledge, that whole mass of results, that whole avaricious harvest that makes up a human being. Then the *decisive inversion* will take place, identifying you as superhuman. You will be aerial, you will surge vertically toward the free heavens.

> Whatever was difficult
> Sank into blue forgetfulness—

Similarly, in a verse from "On Reading and Writing" in *Zarathustra*, when he has conquered the demon of weight, Nietzsche cries out: "now I see myself beneath myself," "*Jetzt bin ich leicht, jetzt fliege ich, jetzt sehe ich mich unter mir, jetzt tanzt ein Gott durch mich.*" I have not translated these lines because I could find no word in French to render the immediacy of the energy and joy in the word "*jetzt.*" What misfortune has caused the French language to be deprived of these words that are indispensable for a psychology of the moment? How can we express the decisive moment of a revolution of being, how can we break the sloth of continuity with words like *maintenant, dès à présent*, and *dorénavant?* The cultivation of the will requires monosyllables. The energy of a language is often as untranslatable as its poetry. Dynamic imagination is first prompted by language.

This *duality of the vertical personality,* especially its *immediate, decisive nature,* cannot be overemphasized. Because of this duality, we live in the air, by the air, for the air. Because of its immediacy, we understand that the transmutation of the being is not a smooth, gradual emanation, but that it is the product of pure will, that is, of instantaneous will. Here dynamic imagination asserts itself over material imagination; cast yourself up, free as the air, and you will become the matter of freedom.

Following this act of the heroic imagination there comes, as though it were a reward, the awareness of being above a universe, above everything. Such a feeling gave rise to this wonderful stanza: "to stand over every single thing as its own heaven, as its round roof, its azure bell, and eternal security." How could this Platonic will, which has the same sense as Platonic love, be better expressed? This will entrusts being to what the being *wants,* to what constitutes the being's future, after erasing all beings from the past, all beings of reminiscence, all sensual desires which feed on a Schopenhauerean will, an animal will.

This tranquillity is certain because it has been *conquered.* We can experience this conquered tranquillity in the following verses:

> Still! Still! . . . As a delicate wind dances unseen on an inlaid sea, light, feather-light, thus sleep dances on me. My eyes he does not close, my soul he leaves awake. Light he is, verily, feather-light.

VI

The human being, alas, experiences the return of confusion and weight. As soon as Nietzschean sleep is materialized by another element, the soul is more uneasy and listless. While so many other dreamers confide their souls with a quiet submission to still water, and so many others sleep gently in the water of dreams, we will feel that pain has returned, penetrating the heroically won happiness in this wonderful Nietzschean passage on the sleep of the sea—a sea heavy with desire and salt, heavy with fire and earth:

> Everything is still asleep now, he said; even the sea is asleep. Drunk with sleep and strange it looks at me. But its breath is warm,

that I feel. And I also feel that it is dreaming. In its dreams it tosses on hard pillows. Listen! Listen! How it groans with evil memories! Or evil forebodings? Alas, I am sad with you, you dark monster, and even annoyed with myself for your sake.

How badly the French *"Hélas"* renders the bitter sigh of the German *"Ach"*! There again the moment of self-disgust, disgust with the universe, requires the simultaneity of a monosyllable. All the sufferings of a person, the suffering of an entire universe, are summed up in the dreamer's sigh. Oneirism and cosmicity here exchange their values. How faithfully Nietzsche translates the nightmare that is intermingled with pleasantness and feelings! "Love is the danger of the loneliest." "What, Zarathustra, he said, would you sing comfort even to the sea?"

But this temptation to love, this temptation to love those who love, to experience their sufferings and to console them, to console ourselves for our own suffering and our own love, is only the nightmare of a night of doubt, a night of the sea's perfidy. The land where the being is his own master is the air of the sky. Nietzsche always returns to it. In the chapter entitled "The Seven Seals," we read these verses filled with *Nietzschean intoxication*, a synthesis of Dionysian and Apollonian intoxications, a whileness made up of ardor and cold, the powerful and the clear, the young and the mature, the rich and the aerial:

> If ever I spread tranquil skies over myself and soared on my own wings into my own skies; if I swam playfully in the deep light-distances, and the bird-wisdom of my freedom came—but bird-wisdom speaks thus: "Behold, there is no above, no below! Throw yourself around, out, back, you who are light! Sing! Speak no more! Are not all words made for the grave and heavy? Are not all words lies to those who are light? Sing! Speak no more!"

This is how the third part of *Zarathustra* ends: with an awareness of aerial and melodious lightness. Nietzsche finds the profound unity of material and dynamic imagination in the substantial song of an aerial being, through the poetry of aerial ethics.

VII

After this unballasting, in which the being throws himself completely *outside himself*, after these liberating flights during which the being can see himself below himself, Nietzsche often gazes into the abyss. In this way, he becomes more aware of his freedom. The depth, contemplated from a height from which he will never again fall, is yet another leap toward the summits. As a result, static images will again acquire a very special dynamic life. Keeping in touch with Nietzsche's work, and reserving the right to return to certain images for broader examination, I am going to look closely at the process of dynamic verticality of images common to Nietzsche.

Here, for example, is the *pine at the edge of the abyss*. Schopenhauer contemplated it. He made of it a testimony to the will to live, describing the difficult symbiosis of the vegetable and the rock, the tree's struggle to resist the forces of gravity. In Nietzsche, the tree is straighter; it is a more vertical being, it scoffs at toppling over:

> —But you, Zarathustra,
> still love the abyss,
> do you love it like the *fir tree?* . . .
> The fir flings its roots where
> the rock itself gazes shuddering
> at the depths—

This shuddering will never become vertigo. Basically, Nietzscheanism is a conquered vertigo. Nietzsche comes near the abyss to find dynamic images of ascent. The chasm's reality gives to Nietzsche, through a well-known dialectic of pride, the consciousness of being a driving force. He could well say, as did Sara in *Axel*: "As for me, I do not deign to punish the chasms—except with my wings."[7]

Now let us follow the example of this Nietzschean tree in greater detail:

> the fir pauses before the abysses
> where everything around it
> wants to descend:
> between the impatience
> of wild boulders, of plummeting streams
> it endures patiently, stern, silent,
> lonely . . .

7. Villiers de l'Isle-Adam, *Axel* (Paris, 1960), 237.

Let me add that it is upright, braced, standing straight; it is vertical. It does not get its sap from subterranean water; it does not owe its solidity to the rock; it has no need of earthly forces. It is not a substance; it is a force, an autonomous force. It finds its power in its own *projection*. Nietzsche's fir tree, on the edge of the abyss, is a cosmic vector of the aerial imagination. We can put it to a very specific use, to distinguish between two types of the *imagination of will* and to see more clearly that will is inseparable from two types of imagination: *will-substance*, on the one hand, which is Schopenhaurean will, and *will-power* on the other, which is Nietzschean will. One wants to remain as it is. The other wants to rise up. Nietzschean will rests on its own speed. It is an accelerated becoming, a becoming that has no need of substance. It is as though the abyss, like a bow that is always bent, helps Nietzsche launch his arrows heavenward. Near the abyss, the plight of human beings is to fall. Near the abyss, the superman's destiny is to spring up, as a fir tree does, toward the blue sky. The feeling of evil tonalizes the good. The temptation to pity tonalizes courage. The temptation of the abyss tonalizes the sky.

I could cite many other passages in Nietzsche's work in which the tree is truly *intoxicated with uprightness*. For instance, in "The Welcome," seeking to convey an image of a lofty strong will, Nietzsche writes:

> A whole landscape is refreshed by one such tree. Whoever grows up high like you, O Zarathustra, I compare to the pine: long, silent, hard, alone, of the best and most resilient wood, magnificent—and in the end reaching out with strong green branches for his *own* dominion, questioning wind and weather and whatever else is at home on the heights with forceful questions, and answering yet more forcefully, a commander, triumphant: oh, who would not climb high mountains to see such plants? Your tree here, O Zarathustra, refreshes even the gloomy ones, the failures; your sight reassures and heals the heart even of the restless.

This straight tree is an axis of will; better, it is the axis of the vertical will that is distinctive to Nietzscheanism. To look at it is to stand up straight; its dynamic image is precisely the will contemplating itself, not in its works, but in its very action. Only dynamic imagination can give us adequate images of will. Material imagination gives us only sleep and dreams of an unformulated will, one that is dulled by evil or by innocence. The Nietzschean tree, more dynamic than material, is the all-powerful link between evil and good, earth and sky. "The more he aspires to the height and light, the more strongly do his roots strive earthward, downward, into the dark, the deep— into evil." There is no ephemeral, fleeting good, no flower that has not been prepared by the work of manure in the earth. Good springs forth from evil.

> Whence come the highest mountains? I once asked. Then I learned that they came out of the sea. The evidence is written in their rocks and in the walls of their peaks. It is out of the deepest depth that the highest must come to its height.

Naturally, themes of ascent are very numerous in Nietzsche's poetry. Certain passages really render a kind of differential of vertical conquest. Such is the case of crumbling earth, of stones that roll under the stride of a mountaineer. We must be able to go up a slope where everything is coming down. The steep path is an active adversary which will meet our dynamism with an opposing dynamism.

> A path that ascended defiantly through stones, malicious, lonely . . . a mountain path crunched under the defiance of my foot. . . . Upward—defying the spirit that drew it downward toward the abyss, the spirit of gravity, my devil and archenemy. Upward—although he sat on me, half dwarf, half mole, lame, making lame, dripping lead into my ear, leaden thoughts into my brain.

Nietzschean images, meditated upon as matter and as dynamism, are inexhaustible. They provide an experimental physics of the moral life. They carefully show us the mutations of images that must induce ethical mutations. This experimental physics is no doubt relative to the individual experimenter, but it is neither artificial, nor gratuitous, nor arbitrary. It corresponds to a nature that is in the act of becoming heroic, or to a cosmos that coincides with heroic life. To live the Nietzschean philosophy is to experience a transformation of energy, a sort of metabolism of cold and air which must, in a human being, produce aerial matter. Its ideal is to make a man as great and as vital as his images. But make no mistake, the ideal is realized, strongly realized in its images the moment that we accept the images in their dynamic reality, as mutations of imaginative psychic powers. The world dreams in us, as Novalis would say; the Nietzschean, all-powerful in his projected oneirism, in his dreaming will, must express himself in a more realistic mode and say: the world dreams in us dynamically.

VIII

It is possible, moreover, to grasp, in certain Nietzschean images, the cosmic work of ascending, or rather the work of an ascensional world whose only reality is energy. For example, in *Zarathustra:* "[The sea] wants to be kissed and sucked by the thirst of the sun; it *wants* to become air and height and a footpath of light, and itself light." In a poem, the dreamer is, in a way, born in the waves; he surges up like an island, thrust upward by erosive forces:

> but even the sea was not lonely enough for him;
> on the island he could climb, on the mountain he became a flame,
> toward the *seventh* solitude
> he searchingly casts the fishing rod over his head.

Earth above water, fire above earth, air above fire, that is the totally *vertical* hierarchy of Nietzschean poetics.

In *Thus Spoke Zarathustra*, Nietzsche came back to that strange image of *fishing from the heights:* "Has a man ever caught fish on high mountains? And even though what I want and do up here be folly, it is still better than if I became solemn down there from waiting, and green and yellow . . ."

In my works on the imagination (cf. *Lautréamont* and *Water and Dreams*) I have frequently recognized a progressive passage from water to air, and I have pointed out the continuous, imaginary evolution from fish to bird. Every true dreamer of the liquid world—and is there an oneirism without liquid?—knows the flying fish.[8] Nietzsche is the fisherman of the air; he casts his fishing rod over his head. He does not fish in a pond or a river, places that belong to horizontal beings. He fishes on the summits, at the peak of the highest mountain:

8. Cf. Audisio, *Antée:*
> The angels' dives raising spray
> Make laughter ring forth from the sea
> In the trees, whose limbs are quivering
> From swimming birds and flying fish!

> Give answer to the impatience of the flame,
> Let me, the fisher on high mountains,
> Catch my seventh, *last* solitude!—[9]

Supreme solitude is in an aerial world:

> *Seventh* loneliness!
> Never did I feel
> nearer me sweet security,
> warmer the sun's gaze.
> Does not the ice of my summits still glow?
> Silvery, light, a fish
> my bark now swims out . . .[10]

The *ship in the sky*, as I have said before, is a dream motif that is found in the work of many poets. For the most part it is the imaginary product of a cradled dream, a dream of being transported. It is the intoxication of passivity. It is a gondola in which the dreamer is not the gondolier. With Nietzsche, despite a few moments of indolence when the dreamer rests "like a ship that has sailed into its stillest cove . . . tired . . . ," cradled and wandering reverie has no trace of a Novalisean or Lamartinean style. It appears that a ship could not be happy with "a horizontal life." In a manner of speaking, it trembles vertically: "till over silent, longing seas the bark floats, the golden wonder around whose gold all good, bad, wondrous things leap . . ." Since it glides, since it is a "golden wonder," it is clear that the bark has gone from the sea to the sky, a sky filled with sunlight. The Nietzschean dreamer sets his course resolutely for the heights, with no thought of returning. He knows that his bark will never again bring him near land.

> Desire and hope drowned,
> smooth lie soul and sea.

Even in the sky, when he has returned to his aerial home, the dreamer looks up:

> I look upwards—
> there roll seas of light:

9. "The Beacon," translated by Philip Grundlehner in Philip Grundlehner, *The Poetry of Friedrich Nietzsche* (New York, 1986), 259.
10. "The Sun Sinks," Ibid., 292.

O night, o silence, o deadly silent clamor! . . .
I see a sign—
out of the farthest distances
a sparkling constellation falls slowly toward me.

. . . .

Loftiest star of being!
Tablet of eternal sculptures!

This account of an exploration of the ethical world is an aerial voyage that yields to the poet constellations of being, the "eternal necessity" of being, the "stellar" witness to his ethical orientation. Matter, motion, valorization are all bound up in the same images. The imagining being and the ethical being are much more inter-related than intellectual psychology believes, since it is always ready to take images for allegories. The imagination, more than reason, is a unifying force in the human soul.

IX

There are of course, in Nietzsche's poetry, images that are more clearly dynamic than the rock in the blue sky, or the upright fir tree that dares the lightning and scorns the abyss, or the path on the mountain tops, or the flying bark. Imaginary air and height are, very naturally, populated by a whole world of birds. Here, for example, is the predatory eagle:

A bird of prey perhaps,
who, joyous of misfortune, clings
to the hair
of the steadfast watcher
with frenzied laughter,
a vulture's laughter . . .

. . . .

one must have wings if one loves the abysses . . .
one must not remain hanging on the cliff
like you, you hanged one![11]

This plumb line, this ridiculous victim of hanging, these passively vertical remains of a heavy man transported in spite of himself; these images underscore very well the transfer of the human power of ascent to the bird of the heights in whom nothing "hangs" or "is

11. "Between Birds of Prey," Ibid., 203.

hanging," unless it is the prey that it has carried away. Conversely, "hair" is, in this poem, the aerial sign of a man who has been forgotten as far as his flesh is concerned. The hair, holocaust of human matter, "light smoke," says an image of Leonardo da Vinci.

The bird in the abstract form of its motion, without ornament and without song, is naturally, for the Nietzschean imagination, an excellent dynamic schema. In "The Seven Seals," we read this true principle: "and if this is my alpha and omega, that all that is heavy and grave should become light; all that is body, dancer; all that is spirit, bird—and verily, that is my alpha and omega . . ."

Here is soaring flight, the restful flight that is so close to oneiric flight, found under the title "Declaration of Love" (where the poet found himself dismissed):

> Wonder! Does he still fly?
> He soars, and yet his wings are still!
> What buoys him up so high?
> What are his goal, his way, his will?
> . . . .
> And high soar all who merely see him buoyed.
>
> O albatross, I'm swept
> Up high, by an eternal impulse spurred . . .

The drama of a flight that has failed or been cut short, recurs quite often. In the "Drunken Song," he is seized with the fear that he has not "flown high enough." The joy of the dance is not enough; "a leg . . . is no wing."

But it must be noted that at the moment when success is unquestioned, Nietzschean flight is characterized by impetuosity and aggressiveness. ". . . I flew, quivering, an arrow, through sun-drunken delight . . ." It seems that the eagle claws the sky: "My eagle is awake and honors the sun as I do. With eagle talons he grasps for the new light." A powerful flight is not a *ravishing* flight; it is flight with the intent to *ravish*. We cannot over-emphasize the importance of the sudden taste for power that the immense happiness felt while flying can take on. Even in oneiric flight, we frequently find that the dreamer demonstrates his superiority to others and glories in his sudden power. The bird of prey is a fatal development of the power of flight. Air, like all the other elements, needs its warrior. Imagination and nature agree on this evolution. The imagination is destined to be aggressive. In "On Old and New Tablets," Nietzsche writes: "Only the birds are still over and above him. And if man were to learn to fly—woe, to *what heights* would his rapaciousness fly?" Birds of prey are the ones that fly the highest. A proud philosopher of the heights will at once admit that the converse is also true. Nietzsche's aerial life is not a flight far from the earth. It is an *offensive* against the heavens. This aggressiveness retells the Miltonian epic of the fallen angels in terms that have the purity of the imaginary and are stripped of all traditional images. Moreover, this is pure aggressive imagination, since it is successful. Listen to the man of the Empyrean sphere holding back his conqueror's laugh: "And often [my broad-winged longing] swept me away and up and far, in the middle of my laughter . . ." The *good* no longer means anything. With this great flight we are in the realm of "wild wisdom." It is by meditating on the concept of "wild wisdom" that we can feel values *shifting*. Ethical truth evolves within a contradiction: delirious wisdom, the heavens attacked, offensive flight, all are so many shifts of values around a central point.

We can see reliable indications in the most minute details. For instance, the eagle's talon tears the light. It is clean, direct, and naked. It is a masculine claw. A cat's claw is hidden, retracted, and hypocritical. It is a feminine claw. In Nietzschean fauna, the cat is the *terrestrial* animal par excellence. It always personifies an attachment to the earth. It represents danger for an aerial being. For Nietzsche —without exception—the *cat* is a woman. Let me give just one example. Faced with the temptation of a warm, consoling love, Nietzsche writes: "You have wanted to pet every monster. A whiff of warm breath, a little soft tuft on the paw . . ." What single image could better describe a cat and a woman at the same time?

Anything that moves through the air is liable to receive a Nietzschean stamp, that unflagging preference for everything that rises. For example, in one poem, lightning can be seen rising from the abyss toward the sky:

> but suddenly, a lightning flash,
> bright, terrible, a strike
> against heaven from the abyss:

—from the mountain itself the entrails
vibrate . . .

This rumbling is not a result, it is the very anger of an abyss that
has just sent lightning, like an arrow, into the sky.

How many references could also be found to prove the dynamic nature of Nietzschean dawns! One passage will suffice to show that the
sky actively prepares a universal awakening within our very being:
"O heaven above me, pure and deep! You abyss of light! Seeing you, I
tremble with godlike desires. To throw myself into your height, that
is *my* depth. To hide in your purity, that is *my* innocence."

This is not a lead-up to a gentle take-off; it is the gushing forth of
being. Before the rising sun, the first Nietzschean sensation is the *inner sensation of will*, the feeling of decision, the feeling that by his own
motion he can receive promotion to a new life, far from the *remorse* of
deliberation, since every deliberation is a struggle against obscure
regrets and against more or less repressed remorse. The rising sun is
innocence of the coming day; the world always rises *new*. *Dawn*,
then, is the coenesthesia of our rising being. Is this new sun not my
sun? "Are you not the light for my fire? Have you not the sister soul
to my insight?" To see so clearly, must I not be luminous?

For the dynamic imagination, from the imagination that fills a
cinematic view of the world with dynamism, the *rising sun* and the
morning being mutually induce each other. "Together we have learned
everything; together we have learned to ascend over ourselves to
ourselves and to smile cloudlessly—to smile down cloudlessly from
bright eyes and from a vast distance when constraint and con-
trivance and guilt steam beneath us like rain." Exactly. No goal. Just
an upsurge, a *pure impulse*. An arrow which is able to kill, of course,
but which takes no interest in its crime. A dynamic tension and a
relaxation filled with laughter. Such are the straight arrows of the rising sun. Down below all those rains with their round drops falling
confusedly smell musty and patter feebly. With the heavens' arrows
the upright being got up and soared upward.

Need we remember the night again?

And when I wandered alone, for *whom* did my soul hunger at
night, on false paths? And when I climbed mountains, *whom* did I
always seek on the mountains, if not you? And all my wandering

and mountain climbing were sheer necessity and a help in my help-lessness: what I want with all my will is to *fly*, to fly up into *you*.

"I want" and "I fly" are both *"volo"* in Latin. There is no way to investigate the psychology of will without going to the very root of imaginary flight.

Of all images, the rising sun gives us an *instant lesson*. It elicits a lyricism of immediacy. To Nietzsche it suggests, not a panorama, but an act. For him, it has to do with decision rather than *contemplation*. Nietzsche's sunrise is the act resulting from an irrevocable decision. It is no more nor less than the *eternal return* of power; it is the myth of eternal return that changes from passive to active. And the doctrine of the perennial return will be better understood if it is attributed to awakenings of the will to power. He who can get up like the sun, with a single beam, can thrust himself into a destiny that is reassumed every day, that is reconquered every day by a young *amor fati*. In his sympathy with the cosmic powers of return, it seems that the Nie-tzschean dreamer can say tonight: "I will make the sun rise. I am the night watchman who will announce the time to wake up. Night is only a long need for awakening." From that point on, the conscious-ness of perennial return is an awareness of a projected will. Our being is what is rediscovered, and it returns to the same consciousness. Our being is what projects the world anew. No one can understand Nietzsche's world without putting *dynamic imagination* in the forefront. If we conceive of it as a mill that endlessly turns and grinds the same grain, we do not see it in Nietzsche's way. Such a universe is dead, annihilated by destiny. A Nietzschean cosmos lives in moments rediscovered through eternally youthful impulses. It is a story filled with rising suns.

X

Besides this dynamic imagination of the moment and this joy that comes from sudden impulses, there are other, even more distinctive, characteristics. If we look more carefully at the temporal fabric of Nietzschean ascent, a profound reason for its discontinuity will soon become apparent. There is not, in fact, an eternal rising up; there is no definitive elevation. *Verticality tears us apart*; it puts both the high and the low within us. We will discover a dialectical intuition that we have already seen in Novalis, one which, in Nietzsche, will join the rhythm of ascent and descent more dramatically.

The *spirit of gravity* mocks Zarathustra by reminding him of the inevitable destiny of the fall:

> "O Zarathustra . . . you philosopher's stone! You threw yourself up high, but every stone that is thrown must fall. O Zarathustra, you philosopher's stone, you slingstone, you star-crusher! You threw yourself up so high; but every stone that is thrown must fall. . . ."

The dialectics of positive and negative, of height and depth, is sensitized to an amazing degree when it is lived with an aerial imagination, like a winged seed which, at the slightest breath of air, is seized with the hope of rising or the fear of falling. In the same way, when we follow the ethical imagination of one like Nietzsche, we realize that good and evil have never been closer—or better, that good and evil, height and depth, have never so clearly been reciprocal causes. Whoever conquers vertigo has incorporated the experience of vertigo into his triumph. If his triumph is not to remain merely a story, every new day brings a renewal of the struggle; the being discovers that he is always being faced with the same necessity to reaffirm himself by rising up. And Nietzsche himself, after his decisive impulses, knew the seduction of the easy way, the *downward slope*: "Not the height but the precipice is terrible. That precipice where the glance plunges *down* and the hand reaches *up*. There the heart becomes giddy confronted with its double will." I spoke earlier of an *ascension differential*. Here is an example of that "double will." Two opposite motions are tied to each other in this passage, fused to each other—hostile, but necessary to each other. The closer the union between vertigo and glory, the more dynamized is the triumphant one. The same *fusion*, the same dynamic complex, can be found in "The Wanderer": "Only now are you going your way to greatness! Peak and abyss—they are now joined together." A soul that is sensitized to the drama of height and depth to this extent does not waver indifferently between grandeur and debasement. It can admit of no mediocre virtues. It is truly the soul of a "weigher." The value belonging to the base alloy will be cast into emptiness. Those who are not suited to flying will be taught by Nietzsche to "fall faster." Nothing escapes this weighing by the soul; everything is value, life is valorization. What vertical life there is in this knowledge of a verticalized soul! Isn't it really the soul "in which all things have their sweep and countersweep and ebb and flood . . ?" The Nietzschean soul is the reactor that precipitates our false values and sublimates the true ones.

In summary, the heightened state of soul is not simply a metaphor for Nietzsche. He calls for a time when

> . . . that very state which has hitherto entered into our soul as an exception, felt with horror now and then, may be the usual condition of those future souls: a continuous movement between high and low, and the feeling of high and low, a constant state of mounting as on steps, and at the same time reposing as on clouds.

Nietzscheans can be recognized by their "need to fly without hesitation whithersoever we are impelled—we free-born birds! Wherever we come, there will always be freedom and sunshine around us."

Let me conclude my discussion on this point by reaffirming that all these remarks that concern the ethical life are far from being mere metaphors, except for those who forget the primacy of the dynamic imagination. Whoever is truly willing to experience images will know the basics of a psychology of ethics. He will be at the center of Nietzschean metaphysics, which is, I believe—although Nietzsche himself was revolted by the word—an idealistic force. Here is the axiom of this idealism: *the being who ascends or descends is the being through whom everything ascends or descends. Weight* does not weigh on the world but on our souls, our minds, our hearts—it weighs on man. To one who triumphs over weight, to the superman, will be given a super-nature—that very nature that is imagined by an aerial psyche.

XI

In a more extensive study of the ascensional imagination, we would have to differentiate constantly among the various types of psyches that are determined by an element as homogenous as air. It is a difficult but indispensable task. No one can be sure that he has grasped *a single unity of the imagination* until he has differentiated it from other unities. Let us review, for the sake of clarity, the differences that separate Nietzsche and Shelley.

Shelley allows himself to be *drawn* to the infinite sky by a slow, gentle aspiration. Nietzsche conquers space and height through an instantaneous and superhuman projection.

Shelley escapes from the earth by intoxicated desire. Nietzsche forbids flight to all those who *wish for* aerial life.

> Do ye not flee from yourselves, O ye climbers?

In the upper regions, Shelley rediscovers the joys of being cradled. Nietzsche finds in heights a "clear, transparent, powerful, and highly electrified atmosphere," a "manly atmosphere." Nietzsche condemns immobility wherever he finds it:

> Now stand'st thou pale,
> A frozen pilgrimage thy doom,
> Like smoke whose trail
> Cold and still colder skies consume.[12]

In the final analysis, it is this cold that is the distinctive quality of Nietzschean Dionysianism, a very strange Dionysianism since it breaks with intoxication and with warmth.

XII

Some might be tempted to explain this lyricism of heights by the reality of mountain life. They might recall Nietzsche's long stays at Sils Maria. They might note that it was there, in 1881, that the idea for Zarathustra came to him when he was "6000 feet beyond men and time!" They might also note that the "decisive chapter" of the third book of *Zarathustra*, "On Old and New Tablets," was composed during the very difficult ascent from the train station to Eza—that wonderful Moorish village in the rocks: "beneath the halcyon sky of Nice" during the brightest of winters.

But such realism does not have the explanatory powers that people attribute to it. It seems that Nietzsche never actually climbed as high as those peaks where "even the chamois lost his trail." Nietzsche was not a mountaineer. In the end, he spent more time on high plateaus than on peaks. As for his poems, he often composed them as he was *coming down* from high places, on his way back to the valleys where men live.

12. "In Lonesomeness," trans. Herman Scheffauer, in *The Complete Works of Friedrich Nietzsche*, 163.

But the *imaginary Climate* plays a much more decisive role than the real one. Nietzsche's imagination is more instructive than any experience. It radiates a climate of imaginary altitude. It leads us into a special, lyrical universe. The first transmutation of Nietzschean values is a transmutation of images. It transforms the riches of the depths into the glory of the heights. Nietzsche is searching for something beyond depth, that is, beyond evil and beyond height; in other words beyond the noble, for he is not satisfied with traditional glory. He stretches *all* ethical forces between these imaginary poles, refusing any form of "progress" that is merely material and utilitarian and that would be merely horizontal progress, with no capacity for modifying our weighty being. Nietzsche has put all his lyrical energy into exchanging what is heavy for what is light, the terrestrial for the aerial. He has made the abyss speak the language of the summits. The cave suddenly gives back aerial echos: "Hail to me! . . . My abyss speaks, I have turned my ultimate depth inside out into the light." Some will still insist on talking about symbols, allegories, and metaphors and will ask the philosopher to point out the ethical lessons first, before the images. But if the images were not one with ethical thought, they would not have such life or such continuity. Nietzschean philosophy, in my view, is a Manichaeism of the imagination. It has a tonic and a beneficial effect since it sets our dynamic being in motion, drawing it along with the most active of images. In actions in which a human being really acts, in an act in which he really engages his whole being, we should be able to discover, if my theories are well-founded, the double perspective of height and depth. Do we not feel a dual will for the abundance and *élan* in this thought from *The Dawn of Day?*

> You know him not! whatever weights he may attach to himself he will nevertheless be able to raise them all with him. But you, judging from the weak flapping of your own wings, come to the conclusion that he wishes to remain below, merely because he does not burden himself with those weights.

In a single great verse in "To Hafiz," Nietzsche has, I believe, shown himself to be one of the greatest philosophers of the ascensional psyche:

> Downward from every height you've sunk,
> And in the depths still shine.

6

The Blue Sky[1]

> One must be able to reflect even the purest things.
>
> GIDE, *Journal*

I

THE BLUE OF THE SKY, if we were to examine its many image values, would require a long study in which we would see all the types of material imagination being determined according to the basic elements of water, fire, earth, and air. In other words, we could divide poets into four classifications by their response to the single theme of celestial blue:

Those who see in an immobile sky a flowing liquid that comes to life with the smallest cloud.

Those who experience the blue sky as though it were an enormous flame—"searing" blue, as the Comtesse de Noailles describes it.

Those who contemplate the sky as if it were a solidified blue, a painted vault—"compact and hard azure," as the Comtesse de Noailles again says.

Finally those who can truly participate in the aerial nature of celestial blue.

Of course, besides the great poets who instinctively follow these basic inspirations, it would be easy to discover, with such a common image, all the rhymers for whom "sky blue" is always a concept, never a primary image. Poetry about the blue sky suffers an enormous loss on this account. We can almost appreciate Musset's scorn when he called "blue" the stupid color. In the works of artificial poets, at least, it is the color of pretentious innocence from which come sapphires or flax blossoms. Such images are not, of course, banned: poetry is just as much the participation of the large in the small as it is the small in the large. But no one experiences this participation by juxtaposing a

1. This chapter appeared in the journal *Confluences*, no. 25.

terrestrial and an aerial name. Only a great poet can discover naturally, without copying a literary example, blue sky in a wildflower.

But, leaving aside facile polemics against false or worn-out images, I would like to reflect on a fact that has often struck me. As I have read many different kinds of poets, what has surprised me was how rare were the images in which the blue sky was truly aerial. This rarity is due, first of all, to the fact that aerial imagination is much rarer than the imagination of fire, earth, or water. But even more important is the fact that, even when the immense, distant blue infinity is felt by an aerial soul, it needs to be materialized in order to be incorporated into a *literary image*. The word *blue* designates, but it does not render. The problem of the image of the blue sky is completely different for the painter than for the poet. For a writer, if the blue sky is not merely a *background*, if it is a poetic object, only a metaphor can bring it to life. The poet's task is not to translate a color, but to make us dream the color. The blue sky is so simple that no one thinks he can *oneirize it* without materializing it. But this process of materialization sometimes goes too far. The blue sky is made too hard, too glaring, too searing, too compact, too burning, and too brilliant. Often the sky looks at us too fixedly. We attribute too much substance and constancy to it because the soul does not become a part of the life of primary substance. We tonalize the sky's blue by making it "vibrate" like a sonorous crystal, whereas, for truly aerial souls, there is only the sound of a breath. Thus, with excessive intensity, the Comtesse de Noailles writes: "Today the blue is so strong that it blinds you if you look at it too long; it crackles, it whirls, it becomes filled with golden tendrils, with hot frost, with sharp and radiant diamonds, with arrows, with silver flies . . . "

The hallmark of what is truly aerial is to be found, in my opinion, in another direction. It is, in fact, based on a dynamics of dematerialization. The substantial imagination of air is truly active only in a dynamics of dematerialization. The blue of the sky is aerial when it is dreamed as a color that pales a bit, like a pallor that seeks finesse, a finesse that we imagine as yielding beneath our fingers like a delicate fabric as we caress, in Paul Valéry's words:

The mysterious texture of the utmost height.[2]

2. Paul Valéry, "Profusion du soir. Poème abandonné," in *The Collected Works of Paul Valéry*, ed. Jackson Matthews, Bollingen Series (Princeton, N. J., 1971), XLV, 42-43.

That is when the blue sky counsels us to be as calm and as light as it is itself:

> The sky above the roof, is
> So blue, so calm!

sighs Verlaine from the depths of his prison where he is still under the *weight* of unforgiven memories. This calm can be filled with melancholy. The dreamer feels that the blue sky will never be a *possessed good.* "What good are the symbols of a basic and comforting mountaineering since I shall not, this evening, reach the blue, that blue which is so aptly called sky blue?"[3]

But it is by following the scale of *dematerialization* of celestial blue that we can see aerial reverie at work. Then we will understand that it is an aerial *Einfühlung*: the *fusion* of a dreamer with as undifferentiated a universe as possible, one that is blue and gentle, infinite and formless, with a *minimum of substance.*

II

Here is a quick survey of four documents from an aerial point of view; none, except the fourth, is absolutely pure.

1.—First, a document taken from Mallarmé in which the poet, living in the "dear ennui" of "Lethean ponds," suffers the "irony" of the azure. He perceives an azure that is too offensive and that wants

> To stop up with untiring hand
> The great blue holes that naughty birds make.

But the azure is stronger, it makes bells ring:

> My soul becomes a voice, the more
> To frighten us with its paltry victory,
> And from the living metal comes out as blue angeluses![4]

How can we fail to feel that the poet, faced with this rivalry of the azure and the bird, suffers from a blue sky that is too hard and that still imposes too much matter on the dreamer in a "paltry victory." Made more sensitive by Mallarmé's poem, the reader will perhaps dream of a less offensive blue, one that is gentler, less vibrant, and in which the bell will ring of its own accord, this time within the

3. René Crevel, *Mon corps et moi*, 38.
4. Mallarmé, "L'Azur," in *Oeuvres complètes*, ed. Henri Mondor, Pléiade edition (Paris, 1961), 37-38.

domain of its aerial function, with no memory of its bronze lip.[5]

2.—In this duel that has begun between the blue of the sky and the objects that are outlined against it, it is often through the *wound* inflicted by things on the immaculate blue that we are able to feel within ourselves a strange longing for the sky to be intact. In a theory of form raised to the cosmic scale, it could be said that the blue sky is an *absolute background*. A passage from Zola renders well the lively sensitivity to this wound. Serge Mouret, forgetful of his past, unconscious even of the spiritual drama that he lived in Paradou, sees the blue sky from his convalescent bed. This is the only motive for his present reverie:

> In front of him there was a broad expanse of sky, nothing but blue, an infinite blue. In it he bathed his pain and abandoned himself as if to a gentle cradling; from it he drank in sweetness, purity, and youth. Only a branch, whose shadow he had seen, stuck out past the window and made a bold green spot on the blue sea. And that was already too much for his delicate condition, as a sick man who was wounded by the dirty spots that swallows, flying on the horizon, made.

Here again, as in Mallarmé's verse, it seems that a bird's vigorous flight wounds a universe that seeks to retain the unity of its simple color, a unity of lightness of being that is like the simplicity and the tranquillity needed for convalescence. This reverie's maxim would be: "Let nothing complicate the blue sky!" The branch, the bird passing by, the overly sharp crosspiece of the window, all disturb aerial reverie and hinder the fusion of being in this universal, incorruptible blue . . . But Zola's passage is cut short. The novelist, entirely devoted to his imagining of the richness of the world of feeling, does not respond to the intuition of an elementary image. Only by accident does Zola limit himself here to images of aerial imagination.

3.—The third document will also be very impure, particularly at the outset. I will set it down here, so that the purity of the fourth one will stand out in contrast. Coleridge (cited by John Charpentier in his study, *Coleridge, The Sublime Somnambulist*) says:

---

5. Cf. La Comtesse de Noailles, who, while listening to "transparent" sounds, thinks of the bell that starts to ring by itself, just as a bird sings, or a flower blooms, because of the fine conditions in the air. *Le Visage émerveillé* (Paris, 1904), 96.

To the eye it [the sky] is an inverted goblet, the inside of a sapphire basin, perfect beauty in shape and colour. To the mind, it is immensity; but even the eye feels as if it were [able] to look through with [a] dim sense of the non-resistance—it is not exactly the feeling given to the organ by solid and limited things, [but] the eye feels that the limitation is in its own power, not in the object.

Unfortunately, comparisons with the goblet and the sapphire "harden" the impression of an indeterminate limit and seem to arrest the great potential for contemplating the blue sky. Nevertheless, if we read Coleridge's passage with a sympathetic feeling for the aerial, we will soon recognize that eye and mind together imagine blue sky without resistance. Together they dream of an infinite matter that has color in its volume without, however, enclosing it, despite the old book image of an inverted goblet. Moreover, Coleridge's passage ends on a note that is very valuable for a psychology and a metaphysics of the imagination: "The sight of a profound sky is, of all impressions, the closest to a feeling. It is more a feeling than a visual thing, or, rather, it is the definitive fusion, the complete union of feeling and sight." This very unusual aspect of the aerial *Einfühlung* requires some meditation. It is a fusion relieved of all the impressions of warmth that a warm heart feels when it tries to equal the ardor of an ardent world. It is an evaporation stripped of the impressions of wealth that this terrestrial heart feels, an "innumerable heart" awed by an abundance of forms and colors. This loss of being in a blue sky expresses an emotional nuance of the simplest kind. It is hostile to "medleys," mixtures, and events. We may truly speak, then, of a "feeling of a blue sky" that would have to be compared to the "feeling of a little blue flower." In this comparison, the feeling of blue sky will appear as a limitless capacity to expand. No one is going to violate a blue sky that is gently blue. The aerial *Einfühlung*, in its *blue* nuance, has no incident, no shock and no history. We have said it all when we repeat with Coleridge: "It is more a feeling than a visual thing." The blue sky, meditated upon by the material imagination, is pure feeling; it is emotionality without object. It can serve as a symbol for a sublimation without goal, for an *evasive sublimation*.

4.—But a fourth document is going to give us so perfect an impression of imaginary dematerialization, of emotive decoloration, that we will truly understand, by reversing metaphors, that the blue of the sky is as unreal, as impalpable, as filled with dream, as the blue of a glance. We think that we are looking at the blue sky. Suddenly it is the blue sky that is looking at us. I am borrowing this document of extraordinary purity from a book by Paul Eluard, *Donner à voir*: "When still very young, I opened my arms to purity. It was only a beating of wings in the sky of my eternity. . . . It was no longer possible for me to fall." The aerial dreamer receives, in all certainty and immediacy, life that is not difficult to live, lightness in which there is no danger of falling, and substance that is one both in color and in quality. The poet thus grasps purity here as an *immediate given of poetic consciousness*. Purity for other imaginations is discursive; it is neither intuitive nor immediate. It must, therefore, be formed by a slow purification process. Conversely, the aerial poet knows a kind of *morning absolute*. He is called to aerial purity "by a mystery in which forms play no part. Curious about a colorless sky from which birds and clouds have been banished, I became a slave to my unreal and innocent eyes, eyes ignorant of the world and of themselves. Peaceful power. I suppressed the visible and the invisible, I lost myself in an unsilvered mirror. . . ." A colorless sky, but still blue, an unsilvered mirror that has infinite transparency is, from this point on, an *object* sufficient for the *dreaming subject*. It unifies the opposite impressions of presence and distance. It would be no doubt interesting to study pancalistic reverie through this simplified thesis. Let us limit ourselves, though, to a few metaphysical remarks.

III

If, as I believe, the meditating being is first of all the dreaming being, a whole metaphysics of aerial reverie can derive its inspiration from Eluard's passage. Here reverie is integrated into its rightful place, i.e., before representation. There, the imagined world takes its rightful place *before* the represented world; the universe takes its rightful place before the object. As is only right, the poetic knowledge of the world precedes rational knowledge of objects. The world is beautiful before being true. The world is admired before being verified. Every primitive condition is pure oneirism.

If the world were not first of all my reverie, then my being would immediately be enclosed in its representations, which are always contemporaneous and slave to its sensations. Deprived of its dream time, it could not be conscious of its representations. To become conscious of its power of representaiton, then, the being must certainly not omit the stage of *pure seeing*. In front of the empty sky's unsilvered mirror, it must bring about pure vision.

With Paul Eluard's passage, then, we have just acquired a kind of pre-Schopenhauerean lesson, which is an introduction—necessary in my opinion—to a doctrine of representation. To convey the genesis of a meditating being, I propose the following sequence to philosophers:

First reverie—or wonder. Wonder is instant reverie.

Then contemplation—a strange power of the human soul capable of recapturing its reveries, beginning its dreams over again, and restoring its imaginary life, despite the accidents of tangible life. Contemplation brings together more memories than sensations. It is history more than spectacle. When one thinks that he is looking at an amazingly rich spectacle, he is actually enriching it with memories of all different kinds.

Finally, representation. This is where the functions of formal imagination come into play: with reflection on recognized forms, with memory, accurate and well-defined this time, recalling forms we have cherished.

Once more, by way of a specific example, I am reaffirming the fundamental role of the imagination in spiritual development. A long imaginative evolution leads us from fundamental reverie to a discursive understanding of the beauty of forms. A metaphysics of utilitarian understanding explains man as a mass of conditioned reflexes. It leaves the dreaming man, man the dreamer, outside of its inquiry. The image must be returned to the primitive psyche. The image for the sake of the image is the motto of an active imagination. It is through this activity of the image that the human psyche receives *future causality* through a kind of *immediate finality*.

Moreover, if we are willing to live, with Eluard, by imagination and for imagination, these hours of *pure vision* in front of the tender and delicate blue of a sky from which *all objects have been banished*, we will be able to understand that the aerial kind of imagination offers a domain in which the values of the dream and of the representation are interchangeable on the most basic level. Other matters harden objects. Also, in the realm of blue air more than elsewhere, we feel that the world may be permeated by the most indeterminate reverie. This is when reverie really has depth. The blue sky opens up in depth beneath the dream. Then dreams are not limited to one-dimensional images. Paradoxically, the aerial dream soon has only a depth dimension. The other two dimensions, in which picturesque, colored reverie plays its games, lose all their oneiric interest. The world is then truly on the other side of the unsilvered mirror. There is an imaginary beyond, a pure beyond, one without a within. First there is *nothing*, then there is a *deep* nothing, then there is a blue *depth*.

If we are willing to meditate philosophically, taking as our point of departure not representation but aerial reverie, then the subject's gain is no less than the object's. In front of a blue sky—one that is a very pale, washed-out blue, purified by Eluardian reverie—we will be able to seize, in all the significant dynamics of its newly formed state, the subject and the object together. Before a sky from which objects have been banished, there will be born an imaginary subject whose memories have been banished. The distant and the immediate form a bond. What is distant from the object is immediate to the subject. This is another proof that the common bond between spirit and matter, which Schopenhauer so often discussed, is even more perceptible if one is willing to take his stand in the realm of the imagination rather than in that of representation, and if he is willing to study—together—imaginary matter and the imagining mind. A dream in the presence of smoke: this is the point of departure for a metaphysics of the imagination. The reverie, a kind of smoke, enters my mind, Victor Hugo says somewhere. Blue air and its dreamer form perhaps an even more perfect parallelism: less than a dream, less than smoke . . . the union of a half dream and a half blue is thus formed at the limit of the imaginary.

To sum up, reverie in the presence of a blue—and only a blue sky—posits in some way a phenomenalism without phenomena. To put it another way, the meditating being finds himself faced with a phenomenalism that is reduced to the very minimum, but which he can still reduce or subdue in color and even *efface*. In such a case, how could he not be tempted by a visual nirvana and by an adherence to a passive power that is peaceably content simply to see, then to see successively the formless, the faded, the unreal. If we were to replace the *method of doubt*—a method which is too virtual and not really suited for detaching us from representation—by a *method of effacement*—which is much more effective because it has in its favor the very gradient that reverie follows—we would see that aerial reverie allows a descent to the minimal state of the imagining being, that is, the minimally minimal state of the thinking being.

Extreme solitude in which matter dissolves and disappears, is lost. Doubt that loses its form when faced with doubtful matter. Such should be, for the solitary subject faced with a colorless universe, the lessons of a philosophy of effacement. I will attempt such a philosophy in another work. To limit ourselves to the problems of the imagination, we must consider the fact that we are working on a difficult paradox here, which amounts to proving the primordial nature of the imagination by describing the activity of an imagination without image that finds its pleasure, even its life, in "effacing images." But the very fact that the problem of imagination can be posed at all in such reduced terms before a world with as few forms as a blue sky, proves, I believe, the psychologically true nature of the problem that I am raising.

All those who enjoy a great reverie, simplified and simplifying, before a sky that is nothing other than "the world of transparency," will understand the futility of "apparitions." For them, "transparency" is more real than appearance. They will come to an inner understanding of lucidity through transparency. If the world is also will, then blue sky is the will to lucidity. The "unsilvered mirror" formed by a blue sky awakes a special narcissism, a narcissism of purity, of sentimental vacuity, and of free will. In a blue and empty sky, the dreamer finds the schema of "blue feelings," of "intuitive clarity," and the happiness that comes in being clear about one's feelings, acts, and thoughts. The aerial Narcissus looks at himself in the blue sky.

IV

The line of dematerialization that we have characterized in some of its phases and in its transcendence, naturally does not exhaust the dynamic reveries that are born before the blue sky. There are some who work over all images with a dynamics of intensification. They experience the most apparently peaceful images with a moving intensity. A Claudel, for example, seeks an immediate and passionate adherence. He will seize a blue sky in its raw material. For him, before this enormous mass where nothing stirs, this mass that is the blue sky or rather a sky overflowing with azure, the first question will be "What is blue?" The Claudelian hymn will answer: "Blue is obscurity become visible." To *feel* this image, I will take the liberty of changing the past participle, for, in the realm of the imagination, there are no past participles. I will say, then, "Blue is obscurity becoming visible." This is precisely why Claudel can write: "Azure, between day and night, shows a balance, as is proved by the subtle moment when, in the Eastern sky, a navigator sees the stars disappear all at once."

A subtle moment, a wonderful moment when everything stirs within us. This moment can be relived, started over, recaptured, through aerial reverie. Even before the most solidly constructed blue sky, the aerial reverie, the least active of reveries, can rediscover the alternation of the obscure and the diaphanous by experiencing the alternating rhythm of torpor and awakening. *The blue sky is our permanent dawn.* We need only look at it through half-closed eyes to rediscover that moment, well before the sun's golden rays, when the nocturnal universe will become aerial. By continually experiencing this value of dawn, of an awakening, we understand the *movement of an immobile sky.* As Claudel says: "There is no immobile color." Blue sky moves like an awakening.

The blue of the sky thus dreamed will take us to the heart of what is elementary. No earthly substance retains its elementary quality in so immediate a way as a blue sky. The blue sky is truly, and in every sense of the word, an elementary image. It provides an unforgettable illustration for the color blue. The first blue is always the blue of the sky. It precedes the word, says Claudel: "All kinds of blue have something elementary about them, and in general something fresh and pure. It suits everything that envelops or bathes. . . . It is the clothing of the Purissima."

A sky that is uniformly blue or golden is sometimes dreamed of in such a unified way that it seems to absorb every other color. At that point, blue is so powerful that it can even assimilate red. D'Annunzio writes in *Leda without a Swan*: "Solar gold and sylvan pollen, intermingled, were, in the palpitation of the wind, no longer two, but one and the same dust. On the tip of every needle, pines have a drop of blue." Is there a better way to express the fact that rustling trees distill blue sky? To make the reader feel in a single phrase, "a drop of azure," that he is participating in a cosmic experience, that is the true function of the poet.[6]

Sometimes it is by contrast that the blue of the sky takes on its blueing function. In verses commented upon by Hugo von Hofmannsthal, we find this powerful reverie of contrast: "The *year of the soul* begins with an autumn landscape." Here is its sky:

> The smile of far, luminous shores,
> The unhoped-for blue of pure clouds
> Lights the ponds and the paths with dappled colors.

> Der Schimmer ferner lächelnder Gestade,
> Der reinen Wolken unverhoffte Blau
> Erhellt die Weiher und die bunten Pfade.[7]

And, in his wonderful *Entretien sur la poésie*, the poet adds: "That is beautiful. You can breathe autumn in it. The *unhoped-for blue of pure clouds* is strong, because, between the clouds, bays of blue are opened that make us think of summer, but it is very true that they are seen only on the edge of *pure* clouds in the autumn sky which is roughly torn to shreds everywhere else. Goethe would have loved these *pure clouds*. And the *unhoped-for blue* is perfect. It is beautiful. Yes, that is just what autumn is like."[8]

"There is truly autumn in this passage, and more than autumn," because the poet has been able to make us feel the unhoped-for memory of the brilliance belonging to a different time, a summer that has now disappeared. In this way, a literary image has one dimension more than a visual image: it has memory. A literary autumn feels that it completes a summer. "Are feelings, even our undeveloped feelings, all the most secret, most profound states of our inner being, not all, in the strangest way, intertwined with a landscape and a season, with a property of air and a breath?" It seems that von Hofmannsthal's landscape is a particular kind of ideality. It is not only a *state of soul*,

6. Gerhart Hauptmann, *The Heretic of Soana*, authorized translation (London, 1923), 103.

7. Stefan George, *Das Jahr der Seele.*

8. Hofmannsthal, "*L'année de l'âme*," in *Ecrits en prose*, trans. Charles du Bos (Paris, 1927), 152-53.

according to Amiel's formula, it is a *former state of soul*.[9] The blue of autumn is the blue of a memory. It is a memory that is becoming blue that life is going to efface. We understand then how von Hofmannsthal can talk about "landscapes of the soul, landscapes that are infinite like space and time (whose) appearance gives rise, within us, to a new sense, one that is superior to all the others." In the same way Milosz writes: "Pure landscapes dream in my memory." These landscapes are almost without features, and they live in a gentle, changing color, like a memory.

V

Sometimes, however, a more recent reverie takes on its original features again. The blue sky is, in this case, a *background* which legitimizes the theory of a cosmic *homo faber*, a demiurge who brutally divides the landscape. In this primitive division, earth is separated from the sky. The green hill stands out against the azure sky like a kind of absolute profile, one that no hand caresses and that no longer obeys the law of desire.

On the cosmic scale, the blue of the sky is a background that gives form to the *whole* hill. By its uniformity, it stands out from all other reveries that live in a terrestrial imagination. The blue of the sky is first of all a space where there is no longer anything to imagine. But when the aerial imagination is awakened, then the background becomes active. It encourages the aerial dreamer to make changes in the terrestrial profile and to take an interest in the point where the earth communicates with the sky. Water's mirror offers a means of converting the blue of the sky into a more substantial blue. A blue motion can spring forth. Here, for example, is the kingfisher: "Of all the birds, it is the one that can be classified the most easily. . . . It is the blue flash that light and water exchange."[10] The most lifeless earth finally moves and takes in air. For an aerial dreamer, it in turn becomes the background, and forces that reach out to it begin to move in the immense unbroken blue. Thus, in the most dream-like and mobile of forms, the imagination finds elements of a Gestalt theory that work in a universe unfolding before us.

9. Byron, before Amiel, had said: ". . . and to me/High mountains are a feeling." "Childe Harold," Canto 3, line 682 in *The Poetical Works of Lord Byron* (London, rpt. 1959).
10. Francis Jammes, *Le Poète rustique* (Paris, 1920), 215-16.

VI

The fact that a blue sky is a space that provides the imagination with no pretext at all for action explains why it goes by another name in the various poetic theories. For Hölderlin, the immense, blue, sun-filled sky is ether. This ether in no way corresponds to a fifth element. It simply represents crisp, clear air sung under a learned name. Geneviève Bianquis is quite correct when she writes in her *Introduction to Poetry*: ether, soul of the world, sacred air, is "the pure, free air of the summits, the atmosphere from which seasons, hours, clouds, rain, light, and lightning descend upon us; the blue of the sky, a symbol of purity, height, and transparency, is, like Novalis' night, a polyvalent myth." And Bianquis cites *Hyperion*, where Hölderlin writes: "Brother of the Spirit which stirs us so powerfully with his flame, sacred Air! how wonderful it is to think that you accompany me wherever I go, omnipresent and immortal." This life in the ether is a return to the protection of a father. *Vater Aether!* Hölderlin's invocation reiterates in a synthesis of happiness and strength. There is no ether without a sort of polyvalence where light and heat, tonicity and grandeur are interchanged. Another poet, during a period of religious exaltation, finds images similar to Hölderlin's for his meditation: "I sank into God, like an atom floating in the heat of a summer day, rises, is drowned, gets lost in the atmosphere, and, when it has become transparent, like the ether, seems as aerial as the air itself and as luminous as light." It would be easy, moreover, to find many other examples that would prove that for poets ether is not a "transcendent" element, but merely the synthesis of air and light.

VII

We can compare the mirage to the blue sky. The mirage appears in reveries that have a connection with reality only through the genius of storytellers. Of all the writers who have used a mirage to enliven a story, is there one in a thousand who has really been seduced by a mirage? Does the storyteller hope to find one reader in a thousand who has had this experience? But the word is so beautiful and the image is so grand that the mirage is a literary metaphor that never wears out. It explains the common by the uncommon, the earth by the sky.

Here, then, we have a phenomenon that belongs almost exclusively to literature, a burgeoning literary phenomenon that has few occasions to be reinforced by something that we actually see. It is a cosmic image that is virtually absent from the cosmos. The mirage is like the vain dream of a cosmos asleep under sweltering heat. In literature the mirage appears as a rediscovered dream.

The mirage belongs to the literature of a blue, sun-filled sky. We cannot deny its aerial hallmark if we think, for example, of the city in "Voyage d'Urien" a mirage-like city on summits that are "lost in the clouds," filled with pointed minarets praising the dawn with the muezzins calling back and forth "like larks."[11]

The mirage can help us in studying the interweaving of the real and the imaginary. It seems, in fact, that in the mirage illusory phenomena are formed on a more solid fabric and, vice-versa, that terrestrial phenomena reveal their idealized form. How many ineffectual images cross the blue sky! That is a fact that gives a kind of reality to this space which already has a color as part of its essence. This may explain how Goethe can speak about the blue of the sky as a fundamental phenomenon, an *Urphänomen*: "The blue of the sky shows us the basic law of chromatics. Do not look for anything beyond the phenomena: they themselves are the lesson." "When at last I rest on the *Urphänomen* it is probably only because I am resigned; but still there is a great deal of difference between resigning myself to human limitations and resigning myself to my own restricted individual limitations." These thoughts of Goethe, quoted by Schopenhauer, seem to me to designate the blue sky as the image that is least relative to the individual contemplating it.[12] It sums up aerial imagination. It determines an extreme sublimation, an adherence to a sort of absolutely simple, indissoluble image. Standing before the blue sky, we are justified in simplifying the Schopenhauerean thought: "The world is my representation" by translating it as: the world is my blue, aerial, distant representation. The blue sky is my mirage. All the formulae that could be supplied by a *minimal metaphysics* in which the imagination, having returned to its elementary life, would rediscover its original powers which compel us to dream.

11. André Gide, "Le voyage d'Urien," in *Oeuvres complètes d'André Gide*, ed. L. Martin-Chauffier (Paris, n.d.), 294.
12. Goethe is quoted by Schopenhauer in his introduction to *Über das Sehn und die Farben*, in *Werke*, (Leipzig, 1977), I:3.

7

The Constellations

Ah what Bull, what Dog, what Bear,
What trophies of victory immense,
Once embarked on resourceless time
The soul imposes on formless space!
PAUL VALÉRY,
Charms, "Secret Ode."

I

MATHEMATICAL REVERIE has drawn diagrams of this immense tableau of a Cerulean night. These constellations are all false, but deliciously false! They have grouped totally foreign stars in a single figure. Between real points, that is between stars that are isolated like diamond solitaires, the dream of constellations has drawn imaginary lines. Dream, that great master of abstract painting, sees all the animals of the zodiac done in a pointillism reduced to the minimum. *Homo faber* —a lazy maker of wheels—puts a chariot without wheels in the sky; the ploughman, dreaming of his harvests, erects a simple golden sheaf. Seeing such luxuriance produced by the powers of projective imagination, how odd this logical dictionary definition seems!

> Constellation: the assembly of a certain number of fixed stars on which has been superimposed a figure, either man or animal or plant, in order to remember them better and to which has been given a name to distinguish them from other groupings of the same kind.

Naming stars to "help remember them," what lack of appreciation for the speaking powers of dream! What ignorance of the principles of reverie's imaginary projection! The zodiac is the Rorschach test for the child Humanity. Why have learned grimoires been written; why has the sky of night been replaced by the sky of books?

There are so many dreams in the sky which poetry, encumbered by old words, has not been able to name. To how many writers of the night would we like to say: "Come back to the principle of reverie; the starry sky has been given to us, not to think about, but to dream"? It is an invitation to constellating dreams, to dream about the easy and ephemeral construction of the thousand forms that our desires take. The mission of "fixed" stars is to fix some dreams, to communicate some, and to rediscover some. They prove to a dreamer the universality of oneirism. This ram, young shepherd, that your hand caresses as you dream—there he is up there, turning gently in the immense night! Will you find him again tomorrow? Point him out to your companion! Then there will be two of you to sketch him, to recognize him, and to talk to him as a friend. You will find that the two of you have the same vision, the same desire, and that even in the night, in the nocturnal solitude, you will see the same ghosts pass by. How much greater life becomes when dreams are bound together!

We will understand to what an extent the imagination of the sky is falsified and impeded by book knowledge if we reread some passages in which writers have blithely lost track of dreams in exchange for "knowledge" that is as poor as it is lifeless. At that stage we will perhaps be justified in suggesting a kind of counter-psychoanalysis that might destroy the conscious mind in favor of an *established oneirism*, which would be the only way to restore a refreshing continuity to reverie. "Knowing" the constellations, naming them as in books, projecting a classroom map of the sky on the sky itself, is brutalizing our imaginary powers and depriving us of the benefits of the stars' oneirism. If we were not burdened with the words that "help our memory"—the memory of words, the great sloth that refuses to dream—every new night would be a new reverie for us, a renewed cosmogony. An ill-formed consciousness or one that is too formal is as harmful for the dreaming soul as an amorphous or warped unconscious. The psyche must find a balance between the imagined and the known. This equilibrium cannot be satisfied by vain substitutions in which, suddenly, the imagining powers find themselves bound up with arbitrary schemata. The imagination is a primary power. It must be born in the solitude of the imagining being. As always, to understand contemplation, we must begin with the Schopenhauerean formula: *the starry night is my constellation*. It makes me aware of my power to form constellations. It puts in my hands, as the poet says, these weightless chalices and these flowers that grow in space.[1]

II

We will find an opportunity to purify the imaginary through counter-psychoanalysis in the works of George Sand, an author who was a great dreamer when it came to things of the heart, but a very poor one where visible things were concerned. I read her works passionately for the genius that she displays in expressing the imagination of simple goodness. Her work can provide us, I believe, with a good example of unfulfilled nocturnal romanticism, that is, an oneirism that is nipped in the bud by an overlay of vague, superficial learning.

It is undeniable that in many passages in George Sand's works reverie before a starry sky degenerates into an astronomy lesson whose pedantry is almost laughable. When André first falls in love with the tender and delicate Geneviève, he first "teaches" her botany, that is to say, the learned name for flowers. Then he explains the mysteries of the nocturnal sky to her:

> André, happy and proud to have something to teach for the first time in his life, begins to explain the workings of the universe to her, taking care to simplify all the explanations and to adapt them to his pupil's intelligence. . . . She grasped it quickly; and there were even moments when André was so carried away that he believed her possessed of extraordinary abilities.[2]

When she was alone again, Geneviève

> sat on a high place planted with medlar trees at nightfall and contemplated the rising of the stars whose course André had explained to her. . . . Already she could feel the effect of these contemplations in which her soul seemed to leave its terrestrial prison and fly away to purer realms.

Thus, imaginary and intellectual activity, which are diametrically opposed, are intermingled in this passage. The writer who owed us a psychological explanation of this liberation of the soul that she

1. Cf. Guy Lavaud, *Poétique du ciel* (Paris, 1930), 30.
2. George Sand, *André*, ed. Calmann-Lévy (Paris, 1976), 85-86.

invokes and of this expansion of soul that a star-filled dream offers us, has given us ideas instead. And what ideas, if we remember for a moment that in her correspondence George Sand wrote without turning a hair: "You ought to study astronomy; you could learn it in a week"! Throughout her work we can see the influence of this "intellectualized star," which she reduces in her thought to a "faraway sun."

In such facile contemplation the constellations will add a name, and little more than a name, to the sky. The beautiful Pleiades, Capella, Scorpio will add a certain sonority to a nocturnal landscape. The name by itself is an astronomy; George Sand sometimes confuses Venus and Sirius; Sirius is her favorite star. It must be present, shining at dramatic moments in her nights. This mania for naming the stars is not, of course, limited to George Sand. We could criticize it in many poets.

Thus, in Elémir Bourges' *The Ship*, innumerable examples may be found of this pathos of the starry sky. The modern author, talking about skies of bygone ages, will not hesitate to distinguish "colossal spheres that attract each other" in the night.

> Adore, like a supreme god, Uranus, who forms the substance of stars, souls, and spirits. See! Thousands of worlds are turning in just one of my rays. Everywhere, your eye can discover, beyond this paltry universe where the earth hangs from its chain, spheres, multicolored fires, which are more numerous than the waves of the rivers or the leaves in the forests. And these colossal spheres are themselves attracted by other spheres that still others carry along, turning amid their phosphorous flames and their stormy typhoons, in the endless dance of their eternal joy.

At no point in his preparation, when he mixes the genres and joins together ancient dreams and Newtonian knowledge, does Bourges get to the place where he participates or succeeds in making his reader participate in a nocturnal life, in the slow cosmogony of night and its lights. Dreamed dynamically, Night is a slow force. The noise and disturbance that are found everywhere in Bourges' work do not belong to it.

It seems to me, then, that true poetry, natural poetry, must leave the great forms of nature anonymous. Whispering the name

Bételgeuse when the star shines in the sky adds nothing to a poet's evocative powers. How do we know, a child asks, that its name is Bételgeuse? Poetry is not a tradition; it is a primitive dream; it is an awakening of primary images.

There is, moreover, nothing absolute about my criticisms. Even in poor uses of an evocative name, we can discern a primary image at work in a modern imagination. Then the constellation appears, removed from all schemata, through a kind of verbal enchantment, as a *pure literary image*, that is, as an image that has value only in literature. When George Sand writes in *Lélia*, "Scorpio's pale stars plunged into the sea one by one. . . . Sublime nymphs, inseparable sisters, they seem to be intertwined and to carry each other along, inviting each other to join in the chaste voluptuousness of the bath," no reader can be expected to recognize the sight that the author is evoking. Does he even know that Scorpio is made up of four separate stars? But by using the images of stars gently carried along in a single motion—an image that can be used only in literature—Lélia's contemplation takes on dynamic value. A true poet sets a poem in motion in a few lines:

> Great waves of constellations
> Awake in the stirring, waning night,

says Charles van Lerberghe.[3] Following the progressive motion suggested by Lélia, the reader feels the stars disappearing in turn into the sea. He sees them moving as a group, and the constellation that is set in motion this way makes the whole starry sky revolve. A writer in a hurry, of course, would tell us that the stars disappear one by one into the sea, and the reader, always ready to ignore the way that books diagram things, would then think only of the coming dawn. Readers "skip the descriptions" because no one has taught them to appreciate "literary imagination."

So, in my view, one of the main functions of the literary image is to follow and to interpret a dynamism that is found in our own imagination. It is more natural for a constellation to set dynamically than for a single star to do so. The imagination needs to prolong the image by slowing it down. In particular, the imagination of nocturnal matter, more than any other, needs this slow motion. How false literature is

3. Charles van Lerberghe, *Entrevisions* (Paris, 1923), 47.

when it hurries everything and does not allow us enough time to read its images. Especially it does not give us enough time to prolong dreams in the way that the reading of any literature ought to create.

III

If we reflect on the precise lesson on imaginary dynamism that constellations provide for us, we see that they teach a kind of absolute slowness. We can say of them, as a Bergsonian would: we perceive that they have turned, we never see them turn. The starry sky is the slowest of all natural motions. On a scale of slowness, it is the first motion. Slowness gives it a gentle, peaceful nature. It is the object of an unconscious adherence that can give an amazing feeling of complete aerial lightness. Images of slowness are connected to images about the gravity of life. As René Berthelot remarks: "The solemn slowness of ritual motions in ceremonies is always compared to the stars' movement."[4]

It seems to me that Maurice de Guérin's prose poem "The Bacchante" gets a great deal of its indefinable charm from the "immobile voyage" of the constellations in the sky.[5] Let us recall this admirable passage. In an aerial life, the being comes alive on the summits.

> I climbed up to the place on the mountain that feels the tread of the immortals; for some among them enjoy traveling over the mountain chain steering their unshakable stride along the waving tree-tops. When I reached those heights, I received the gifts given by night, calm, and sleep. . . . But such rest was similar to that of the birds who are friends of the winds and always borne along on their course.

It seems as though the dreamer is sleeping the sleep of high foliage, which even in its sleep enjoys the "attacks of the winds" with a soul that "opens to the slightest breaths that reach the high points of the woods."

It is at this point, then, that the being sleeping *in the heights, in true aerial sleep* will revive the myth of Callisto, who was beloved of Jupiter and who was carried into the sky through the god's kindness.

4. René Berthelot, "L'Astrobiologie et la pensée de l'Asie," *Revue de Métaphysique et de Morale* (October 1933), 474.

5. Maurice de Guérin, "La Bacchante," in *Oeuvres complètes* (Paris, 1947), I:17-18

Jupiter . . . took her away from the woods in order to join her to the stars, and he guided her destiny in a sleep from which it could no longer break away. She was given a home in the depths of the dark sky. . . . The sky arranges the oldest of its shadows around her and has her breathe in all that it still possesses of life principles. . . . Permeated by an eternal intoxication, Callisto remains tilted on the pole, while the whole order of constellations pass by and lower their courses toward the ocean; this is how I remained during the night, immobile on the summit of the mountains.

Here we are once more in the presence of an *absolute literary image.* The constellation, Callisto, is not in fact evoked as a form; the poet takes care not to comment on the legend that would take us back to the mythology that we learned in school. He barely mentions that while Callisto was living her life on earth, "Juno, in her jealousy, dressed her in a wild form." Neither does the poet make this constellation's lights shine. All of the image's life, in Guérin's poem, belongs to *dynamic imagination.* In this poem, then, the constellation is an image intended for closed eyes, a pure image of slow, peaceful, celestial motion, one without change or end, one that is alien to the ravages of destiny or to the lure of goals. As he contemplates, the dreamer learns to find his rhythm within himself and to regulate his living by this constant time, time without *élan* or shock. This is *night's time.* In this image, dream and motion provide us with proof of their temporal harmony. Day's time, always filled with a thousand tasks, frittered away and lost in futile activity, lived and relived in the flesh, appears in all its vanity. The one who dreams in the serenity of the night finds the marvelous web of *time that is resting.*

When it is lived in such a reverie as this, the constellation is a hymn rather than an image. And only "literature" can sing this hymn. It is a hymn with no cadence, it is a voice with no volume, a motion that has transcended its goals and found the true matter of slowness. You will hear the music of the spheres when you have collected enough metaphors, the most varied kinds of metaphors—that is, when the imagination has been re-established in its vital role as a guide for human life.

If we reread Guérin's "The Bacchante" with the themes of aerial and dynamic imagination in mind, we will find that it is an example of a work that owes nothing to the inspiration of the Ancients but that is, instead, completely contemporary and alive. In the closing lines we can grasp the action of an image that is neither drawn nor desired in its form and that is operative only because of its imaginary induction. It is in fact the constellation's purely dynamic induction. Through it, the dreamer is able to relate to the motion and destiny of the starry sky. "I rose, following the tracks of this bacchante who was walking ahead of us like the Night, when, head turned aside to call the shadows, she moved toward the West."

IV

The best way to convince ourselves of the dynamic beauty of Guérin's image is, perhaps, to compare it to a frantic image, the kind that is so common in Elémir Bourges' *The Ship*:

> I am speaking to you who lead this unreined bird-horse with the eagle's pinions in the midst of the starry chasms. Since I hear your cries, certainly mine will carry to where you are. Who are you, warrior? A man? A god? A demon that falls somewhere between the two? Answer! What celestial enemy hurls the blazing wake of your flight through Uranus? Do you live at peace with the earth? Are carnage and terror seated on the tip of your lance?

And in another place this too colorful Bellerophon calls out: "Ha! ha! ha! my shield on which the flaming lightning-serpent writhes is burning my flesh down to the bone. The blazing star lighted at the crest of my brass helmet clings to my bubbling brain. . . . My eyes start out of their orbits. I am panting . . ." If we judge this production of "Uranian monsters" by applying the principle that Maurice Boucher, with a great deal of insight, calls the four dimensions of the poetic word: the meaning, the aura, the valence, and the life, we will recognize that Bourges' Bellerophon lacks this fourfold depth. Contrary to Guérin's bacchante, tradition confuses life in this image. The allusions come from books. The frenzied movement does not follow the valence of night. The meaning and the oneiric aura are so completely lacking that no reverie can develop in the reader's soul. Elémir Bourges appears not to have lived in his imagination any of the powers of the Uranotropism that is so characteristic in true dreamers of the night.

V

The gentle shining light of the stars also stimulates one of the most persistent and regular of reveries: the reverie of the gaze. We can sum up all of its aspects in a single law: *in the realm of the imagination, everything that shines is a gaze.* Our need to be on familiar terms is so great, and contemplation is so naturally a confidence, that everything that we gaze upon passionately, either because of our distress or our desire, looks back at us familiarly, with either compassion or love. When we fix upon one star in the anonymous sky, it becomes *our* star; it twinkles for us; a few tears gather around its fire, and aerial life brings us some comfort for the suffering that we endure on earth. Then it seems that the star is coming toward us. We are unmoved by reason, which tells us that it is lost in the immensity of space; personal dream puts it in touch with our heart. Night isolates us from earth, but it gives us back our dreams of kinship with air.

A psychology of the star and a cosmology of the gaze could be developed at length in reciprocal exchanges. This would take place within a curiously unified imagination. An examination of this imaginary unity would require lengthy studies. It would not be difficult to find many references in poetic works from every country and every era. We will look at only one example in which the dream of the star's gaze attains its greatest cosmological power. It comes from a book by O. V. de L. Milosz, *Epistle to Storge*, following a meditation on infinity occasioned by *stellar space*. There suddenly arises this proof of a joining of two gazes:

> In our small astronomical sky, I know two particularly brilliant stars, two pure, beautiful, faithful confidants, which I believed were separated from their friend by unimaginable distances. Well, the other evening, a huge moth fell from the lamp onto my hand and I was moved to question its blazing eyes.[6]

Yes, we immediately perceive two twin stars as a face looking at us, and, in an even exchange two eyes that look at us, no matter how far-removed they may be from our own lives, immediately exercise a stellar influence on our souls. In a flash they break our solitude. The act of seeing and gazing here exchange their dynamics: we receive and

6. O. V. de L. Milosz, "Epître à Storge" in *Ars Magna* (Paris, 1924), 16-17.

we give. Distance is abolished. An infinity of communion erases an infinity of size. The world of stars touches our soul: it is a world of gazing.

8

Clouds

The clouds' play—nature's essentially
poetic game . . .

NOVALIS, *Fragments*

I

CLOUDS ARE NUMBERED among the most oneiric of "poetic things."
They are the objects of daytime oneiric experience. They call forth
easy, ephemeral reveries. In an instant we are "in the clouds," and
then we come back down to earth, gently teased by positivists. No
dreamer attributes to clouds the solemn significance of other sky
"signs." In short, the reverie of clouds has a particular psychological
characteristic: it is a *reverie without responsibility.*

The first thing that we notice about this reverie is that it is, as has
so often been said, an easy play of form. Clouds provide imaginary
matter for a lazy modeler. We dream them as a light cotton batting
that rearranges itself. Reverie—as children often practice it—controls
a changing phenomenon by giving it a command that has already
been carried out or is being carried out. "Great elephant! Stretch out
your trunk," says the child to the cloud that is growing longer. And
the cloud obeys.[1]

To account for the importance of the cloud in religious themes in
India, Bergaigne writes quite correctly: "The cloud that envelops
these waters is not only billowing and dripping, but even moving,
and seems quite ready to play animal games."[2] If the night's zoomorphism is stable in the constellations, the day's zoomorphism is
undergoing constant change in the clouds. The dreamer always has a
cloud to transform. The clouds help us to dream of transformation.

The *authoritarian* nature of reverie cannot be overemphasized; it is

---

1. Johann Ludwig Tieck, *Das alte Buch und die Reise ins Blaue hinein* in *Ludwig
Tiecks Schriften: Gesammelte Novellen* (Breslau, 1838-42), 8:10.
2. Abel Henri Joseph Bergaigne, *La Religion védique* (Paris, 1878-83), I:4.

given as the most effortless of creative powers. This reverie works by way of the eyes. Meditated in the right way, it can shed light on the close relationship between will and imagination. Faced with this world of changing forms in which the *will to see* goes beyond passive vision and projects the most simplified of beings, the dreamer is master and prophet. He is the *prophet of the moment*. He tells, in a prophetic voice, what is currently going on before his very eyes. Should there be, in some corner of the sky, matter that will not conform, other clouds have already prepared the preliminary outlines that the *imagination-will* eventually completes. Our imaginary desire is attached to an imaginary form filled with imaginary matter. All the elements, certainly, are good for healing reverie. The whole world can be brought to life by the command of a hypnotic gaze. But with clouds the task is grandiose and easy at the same time. In this globular mass, everything rolls on just as you please. Mountains glide, avalanches fall and then regain their composure; monsters swell up and devour each other; the whole universe is governed by the will and by the imagination of the dreamer.

Sometimes the modeler's hand accompanies the reverie of modeling up to the heavens. The dream "takes a hand in the work" in an enormous, even demiurgic task. Jules Supervielle, in his *Drinking at the Spring*, follows in the sky of Uraguay animals that are more beautiful than those found on the pampas, ones that

> do not die. You merely see them disappear before your eyes, without suffering. Their forms are not fixed, they are ever-changing, but so soft to the hand that caresses them. This is what I would like to say if it were not completely mad! Clouds.

And Christian Sénéchal, who quotes this text, adds:

> This expression is one that we should remember and add to the other very numerous examples of taking possession of the world with the hands. Jules Supervielle has the gift of caressing clouds like the sculptor who models with his hands contours that are invisible to others' eyes.[3]

Sénéchal, we may note, asks literary criticism not to limit itself to the common distinction between visual and auditory imagination, which

3. Christian Sénéchal, *Jules Supervielle, poète de l'univers intérieur* (Paris, 1939), 142.

is an unwarranted distinction that alienates us from so many profound statements on the imaginary life and so many direct, dynamic intuitions. Without an imagination properly attuned dynamically, formed by the dynamics of the hand, how can we understand these lines by Supervielle:

> Hands give their name to the sun, on a lovely day
> They call it "trembling," that slight hesitation
> That comes to them from the human heart at the other
> end of the warm veins.

We see the same thing again in *Love and Hands*:

> And holding your hands prisoner in my own
> I shall remake the world and the gray clouds.

These passages are all the more important since we may find in them proof that hands are not necessarily *terrestrial* and are not necessarily linked to the geometry of the tangible, close, resistant, object. With an immense hand, the modeler of clouds may seem to us a specialist in aerial matter. That is exactly what Sénéchal is trying to show us in his book about Supervielle, i.e., that he is a personality "eager to seize the invisible world in his *hands* and yet capable of the most aerial and subtle *fantasy* and of a *dream* that is entirely free of the constraints imposed by earth."[4]

Supervielle's images are really built upon deliberate, subtle manipulation; they invite the reader to take his turn at building them without accepting ready-made visions. For example, we read in *Native City*:

> Children and women in the street
> Like beautiful clouds,

4. The cloud modeler has another great advantage: he has an abundance of cosmic matter. He can pile Pelion on Ossa.

> Contemplator enim, quum montibus assimilata
> Nubila portabunt venti transversa per auras
> Aut ubi per magnos montes cumulata videbis
> Insuper esse aliis alia . . .
> Consider, when the winds have carried the clouds
> Like mountains through the air in a slanting course
> Or when you see them pile one on top of the other
> On the sides of great mountains, and pressing down from above . . .

Lucretius, *The Poem on Nature*, trans. C. H. Sisson (Manchester, England, 1976), 182.

Gather to search for their souls
And pass from shadow into sunlight.[5]

Anyone who grasps these lines *dynamically* will feel his hands *modeling eiderdown*. First, on a lovely summer's day, he will take a forgotten tuft from the bottom of a basket. In his reverie of unfolding and aerating an over-compressed matter, he will give to burgeoning matter its share of white light; he will dream of the lamb, the child, the heavenly swan. Then he will reread, with greater appreciation, a preceding stanza:

The palm trees, when they found a form
Where their pure pleasure could sway,—
Called the birds from afar.

In the same way the cloud summons all feathery tufts of wool, all white down, all artless wings. The spinner's dream unreels up to the sky. If we reread George Sand's tale, *The Cloud-Spinner*, we will see that the dreaming spinner's secret or hope is to spin as fine a thread as the clouds that soften and subdue the sky's light.[6]

D'Annunzio has developed this image in his "Poems of Love and Glory" in *Evening in the Alban Hills*:

Last clouds, light woof through which the slender crescent moon passes like a golden shuttle.
The aerial shuttle does its work in silence; sometimes it is hidden, sometimes it flashes between widely spaced threads.
The pensive woman silently follows it in the sky with pure eyes that see further:—further than life, but in vain!

The image of birds—often swallows—that spin invisible threads in the blue sky seem to be a synthesis of wing movement and the puff of a cloud. In *The Heretic of Soana*, we read:

And the voices of the birds . . . joined above the rocky hollows of the mighty valley, as though infinitely held in a net of invisible thread. . . . And wasn't it miraculous that this woof, when it

5. Jules Supervielle, *Gravitations* (Paris, 1966), 110.
6. Friedrich Lebrecht Wilhelm Schwartz notes many myths in which cloud material is spun. With his complete confidence in naturalistic mythology, Schwartz places the three Fates in the sky; the three spinners represent Dawn, Day, and Night. *Wolken und Wind, Blitz und Donner* (Berlin, 1864), I:6.

disappeared or was torn, was reestablished as though by the tireless shuttle of rapid flight? Or did the tiny weavers have wings?[7]

When we have learned the themes of aerial imagination by reading such passages in which the images seem somewhat overemphasized, we will be better prepared to appreciate the amazingly subtle aerial charm of Paul Valéry's "The Spinner." It seems as though a little of the sky's matter comes down to work on earth:

> Seated, the spinner in the blue of the windowpane
> . . . .
> Sated with azure, weary . . .
> . . . .
> . . . the pure air and a shrub contrive a living spring
> A stem, where the vagabond wind comes to rest,
> Bows with the vain curtsey of its starry grace,
> Vowing the splendid rose to the antique spinning wheel.

In each stanza there is a bit of pure air, a bit of blue air, a patch of it come to rest . . .

II

We can grasp the form-producing power of what is originally amorphous, what we feel at work in "cloud reverie," and the absolute continuity of the process of deformation only if we truly participate dynamically in them. "It is not far, as a bird flies, from cloud to man," says Paul Eluard.[8] This is true on condition that to a bird's linear flight we add global flight, flight that rolls and is round, like light bubbles. Dynamic continuity replaces discontinuities of static beings. Distinctions among different things are clearer, and things themselves are more alien to the subject when they are motionless. When they begin to move, they move in us by arousing our latent desires and needs. "Matter, motion, need, and desire are inseparable. The honor of living is well worth the effort we make to awaken to life," Eluard concludes. To put it as Supervielle would: "Faced with the clouds' slow movement, we suddenly know 'what goes on behind immobility.' " Motion has more oneiric homogeneity than does the

7. Gerhardt Hauptmann, The Heretic of Soana, authorized translation (London, 1923), 98.
8. Paul Eluard, Donner à voir (Paris, 1939), 97.

being. It brings together the most diverse beings. Dynamic imagination puts seemingly unrelated objects "into the same motion," not "into the same slot," and suddenly a world forms and becomes one before our very eyes. When Eluard writes "We often see clouds on the table. We often see glasses, hands, pipes, cards, pieces of fruit, knives, birds, and fish too," he frames immobile objects with mobile beings in his oneiric inspiration. At the beginning of his dream only the clouds induce motion, while at the end fish and birds do too. The clouds on the table will fly and swim with the birds and fish in the end, after they have gently set the lifeless objects in motion. The poet's first responsibility is to release within us matter that will dream.

During our endless dreams before the sky, as soon as the clouds come down onto the stone table or into the hollow of our hand, it seems that all things become a little rounder and that crystals are clothed in a white half-light. We and the world are the same size; the sky is on the earth; our hand touches the sky. Supervielle's hand will knead the cloud. The cloud is going to come and take shape in Eluard's musing hand. The reason that literary criticism fails to understand so many poems of this generation is because it judges them by the standards of forms, whereas they constitute a world of movement, a poetic becoming. Literary criticism has forgotten Novalis' great teaching: "Poetry is the art of psychic dynamism (*Gemütserregungskunst*)." Let us now leave aside vain forms and go beyond the game that I myself described. The cloud, a slow, round motion, a white motion, one that silently collapses, awakens in us a soft, round, pale, silent, fluffy, imaginative life. . . . In its dynamic intoxication, the imagination uses the cloud like an ectoplasm that sensitizes our mobility. In the long run nothing can resist the invitation of the clouds to travel as they patiently float by, again and again, far up in the blue sky. It seems to the dreamer as if the cloud could carry everything away with it: sorrow, steel, screams. About the fragrance of "wild strawberries," Supervielle asks:

> How can one take it along when one is only a cloud
> With holes in his pockets?
> But nothing seems amazing to this little bit of
>   nothingness that glides.
> Nothing seems so heavy that it cannot be taken along.

In another of Supervielle's poems, elastic men, tired of weight, embark upon a whole universe:

> From three masts a few waves take wing, at their flanks
> Hamlets, watering and washing places, will go skyward,
> Wheat fields, amid the poppies' laughter;
> Giraffes vying with each other in the bush made of clouds,
> An elephant will climb the snow-capped summits of air;
> In celestial water will shine porpoises and sardines
> And the barks sailing up to the angels' smiles . . .

The passage ends with an awakening of the dead. They are drawn by the aerial dynamics of the living and guided by the clouds rising up in the blue sky. Then, as Anna de Noailles says: "The azure, the wave, the earth, everything is in flight."

The cloud is also taken as a messenger. Among Indian poets, it is sometimes, as Gubernatis tells us, "represented as a leaf that is carried off in the wind," and he adds, in a note, "Schiller, in his *Maria Stuart*, was certainly influenced by an old popular idea when he addresses the wishes and regrets of a captive queen to a cloud."

III

To answer anyone who would deny the role of dynamic imagination in imaginary life, it would be enough to seek an analysis of the heavy cloud and the light cloud, the cloud that oppresses us and the cloud that draws us up to the highest point in the sky. On one side, in an immediate dialectic, we would place Supevielle's comment that "Everything is a cloud to me, and I am dying of it," and, on the other, Baudelaire's prose poem—the first, which opens his collection:

> —Well! what do you enjoy, then, incredible stranger?
> —I enjoy clouds . . . clouds that go by . . . out there . . . out there
> those marvellous clouds!

Quite directly, without any descriptions, one cloud strikes our fancy, another strikes us down. Clouds, like those in the evil storm of *Princess Maleine*, do not need lightning or thunder to shake the cursed castle "from basement to attic."[9] A black cloud is enough to make unhappiness *weigh down* the whole universe.

If we want to experience the feeling of suffocation created by a low-

9. Maurice Maeterlinck, *La Princesse Maleine* (Bruxelles, 1908-09), 157.

hanging sky, it is not enough to link the concepts of low and heavy. Imaginations's participation is more personal. The heavy cloud feels like evil sent down from heaven, an evil that will overwhelm the dreamer and of which he may die.

To understand the imaginary essence of the sickness brought on by heavy, low-hanging clouds, we must consider it in relation to the truly active function of the imagination of clouds. In its positive imaginary aspect, the function of the imagination of clouds is an invitation to ascend. Normal reverie follows the image as if it were a substantial rising that finally attains the highest sublimation by disappearing at the highest point in the blue sky. True clouds, little clouds, disappear in the heights. We cannot imagine a little cloud disappearing while it is falling. The little, light cloud is the most regular and dependable theme of ascent. It is a constant reminder of sublimation. In William Blake's "The Book of Thel," the little cloud says to the Virgin: ". . . when I pass away,/It is to tenfold life, to love, to peace, and raptures holy."[10]

In the illustrations, the formal imagination, which is often naively materialistic, suggests long paths lost in the clouds where processions of the elect make their way up to heaven. But these images created by the formal imagination are deeper when rooted in dynamic and aerial imagination. The soul that dreams before a light cloud receives at once the image of effusive matter and the dynamic image of ascent. In such a reverie about losing a cloud in the blue sky, the dreamer participates with all his being in a total sublimation. It is truly the image of absolute sublimation. This is the ultimate voyage.

IV

Goethe has written a passage in which he gives a detailed analysis of the imagination of clouds. After lengthy reflections on the work of Howard, the English meteorologist, the poet seems to be drawn to another view of nature through poetic inspiration. Stratus, Cumulus, Cirrus, and Nimbus provide us with four direct images that are experienced in a manifest ascensional psychology.

> *Stratus.* When from the water's peaceful mirror a mist arises and unfolds as a single lament, the moon, linked with the watering phenomenon, seems like a phantom that creates other phantoms:

10. Blake, "The Book of Thel," Plate 3, lines 10-11, 4.

then, o nature, we are all entranced and delighted children, we admit it. Then it rises next to the mountain, piling up layer upon layer, it casts a shadow at a distance over all of the middle region, as ready to fall in the form of rain as it is to rise as a vapor.

Cumulus. And if the imposing mass is called into the upper regions of the atmosphere, the cloud stops in a magnificent sphere. In its determined form it proclaims its power to act, and what you fear and even what you experience is a threat above; below it is trembling.

Cirrus. But a noble impulse makes it rise even higher. An easy, divine constraint delivers it. A mass of clouds is broken up into flakes, like bounding sheep, a lightly combed multitude. Thus, what comes gently to life down here, up above finally flows with no sound into the lap and the hand of the Father.

Nimbus. And what is amassed up above, drawn by the earth's force, is hurled down in the fury of thunderstorms, spread out and dispersed in legions. The active and passive destiny of the earth! But lift up your gaze with the image: the word descends, for it describes. The spirit wants to rise to where it lives forever.

Gift. And when we have made this distinction, we ought to attribute the gifts of life to the thing that has been separated out and rejoice in a continuous life.

Therefore, if the painter or the poet, familiar with Howard's analysis, contemplates the atmosphere in the morning and evening hours, he allows its nature to subsist; but aerial worlds give him sweeter, more varied tones that can be grasped, felt, and expressed.[11]

The reader may be disturbed by the mixture of abstract ideas and images that are found in this passage. But looking at it more closely, he will be struck by the pluralism of the cloud's imaginary substance. By pursuing this pluralism even further, he can truly relate to the life of clouds. In this way, reverie can establish a further distinction between *rolling cumulus* and *rumbling cumulus*, namely a distinction between game and threat.[12] In the *Nimbus*, caught between rising and

11. "Howards Ehrengedächtnis" in *Goethes Werke* (Hamburg, 1949, rpt. 1964), I:350-51.
12. For example, the happy reverie of Jules Laforgue, correctly feeling that a cloud is a motion, will produce this line: "Cumulus: Indolent rolls, that a wavering wind/Guarded one fine evening." "Complaintes des Voix," in *Oeuvres complètes de Jules Laforgue* (Paris, 1909), 69.

falling, many different reveries are also in preparation. In any case, in reading Goethe, we should recognize that contemplating a cloud's form is not enough for a complete analysis of cloud reverie. Cloud reverie is a more profound participation; it attributes to the cloud a material that is either gentle or menacing, a potential for action, or for self-effacement and peace.

Goethe seems to have wanted to put objective knowledge at the very basis of these poetic images.

In particular, cloud reverie sometimes allows the accumulation of more heterogenous images. The stormy sky, with its motion, its clamor, its lightning flashes, is expressed in two short stanzas in one of Lenau's poems: the clouds are flocks, clouds rounded up in galloping circles, while the wind, like a good rider, urges them on by cracking his "lightning whip." We might say that the contemplation of clouds brings us face to face with a world where there are just as many forms as there are motions. Motion produces form, forms are in motion, and motion constantly deforms them. This is a world of forms in constant transformation.

The most varied poetic temperaments can harbor "these meterological forms of beauty," as Baudelaire puts it.[13] Studying the sky painted by a landscape artist, Baudelaire writes:

> All these clouds, with their fantastic and luminous forms, these chaotic shadows, the huge green and pink spaces, hanging suspended and piled one on top of another, these gaping furnaces, these firmaments of black or violet satin, wrinkled, rolled, or torn, these horizons draped in mourning or dripping with molten metal, all of these splendors go straight to my head like a heady wine or the eloquence produced by opium.

Baudelaire, who was a man of the city and a poet of human things, is suddenly seized by the power of cosmic contemplation and adds, "One thing is odd, looking at this liquid or aerial magic, not once did it occur to me to complain that man was not present."

V

To be more specific, the dynamic imagination of the cloud seems to me the only means of providing a psychological explanation of the

13. Baudelaire, *Curiosités esthétiques* (Lausanne, 1956), 369.

poetic myths that use a *magic carpet* or a *magic cloak*. Many storytellers have accepted them ready-made—without really following the laws of the imagination—from among the bric-a-brac of an Oriental bazaar. These writers are always in a hurry to tell us about things human—far too human. For them, the cloud is a means of transportation that will carry us to a land where we will see a new act in the old human comedy. The oneiric power of the trip is completely lost. In the beginning, however, the image is powerful. We want it to be well-developed and multi-faceted. Alas! the magic cloak is a ready-to-wear coat! The psychologist who wants to study its natural dream function is forced to rely on a few brief comments. Let me give a few examples, which should be enough to show the connection between oneiric flight, travel on a cloud, and a magic cloak. This will allow us to better understand the creative role of dynamic imagination.

In *Merlin the Magician*, Edgar Quinet writes that the magician "was enveloped in a cloak wrapped around him and with one bare foot he pressed down on the clouds that were carrying him along with the speed of eagles." As we can see, the oneiric wealth is no doubt too concentrated here. An analyst of the imaginary would prefer that the oneiric flight be described in full, beginning with the first time the heel strikes the earth; but here already the dreamer is walking on a cloud; he is asking the cloud to send him upward. The cloud is what is carrying him like an enveloping cloak, one that soon becomes a wing, an eagle's wing. Everything at once participates in the flight, in a cluster of aerial images or of flying powers. A literature that would place images before ideas would give us time to live such wonderful metamorphoses. This is where the real magic lies! But the writer gives us only an enchanting sight. A writer who has had the experience of the real voyage-in-itself gives us only a voyage to contemplate.

The same could be said for *Helen's robe* in the *Second Faust*:

> . . . . Make use of the exalted
> Inestimable boon and rise aloft,
> It [Helen's robe] bears you swiftly over all that is base
> Across the ether, for as long as you may endure.

The philosopher's desire to manipulate intellectualized symbols leaves the poet no leisure for living his images oneirically. He has deprived us of the first impulses of his reverie. Nevertheless, it is the moment when the dream detaches us from reality that it is most beneficial.

VI

Since I have felt obliged to take my examples in this work primarily from consciously written literature, I have had to leave Michel Bréal's admirable thesis out of this dissertation. Bréal presents the legend of Hercules and Cacus as a true myth of the cloudy sky. Bréal's explication of the myth is, of course, basically linguistic. In his view "the heavenly cows [of Geryon] are a linguistic creation. . . . " In Sanskrit, the verb root that formed the noun *go* (*boeuf* [cattle]) comes from a root that means *to go, to walk*. The clouds run through the sky. Therefore, there was really no metaphor involved in "calling the clouds *gavas, those that walk*. . . . " "Language, which was still in a state of flux and unable to be certain with regard to word choice, named different objects for a common attribute: it created two homonyms." Let us note, however, that this same attribute is purely and simply *a movement*. It is *dynamic imagination* that is at work here. I therefore feel justified in speaking of a *homonymous dynamics*.

Reading Bréal's thesis, pen in hand, a reader will see that the phenomena of a cloudy sky explain all of the adventures found in the legend of Geryon. Mythology is a primitive meteorology.

9

The Nebula

At a quarter past midnight; what shores
see you pass, in the anonymous nights,
Mother Nebula?
                          JULES LAFORGUE
                    Autobiographical Preludes

I

THE DREAM is an evening's cosmogony. The dreamer begins the world over again every night. Anyone who can detach himself from the worries of the day and give his reverie all the powers of solitude gives back to reverie its cosmogonic function. He can appreciate the truth of O. V. de L. Milosz's statement: "The cosmos, in its entirety, courses physically through us."[1] The cosmic dream, in the half-light of sleep, has a kind of primitive nebula from which forms without number can come forth. If the dreamer should open his eyes, he will see once more in the sky that substance of nocturnal white—even more easily manipulated than a cloud—with which one can shape worlds without end. Therefore, how easily erudite thought accepted the cosmogonic hypotheses of modern science which have it that worlds emerge from a primitive nebula! And what success a simple image of the sky with its swirling nebulae can bring to a book for a popular audience! This is because the dynamic imagination is at work beneath such images. Whereas the stars, so often compared to golden spikes, are symbols of fixity, the nebula, on the other hand, the Milky Way—to which a thoughtful view should attribute the very same fixity as it does to the stars—is, during an evening's contemplation, the theme of constant changes. Its image is contaminated by both cloud and milk. Night takes on life in this milky light. An imaginary life is formed in this aerial milk. The moon's milk comes down and bathes the earth; the milk of the Milky Way stays in the sky.

1. O. V. de Milosz, *Ars Magna*, 37.

Lafcadio Hearn experienced the Milky Way's celestial outpouring. He comments on a number of Japanese poems on this "River of Heaven," where we see "the water grasses of the River of Heaven bend[ing] in the autumn wind . . . and on the River of Heaven the sound of the rowing of the night boat is heard, and the splash of the oar resounds."[2] He concludes, experiencing the usual rationalization inversely and following a way of thinking that would have to be called derationalization:

> Then I no longer behold the Milky Way as that awful Ring of the Cosmos whose hundred million suns are powerless to lighten the Abyss, but as the very Amanogawa itself, —the river celestial. I see the thrill of its shining stream, and the mists that hover along its verge . . . and I know that the falling dew is the spray from the Herdsman's oar.

In this way, beyond all objective knowledge, despite an unemotional examination, the imagination regains its rights; it sets the most static images in motion and revitalizes the most lifeless ones. The imagination makes the sky's matter flow. When Descartes sets forth his learned cosmology where "the skies are liquid," we will be able to see in it the rationalization of a forgotten reverie.

We could, moreover, state the following proposition as a true postulate of the material and dynamic imagination: *what is diffuse is never seen as motionless.* D'Annunzio says in *The Dead City:* "The Milky Way seems to wave in the wind like a long veil." Any amorphous mass made up of many parts gives the impression of a swarm. Victor Hugo called the Milky Way "heaven's anthill." Along the same lines of this proposition, a glow for the dreamer is greater than light, because it is a glow's imaginary nature to spread and become diffused far from the confines where it seemed at first glance to be located. Also, in contemplating the Milky Way, the imagination can experience a gentle cosmic force. Gustave Kahn provides us with an example of the gently expanding vision: "The Milky Way's gentle radiance fell over an even greater space with more faraway worlds, vibrating silver, unknown things, and sweet, vague promises."[3] The

---

2. Lafcadio Hearn, "The Romance of the Milky Way," in *The Romance of the Milky Way and Other Studies and Stories* (Freeport, New York, n.d.), 38.
3. Gustave Kahn, *Le Cirque solaire* (Paris, 1899), 110.

dreamer lets himself be cradled in these wholly imaginary vibrations. He seems to rediscover the confidence of a distant childhood. The night is a swollen breast.

In some cases, the reverie of the Milky Way takes on such importance in a work that it is the explanation for an entire aspect of it. Such is the case in the work of Jules Laforgue, for example, which could be organized as a *Literary Cosmos of the Nebula*. That is no doubt the origin of the work. In *Letters to a Friend*, which were written, it so happens, to Gustave Kahn, we read: "I must say ... that before being a dilettante and a clown, I spent some time living in the cosmic."

In nature, Jules Laforgue loves soft, burgeoning matter, and in poetic alchemy he, like Faust's son, was very familiar with barely perceptible transformations:

> If you only knew, Mama Nature . . . .
> If you only knew how well I know
> The Table of your Contents!
> You would hold me an accountant
> accountable to death!

Science tells us that real life began in the sea. The life of dreams begins in a kind of celestial sea. In his *Litanies of Wretchedness* Laforgue evokes:

> The life-giving forces of the Sun, traveling in the blue heavens
> An incandescent lake falls, then scatters.

They are the source of early seas . . . then the groaning of the woods and all the outcries of the world.

And his unending reverie asks:

> O! far out there, out there . . . in the night of mystery
> Where have you been, for so many stars and now . . .
> O chaotic river, O mother-nebula,
> From whom emerged the Sun, our powerful father?

The cosmic meaning of Laforgue's poems may appear to some readers veiled by their disillusioned tone. In many respects, Laforgue's cosmos viewed subjectively might pass for a cosmos of the disheartened. But a detailed analysis of the images allows us to grasp the filiations that lead from the discouraged dreamer to congealed lights, and to nights churning erratically in strange vortexes, and to pale, gelatinous moons. All of these are adjectives that a psycho-analyst would have no trouble classifying. I am putting them together only to show how matter invades the dreamer's sky. The sky is truly a "dream machine" for Laforgue. Every night, he is there, "drinking in the stars themselves, O mystery!" and "dredging the stars' paths." And it is to the Milky Way that he repeats his wish: "Become plasma again."

It is the same in the skies as on earth: everything that is vague and round swells as soon as reverie intervenes. An overly active imagi-nation will not be satisfied with swelling and flowing. It will see and experience a bubbling over. This passage, from Bourges' *The Ship*, is an example of one that is overly colorful, too forced in its force. From the high clouds, "vortexes of gold escape in rushing floods; and, in its opening depths are vaguely seen, palpitating amidst the blazing foam, the rumbling, boiling, golden mists, new forms of divine animals: the eagle, the bull, the dazzling swan. . . . " This excessive rumbling of round matter is present in a contemplation of a very peaceful night: "The whole ether forms flakes, seeded with this gilded snow." The same impression is conveyed by this passage in which André Arny-velde dreams of participating in the life of a nebula:

> I saw a kind of spasmodic incandescent chaos, a substance made of fire-clouds that were constantly changing their lines, extent, and density. Tresses, ruffled plumes, flowing manes of flame stretched out in all directions; and their furious flux, encountering the cold-ness of space, disappeared into the air or fell down in fiery rain.[4]

These amplified voices do not allow us to hear the silence of the night. How much better O. V. de L. Milosz understands creative powers:

> So, put your ear next to my temple and listen. My head is like the stone at the cosmic crossways or of the cosmic torrent. Here they are. The great silent black chariots of Meditation are going to pass by. Then there will be fear like an outpouring of primordial water. And all will be silence.[5]

Within the creation of the nebula, the Night silently meditates and

4. André Arnyvelde, *L'arche* (Paris, 1920), 36.
5. O. V. de Milosz, *Ars Magna*, 35.

the primordial clouds slowly assemble. It is this slowness, this silence, that a great poet must preserve.

II

Imaginary power and the plasma of image exchange their values in such contemplation. Here we find a new application of what I have called, in the preceding chapter, *general imagination* in order to characterize images in which the imagined and the imagining are as completely bound together as are geometric reality and geometric thought in *general relativity*. The power to imagine becomes one with its images when the dreamer touches upon celestial matter. The magic that normally tries to act on the universe gives way to a magic that works on the very heart of the dreamer. Extroverted magic and introverted magic join in an equal reciprocity. Total poetry, *perfect poetry*, as Hugo von Hofmannsthal says,

> is the body of an elf, which is as transparent as air; the vigilant messenger who carries a magic word through the air. As he goes by, he grasps the mystery of the clouds, the stars, the treetops, and the winds. He faithfully transmits the magic formula; however, it is mixed with the mysterious voices of the clouds, the stars, the treetops, and the winds.[6]

The messenger is now one with the message. The personal world of the poet rivals the universe. The soul's landscapes are more marvelous than the landscapes of the starry sky. They have not only Milky Ways made up of millions of stars, but even their dark abysses are living, embracing an infinite life whose very overabundance darkens and stifles. And these abysses where life is consumed can in a moment be illuminated, liberated, and changed into Milky Ways.

6. Hugo von Hofmannsthal, *Ecrits en prose*, 169, 171.

10

The Aerial Tree

> The tree endlessly surges up and there is
> a rustling in its leaves, its innumerable
> wings.
>
> ANDRÉ SUARÈS, *Rêves de l'Ombre*

I

THE IMAGINARY LIFE that is lived in sympathy with the vegetable world would require an entire book. Its general themes, curiously dialectic, would be prairies and forests, grass and trees, clumps and bushes, green leaves and needles, creepers and vine-stocks, flowers and fruits —then the being itself: root, stem and leaves—then its development, marked by the seasons of flowering or dying—and then its potential: wheat and olives, roses and oaks—the vine. Until such a systematic study of these basic images has been done, the psychology of literary imagination will lack the elements it needs to form a doctrine. It will remain dependent on the imagination of visual images, believing that the writer's task is to describe what the painter would paint. Yet how can we fail to understand that attached to the vegetable world is a world of such characteristic reveries that we can consider vegetables as inducers of a particular kind of reverie. Vegetable reverie is the slowest, most tranquil, most restful of all reveries. If only we could get back our gardens and meadows, riverbanks and forests, we could re-live our childhood happiness. The vegetable world faithfully retains the memories of happy reveries. It gives them new life every spring. And, in exchange, it seems that our reverie gives it greater growth, more beautiful flowers, human flowers. "Trees of the forest, you know that you are protected from me by your mysterious plant life—but I am the one who nourishes you . . . "[1]

But a dream botany has not yet been created. Poetry is encumbered by false images. Copied and recopied, lifeless images run throughout

1. Patrice de La Tour du Pin, *Psaumes* (Paris, 1938), 87.

literature, giving little satisfaction to the imagination attracted to flowers. It burdens descriptions that it intended to animate. These burdens can be felt in the *Paradous*, bravura that are easy to write with a scientific flower guide in hand. But it seems that calling a flower by its name is taking a liberty that disturbs reverie. Flowers, like other things, must be loved before they are named. If we were to give them the wrong name, too bad. It would be surprising if any attention were paid to the names of flowers in dreams.

Although I cannot organize the whole "jungle," I would like, in these few pages, merely to emphasize the profound and living unity found in certain vegetable images. I will take the image of the tree as my example and will examine it according to the principles of the material and the dynamic imagination, concentrating on essentially aerial images. The *terrestrial* nature of the tree and its subterranean life should certainly be studied as part of the imagination of earth.

II

In the chapter devoted to Nietzschean energetics, I have already shown that, for the imagination, the pine tree is a true axis of dynamic reverie. Every great dynamized dreamer benefits from this *vertical image*, this *verticalizing image*. The upright tree is an obvious force that carries terrestrial life into the blue sky. De Gubernatis retells a tale that points up very well this power of verticality:

> In Ahorn, near Cobourg, a terrible wind called up by a witch bent the church's bell tower; everyone in nearby towns made fun of it; to free the village from such a shame, a shepherd attached a heavy rope (between the bell tower and a pine tree that is still marked) and by dint of magical invocations and imprecations managed to straighten the tower.[2]

What better way to learn the dynamic lesson of the *pine* tree: "Come, be upright like me," says the tree to the depressed dreamer, "straighten up."

The tree unites and organizes the most disparate elements. The pine tree, says Claudel,

> rises through its own efforts, and, while it remains attached to the earth through the joint effort of its roots, its many and divergent

2. Angelo de Gubernatis, *La Mythologie des plantes* (Paris, 1878), II:292.

branches—tapering to the fragile, sensitive fabric of its leaves, through which it can seek its support in the light and air itself—give it not only its movement, but its essential act and necessary conditions of its stature."[3]

This is the most condensed way of expressing the tree's movement, its essential vertical act, its "aerial, suspended" nature. It is so straight that it gives stability even to the aerial universe.

In the work with the over-playful title "Madness in Vegetables," Francis Jammes sympathizes with the tree's uprightness:

I am dreaming of the trees that devote themselves to an unending search for their aerial balance. . . . Such is the life of a fig tree, like a poet's: the search for light and the difficulty of *remaining in it*.

There are apple trees that prefer the beauty of their fruit to the maintaining of their balance and so break. They are mad.[4]

Moreover, from this vertical life, the most diverse imaginations, whether they be of fire, water, earth, or air, can relive their favorite themes. Some, like Schopenhauer, dream of the pine tree's subterranean life. Others, of the wind and the angry rustling of pine needles. Others experience powerfully the preeminence of water in vegetable life: they "hear" the sap rising. In this exaggerated sympathy with the vegetable world, the hero of Gerhardt Hauptmann's novel "touches the trunk of a chestnut tree" and feels "the nourishing sap that it made rise in him."[5] Finally, others know, as if instinctively, that the tree is the father of fire; they dream endlessly of warm trees in which the joy of burning is immanent: of laurels and mistletoe that crackle; of vines that twist in the flames; of *resin*, the material of fire and light whose scent already seems to burn in the summer's heat.

Thus a single object can give "the total spectrum" of material imaginations. The most disparate dreams cluster around a single material image. It is even more striking to think that these disparate dreams, before a tall, upright tree give themselves over to a certain orientation. Vertical psychology imposes its primary image.

Even motifs like those awakened by woodworking never completely eliminate the image of the living tree. In its fiber, the wood

3. Paul Claudel, *La Connaissance de l'Est*, in *Oeuvres poétiques*, Bibliothèque de la Pléiade (Paris, 1962), 79.
4. Francis Jammes, *Pensées des Jardins* (Paris, 1906), 44-45.
5. Gerhardt Hauptmann, "The Heretic of Soana," 97.

always retains memories of its vertical vigor, and without con-
siderable skill, one cannot go against the grain of the wood. Thus, for
some psychic systems, wood is a kind of fifth element—a fifth matter.
It is fairly common, for example, to find wood ranked among the
basic elements in Oriental philosophies. But such a designation implies working with wood; this is, in my opinion, a reverie of *homo
faber*. It should give added meaning to a psychology of the worker.
Since in this book I am limiting myself to a psychology of reverie and
dream, I must recognize that wood is of little importance to our truly
profound oneiric state. While trees and forests play such a large role
in our nocturnal life, wood itself scarcely ever appears. The dream is
not an instrument. It is not a *means*; it lives directly in the realm of
ends. It needs no intermediary to imagine the elements, but is a part
of the elemental life. In our dreams, we float without a boat, without
a raft, without needing to hollow out a canoe from the trunk of a
tree. In the dream, tree trunks are always hollow. They are always
ready to envelop us and let us stretch out to sleep a long sleep after
which we are sure of a youthful, vigorous awakening.

A deep sleep does not damage the tree.

III

Now let's allow our reverie to follow the images of the tree.

How quickly these images lose interest in shapes! Trees have such
diverse shapes! They have so many and such different kinds of
branches! The unity of their being will seem therefore all the more
striking, as is their unity of motion and their bearing.[6]

This *unity of being* seems at first glance to come from the trunk,
which stands alone. But the imagination is not satisfied by this unity
of isolation, which is a formal and exterior unity. Let it grow, let it
live, and little by little, by way of our imagination, we will feel within
ourselves that the tree, the static being par excellence, becomes

6. It must be noted, however, that a tree's "shape" is untranslatable in literature.
As a matter of fact, no one tries. When the gardener—*homo faber* of the pruning
shears—claims to give a geometrical form to the yew or the arbor vitae, reverie takes it
as a joke. If comedy consists of something mechanical being added on to what is living, then we reach the height of the ridiculous when something geometrical is applied
to the vegetable world. That is how what Nietzsche calls "the rococo in horticulture"
is formed. *The Dawn of Day*, in *The Complete Works of Friedrich Nietzsche*, trans. J. M.
Kennedy, IX:311.

marvelously and dynamically alive. A silent, slow-moving, and invincible upthrust! It is a conquest of lightness and the creation of flying things—aerial, rustling leaves! How the dynamic imagination adores this being that is always upright, this being that never lies down! "In all of nature, only the tree, for symbolic reasons, is upright like man."[7] The tree is an ever-present model of heroic uprightness: "What Epictetuses these fir trees are. . . . How these slender slaves cling to life and, even in their distress, how content they seem to be with their lot in life!"[8]

This vertical dynamism is precisely what forms the basic dialectic between grass and trees in the vegetable imagination. However upright the umbel at harvest time, it retains a little of the meadow's horizontal lines. Even though it has flowers, it is still the spray of a green sea that ripples gently on a summer's morning. Alone, the tree firmly holds its vertical position for the dynamic imagination.

IV

But to get a good feeling for the action of an imaginary power, it is still best, however paradoxical it seems, to catch it when it is just hinting, when it is least in its early, formative stage. With this in mind, we will consider one of the most leisurely and friendly implications of the tree's dynamics: the dreamer sitting comfortably against a tree.

Let us now reread the passage from Rilke:

> Walking back and forth as was his habit, with a book in his hand, he happened at a given moment to find a resting place about shoulder height in the fork of a tree, and at once he felt so pleasantly supported and so completely relaxed in this position that he stayed there, not reading, completely enclosed in an almost unconscious contemplation.[9]

Thus begins a purely dynamic contemplation, as a gentle exchange of powers between dreamer and cosmos, when nothing takes on color or contour under his dreaming gaze, a gaze that is very aptly called *absent.*

7. Paul Claudel, *La Connaissance de l'Est*, 790.
8. Joachim Gasquet, *Il y a une volupté dans la douleur* (Paris, 1921), 27-28.
9. Rainer-Maria Rilke, *Fragments en prose*, 109-10.

It was as if almost imperceptible vibrations came from the inside of the tree and passed over into his body. . . . He felt as though he had never been moved so gently, as if his body had been in some way treated like a soul and prepared to receive an influence whose degree, in ordinary clear-cut physical conditions, would not even have been perceptible at all. To this first impression was added the fact that for the first few minutes he could not determine through which of his senses he was receiving this subtle, yet pervasive message. Moreover, the condition that this contact produced in him was so complete and so consistent—different from any other, but impossible to imagine as either a reinforcement or a reaction to previous events in his life—that despite his fascination, it could not be called a pleasure. No matter. Endeavoring to become aware of the slightest of these impressions, he wondered over and over what had happened to him and, almost at once, found an explanation that satisfied him. He told himself that he had been carried to the other side of nature.

A wonderful passage in which the person, finding peace in a very ordinary fork of a tree, barely aware of the attraction of an almost imperceptible life, without taking anything more from the substance of the world, feels that he is on the other side of the world, very close to the slow general will and in tune with the slow pace of time, stretched out on the wood's smooth grain. The dreamer is then simply a phenomenon of the tree's vertical thrust. His only thought now is of "standing in (his body) while looking elsewhere." And Rilke ends with this completely pure expression of dynamic imagination: the dreamer's body that found the tree's support is "still good, at the least, for standing upright against it, pure and prudent." Man, like the tree, is a being in whom undefined forces stand upright. The dynamic imagination asks no more than this to begin its aerial dreams. Then everything is arranged with this assured verticality. Without this induction, the reader cannot truly link the images, and Rilke's passage remains meaningless and lifeless. Conversely, by following the teachings of the dynamic imagination, we realize that Rilke's passage is above all an *image of motion*, advice from the movement of the vegetable world.

We can compare Rilke's passage—explaining one poet by another —to a beautiful image of vegetablism found in Maurice de Guérin's *Journal:*[10]

10. Maurice de Guérin, *Journal. Morceaux choisis*, in *Oeuvres complètes* (Paris, 1947), I:236-37.

Who can say that he has found a refuge if he is not on some height, the highest one to which he can possibly climb? . . . Supposing I swept away these heights! When will I find myself surrounded by calm? Long ago, the gods had plant life grow up around (certain wise men) and, as it grew higher, it enveloped their old bodies in its embrace and substituted for their life, weakened by extreme old age, the vigorous, silent life that is to be found under the bark of the oak trees. These mortals, having become immobile, no longer moved except at the very tips of their branches that were stirred by the winds. . . . To be sustained by a sap that one chooses from the elements, to be enveloped, to appear powerful to men because of one's roots, and completely indifferent—like the bases of trees that we admire in the forests— returning at random only the vague but profound sounds similar to those of certain thick treetops which imitate the sea's murmurs. This is a way of life that seems to me worthy of our efforts and a very suitable one for opposing men "and the vicissitudes of life."[11]

This vegetablism of the summits clearly shows that for Maurice de Guérin imagination is life in the heights. The tree helps the poet "to sweep away the heights," to go beyond the treetops, to live a well-aired, aerial life. Quite surprising, then, is the criticism that Sainte-Beuve made of this passage, which is so faithful in its vegetable reverie: "(Maurice de Guérin) was dreaming about goodness knows what tree metamorphosis." This is not merely a mistake about a detail, because there are no mere mistakes in details when a judgment is being made on a poet's imagination of the elements. It certainly appears that the dynamic imagination that gives life to so many passages in the works of the hermit of Gayla remained totally foreign to Sainte-Beuve. To bring this idea to a conclusion, Sainte-Beuve does not hesitate to add: "But this destiny for an old man, the end that might be worthy of *Philemon* and *Baucis* would be, at best, good for a Laprade's wisdom."

We will be less harsh than Sainte-Beuve if we compare the gentleness of Guérin's vegetablism with other very artificial uses of the legend of Philemon and Baucis. For instance, in Nathaniel Hawthorne's "The Miraculous Pitcher" there is nothing oneiric at

---

11. A book published anonymously in Rouen in 1723 under the title *Principales merveilles de la Nature* still shows the *trunk* of a tree which is completed by the *trunk* of a man. Oneiric activity demonstrates this etymology better than any discussion of concepts.

work when two old men are suddenly transformed into oak and linden trees.[12]

In the work of D. H. Lawrence we can find many passages in which the dreamer experiences being metamorphized into a tree. For example, in *Fantasia of the Unconscious*: "I would like to be a tree for a while. . . . He towers, and I sit and feel safe. I like to feel him towering around me." Lawrence likes to

> sit among the roots and nestle against its strong trunk, and not bother. . . . Here am I between his toes, like a peabug, and him overreaching me, and I feel his great blood-jet surging. . . .(But) he turns two ways: he thrusts himself tremendously down to the middle earth, where dead men sink in darkness, in the damp, dense undersoil, and he turns himself about in high air. . . . So vast and powerful and exultant in his two directions. And all the time he has no face, no thought . . . where does he keep his soul? Where does anybody?"[13]

V

Why must the word *perched* be good only for jokes? And what is the cock doing on top of the steeple? What is the bird doing on the great stone tree? Is he not adding his wing to motionless height? Rigid treetops are not entirely aerial. The dynamic imagination wants everything in the heights to move. Under the heading *reverie of perching*, I will present a kind of dynamic reverie which, as it passes from the real to the imaginary, will allow us to follow the transition from the imagination of summits to the imagination of a swinging motion.

An example of this *reverie of perching*, which is presented as a familiar and positive experience, may be found in Jean-Paul Richter's *Titan*:

> Often, in the month of May, he sought refuge in the topmost parts of an enormous apple tree whose branches seemed to form a study

12. Nathaniel Hawthorne, *A Wonder Book* (New York, n. d.), 231-33.
13. Other passages in Lawrence's work should be examined for a terrestrial reverie about the tree. Lawrence participates in the life of roots as a terrestrial being. In short sentences he notes: "The great lust of roots. Root-lust." He thinks that the tree's upward thrust owes everything to the earth: "A tree grows straight when it has deep roots . . . ." This "deep" life is what makes him afraid: "I used to be afraid. I used to fear their lust, their rushing black lust." "The will of a tree; something that frightens you."

in green; he liked to feel himself rocked there, sometimes gently, sometimes in violent bursts. At times, the high branches that he occupied were struck by a whirlwind and bent to caress the green grass of the meadow; then suddenly they straightened up forcefully and reclaimed their rightful place among the clouds. This tree seemed to him a part of eternal life; its roots touched the underworld; its proud crown asked questions of the skies, and he, the innocent Albano, alone in his aerial summerhouse, living in a fantastic world created by his imagination's magic wand, nonchalantly obeyed the storm that moved the roof of his palace from day into night and from night into day.[14]

Everything in this text increases in size, as is only fitting in a realistic passage on the *Imaginary*. The tree joins heaven and hell, air and earth; it swings from day to night and from night to day. Its swinging motion also aggravates the storm: the treetop bends toward the meadow! Then immediately, how forcefully the ideal inhabitant of the branches is returned to the blue sky!

Anyone who has read and dreamed above the earth, in the fork of an old walnut tree, will recapture Jean-Paul's reverie. The exaggeration of the motion will not bother him, because it is done in order to awaken basic urges. He will understand that the tree is truly a dwelling, a kind of dream castle. He will read, dynamically and oneirically, the great rhythms of Chateaubriand, whose profound nature was demonstrated by Pius Servien: "When the winds came down from heaven to sway these great cedars, how the aerial chateau, built on its branches, went floating away with birds and passengers asleep in its shelters; and how a thousand and one sighs arose from the corridors and the arches of this moving structure."[15] Are not the motion of an aerial being and the voice of a poet so closely bound together in Chateaubriand's prose that they can be considered an excellent example of dynamic poetry and the poetry of breathing?

We can compare the reverie of perching with the image of a *nest in the highest treetops*, a nest that does not have the same warmth as terrestrial nests. We can find an example of this in the passage in

14. Jean-Paul Richter, *Werke* (Munich, 1969), II:73-74.
15. Pius Servien Coculesco, *Lyrisme et structures sonores. Nouvelles méthodes d'analyse des rythmes appliqués à l'Atala de Chateaubriand* (Paris, 1930), 81.

which Jack London thinks that he recognizes a memory dating from prehistoric man:

> The commonest dream of my early childhood was something like this: It seemed that I was very small and that I lay curled up in a sort of nest made of twigs and boughs. Sometimes I was lying on my back. In this position it seemed that I spent many hours watching the play of sunlight on the foliage overhead and the stirring of the leaves by the wind. Often the nest itself moved back and forth when the wind was strong.
>
> But always, while so lying in my nest, I was mastered by a feeling as of a tremendous space gaping beneath me. I never saw it. I never peered over the edge of the nest to see; but I knew and feared that space which was just beneath me, which threatened me without respite, like the maw of some devouring monster.[16]

Need the metaphor of the abyss as a devouring maw be underscored once again in passing? It is an image that recurs in the most diverse writers.

"This dream," London continues, "in which I was quiescent and which was more like a condition than an action, I dreamed very often in my early childhood." It is on this oneiric basis, then, that Jack London writes his prehistoric novel. Its incidents soon become too human; but the dream element has a basic form. The reverie explains the image of the nest in all of its privileged meanings. The nest—one of the most valorized words in any language—here maintains its latent drama. It has neither the security of the den nor of the cavern. In the tree, cradling remains a danger as long as the creature is not conscious of his agility, his lightness, his ability to "clutch at branches." Life in the tree is thus both a refuge and a danger. We often dream about it, and always in the same way. It is one of the great natural reveries.[17] It is at one and the same time a special kind of solitude and a strong attraction to a clearly dynamic, aerial life.

Then too, without the dynamic imagination, how could we attribute strength to the virile and paternal oak tree? In Strindberg's *Swanwhite*, when the duke protects his daughter against her stepmother, the dynamic image immediately appears, without warning, right in the middle of the first dramatic scene:

16. Jack London, *Before Adam*, 22-23.
17. Cf. George Sand, *Le Chêne parlant* (Paris, 1981), 92.

Swanwhite (runs into the Duke's arms): "Father! What a kingly oak art thou! Embrace thee I cannot, but I can hide myself under thy foliage from the rough showers." (She hides her head beneath the hero's beard, which reaches to his middle.) "And on thy limbs will I swing like a bird! Lift me up, then I can climb to the top." (The Duke stretches out his arms like the branches of a tree.)

Swanwhite climbs up and sits on his shoulder.

"Now I have the earth under me and the air over me; now I see out over the rose garden, the white sand dunes, the blue sea, and seven kingdoms."

Such an image has no meaning in the realm of forms; nor is the tranquil oneirism of the vegetable world able to endow it with its precise vigor. Only dynamic imagination can take the tree as a *theme of exaggeration*. To the shadows it relegates images of impoverished formal value, ridiculous images like the beard that gives protection from the storm. Everything is swept along by the motion that imagines and by the ascensional force that dynamic reverie draws from the majestic oak. A few pages later, the old duke, or the old oak, seizes Swanwhite in his arms, throws her into the air, and catches her again (Swanwhite is not a child, she is a young lady): "Fly, little bird; hold thyself high over the dust and always have air under thy wings!" To live in a great tree under its enormous leafy crown is always, for the imagination, to be a bird. The tree is a source of power for flight. "The bird," says Lawrence in *Fantasia of the Unconscious*, "is only the topmost leaf of a tree, fluttering in the high air, but attached as close to the tree as any other leaf." Is it not, in fact, always bound to return to the nest? The tree itself is a huge nest swaying in the winds. We feel no nostalgia for it as we do for a warm and sheltered life. We remember its height and its solitude. The nest in the treetops is a dream of power: it gives us back the pride of our youth whenever we think that we are made to live above "the seven kingdoms."

Of course, when a poet confides to us, as though it were truly a reality, a memory of time spent in foliage, we must often read him from the perspective of the imaginary. The country child who dares to climb up into poplar trees is so rare that we must, I think, consider Maurice de Guérin's reminiscence to be imaginary: "I climb to the tops of the trees, the crowns of the poplars swing me back and forth above the birds' nests."[18] Only someone caught up in an all-powerful

18. Maurice de Guérin, *Morceaux choisis*, 158.

reverie can want to sway, like a super-bird, at the very top of the largest tree.

Swaying in the treetops is, moreover, admirably rendered in its *cosmic tonality* on one page of Maurice de Guérin's *Journal*. It is the month of May, the trees' blossoms have faded; at the ends of the branches the fruit, which is breathing in vital energy, is set. Then,

> a generation of countless beings is suddenly hanging on the branches of all the trees. . . . All these seeds, whose number and diversity cannot be reckoned, are there, suspended between heaven and earth, in the cradle and consigned to the wind which is responsible for rocking these creatures. Future forests imperceptibly sway in the living forests. Nature is completely involved in her enormous maternal duties.

It should be noted in this passage that the old adage about universal motherhood has taken on a new shade of meaning: it comes to life as it is rocked in the treetops. The forest is only a cradle. No cradle is empty. The living forest rocks the future forest. From that point on, we should understand that it is the same motion, the primitive motion of the cradle, that gives happiness to the branch, the bird, and the dreamer. We read another passage by Guérin in its perfect continuity: "The flowering branch, the bird who perches there to sing or to build its nest, the man who is watching the branch and the bird, are all moved by the same principle at different degrees of perfection." We see that unity is established in the contemplation of a single motion, the primitive motion of rocking. Let us take one more step and instead of watching, let us dream: above the green tree, higher than the highest treetop, more attentive than the singing bird, we will know aerial life in its highest degree of perfection.

VI

Thus the tree offers many images for the development of a psychology of vertical life. At times, the tree is only a simple line, reminding and guiding the aerial dreamer. In *Verses from Valais*, Rilke points out the essential lines of a vertical design in this way:[19]

19. Renan has stated this need for the vertical very well in *Patrice*: "There are many, many countrysides that owe their charm to the bell that dominates them. Would our rather unpoetic cities be bearable if tall spires or majestic belfries did not rise above the mundane roofs?" Ernest Renan, *Oeuvres Complètes* (Paris, 1960), 9:1535.

Poplar, in its rightful place
which puts its upright line
against the slow, but robust greenery
that stretches up and spreads out.

The more isolated the tree is, the better we can feel the vertical action of contemplating it. It is as though the isolated tree were the only vertical destiny of the plain or plateau.

All alone

. . . .

It imposes its great and sovereign life
On the plains.[20]

In other poems from "Groves" (cf. "The Walnut Tree," II, p. 32), Rilke clearly feels that in a landscape it is the tree that is the axis by which the dreamer normally passes from the terrestrial to the aerial:

There is the meeting of what we have left
What weighs down or what nourishes
And the clearly marked passage of infinite tenderness.

Even the walnut tree, the rounded tree, the one "turned toward everything," evoked by an aerial being:

. . . savors the whole vault of the skies.[21]

In beautiful, calm weather, a thousand palm leaves are aroused, as a new heart is awakened by thousands of nebulous affections. Shelley said it well, as Rabbe quotes him in *Shelley: The Man and the Poet*: "In the motion of the very leaves of spring, in the blue air, there is then found a secret correspondence with our heart." It is the advantage of the imagination that has been analyzed to be able to live this "secret correspondence" in all its details. A reader in a hurry sees in these lines only a worn-out topic. He does not sympathize in a Shelleyan way with this confused but happy movement of springtime foliage and with the emotion of the first unfolded leaf, which only yesterday was a hard bud, a thing that had sprung from the earth.

As it wraps itself in a light mist in the evening, the familiar tree, the being with no face, will take on an expressive quality which, with its

20. Emile Verhaeren, "L'Arbre," in *La Multiple splendeur*, 14th ed. (Paris, 1917), 87.

21. Rainer-Maria Rilke, *Sämtliche Werke* (Wiesbaden, 1957 rpt. 1963), II: 658.

muted tones, will have great power. Joachim Gasquet, dreaming in the twilight in a restful atmosphere after a day in the scorching heat of a Provençal sun, after the ardent struggles of green and gold, writes: "The translucent flesh of things creates an aura and mingles appearances. From among their roots, the idea of trees evaporates. Like a more chaste sun, the moon illuminates the sea."[22]

The same vertical *élan* and the same work of beauty in the sky are experienced in this passage by Paul Gadenne:

> This tree lived by virtue of its strong, sprawling branches; it had its own way of taking hold of the sky and calling all of nature to witness its fervor. It described a single movement with masterful ease so as to rise into space and seize it. Its proud, impatient trunk divided into as many branches as needed in order to absorb nourishment from the air and to yield its beauty. On top could be seen the flowering, like a bouquet, of its rounded crown, on the same scale as the sky . . .

In a storm, too, the tree, like a sensitive antenna, sets the dramatic life of the plain into motion. It is noted in Gabriel d'Annunzio's *The Triumph of Death*:

> The little tree could be seen moving in an almost circular fashion, as though it were being pulled by a hand that wanted to uproot it. For a few minutes they both watched this furious shaking, which, in the pale, denuded, lifeless torpor of the countryside, took on the appearance of conscious life . . . The imaginary suffering of the tree brought them face to face with their own suffering.

In another work, the poet imagines a struggle between the tree and the cloud:

> All around us, strange trees sprang up out of the earth as if they were trying to seize the delicate clouds in their monstrous arms.
> The nimble clouds fled this terrible embrace, leaving to their savage assailant gliding golden veils.[23]

Thus the tormented tree, the shaken tree, or the ardent tree can provide images of all the human passions. How many legends have shown us the bleeding tree, the tree that weeps?

22. Joachim Gasquet, *Il y a une volupté dans la douleur*, 72.
23. Gabriele d'Annunzio, "Villa Chigi III," in *Versi d'Amore e di Gloria*, 4th ed. (Verona, 1964), 337-38.

At times it even seems as though the moaning of the trees is closer to our souls than the distant howling of an animal. It groans in a more muted way; its pain seems more intense. The philosopher Jouffroy put it very simply: "We cannot remain untouched by the sight of a tree on a mountain whipped by the winds: the sight reminds us of man, the pain of the human condition, and a host of other unhappy thoughts . . ." The simplicity of the sight is exactly what moves the imagination. It makes a profound impression, and yet the expressive value of a tree bending under the force of a storm is insignificant! Our whole being trembles in primitive sympathy. Through this sight, we understand that pain is in the cosmos, that the struggle is *in the elements*, that things have opposing wills, that repose is ephemeral. The suffering tree is the epitome of universal pain.

VII

We have judged too hastily when, in all these images in which the tree is stirred up or calmed down, we see only a manifestation of poetic animism. Literary critics too often evoke, in *general terms*, a poetic animism that has meaning only when it is expressed in its own particular images. A poet must be able to go to the source of present-day images to discover the principles of life as it is expressed in images. If we go along with him, we will discover that *primary images* are not very numerous. The tree is one of them. It is the model for a whole series of dreams in which we see the tree forming its trunk and branches.

For example, in a chilly October when potato tops are being burned in the open fields, who has not dreamed that he saw tree shapes forming in the smoke? Instead of a column of flame, instead of vivid, crackling flowers that leap up from dry wood, here we have the sprouts, then the trunk, then the first branches, and then, high up in the sky, the palms and the wreaths. Spreading slowly, the smoke rises in the evening air. An ethereal tree, all blue and grey, grows effortlessly. A little of the smell of death has passed through the night. . . . Something lives and dies before our eyes, and our dreams continue on forever. The tree of smoke is on the border between ethereal and living motion.

From this tree, still too clearly outlined and too much affected by the limitations of our vision in colors, a great poet will create the im-age of a destiny in which the many seductions of an aerial Einfühlung are revealed:

> Toward an aromatic future of smoke,
> I felt myself led, offered, and consumed,
> Completely, wholly promised to the happy clouds!
> And even, I seem to be that misty tree
> Which, as its majesty is lightly lost,
> Abandons itself to love along all its length.
> The great being has won me over.[24]

Continued by a dream, the tree of smoke fills the sky. Charles Ploix notes that "in Vedic mythology. . . the canopy of clouds that en-velops and darkens the earth is likened to an enormous plant world." The dreamer sees this great canopy of clouds forming on the earth. It is the column of smoke rising from his own hearth in the evening. It is flattened and spread out over the vault of the sky, the dark foliage of the tree at twilight.

VIII

If we acquire the habit of allowing great images to mature slowly within us, of following natural reveries, we will better understand the relationships among certain myths. Thus, the imagination, studied in its dynamic principle, will make the theme of *the cosmological tree*, which at first glance seems so odd, more natural. How can a Tree ex-plain the formation of a World? How can a single object produce a whole universe?

In a time of general pragmatism, no one hesitated to explain things by their usefulness. Having completed a botanical study of the flora of Mesopotamian monuments, Bonavia claimed that:

> the sacred tree of Assyria is quite simply a synthesis of all the plants venerated in the region in former times because of their usefulness to man: the palm tree for its dates, the vine for its juice, the pine or the cedar for its wood for building and heating, the pomegranate for its role in the production of tannic acid and in the creation of sherbets.[25]

24. Paul Valéry, "La Jeune Parque," in *The Collected Works of Paul Valéry*, ed. Jackson Mathews (Princeton, N. J., 1971), I:96-97.
25. Eugène Félicien Albert Goblet d'Alviella, *La Migration des symboles* (London, 1894), 141.

Such a conglomeration of useful characteristics might determine a concept of utility, but these useful functions are insufficient to explain the original power of the mythical dream. Goblet d'Aviella, although he does not reject Bonavia's thesis forcefully enough, still sees the sacred tree in a truer light. "It may be the vegetable symbol of a powerful divinity . . . or the simulated shape of a mythical plant, like the winged oak on which—according to a Phoenician tradition brought back by Pherecydes of Syros—the supreme god has woven the earth, the starry sky, and the ocean."

De Gubernatis studies at great length the myths of cosmogonic trees, anthropogonic trees, trees related to rain or clouds, and phallic trees. All these myths accustom us to attaching grandeur and power to the images of our reverie. If the Pipal, the cosmogonic tree of the *Rig Veda*, is visited by two birds, a day bird and a night bird, and by the sun and the moon, there is nothing that deviates from the scale of dreams, though it might disturb rational and objective thought. If the rain tree attracts rain, produces rain or associates with the thunder-cloud, there again is the effect of the power of dreams.

It seems to me, then, that simple studies of present-day imagination can help us rediscover the oneiric principles of certain myths. If symbols are so easily transmitted, it is because they grow in the same soil as dreams. Everyday life might often seem to prove them wrong. Reverie constantly nourishes them. Throughout all of my studies on primary images, I have always found that, because of the growth that takes place in dreams, a primary image is bound to rise to a cosmic level. The tree, like all unified themes in reverie, can therefore acquire, normally as it were, cosmogonic power. Goblet d'Alviella, while he did not hide his surprise very well, had an inkling of this power. He recalls that "the Chaldeans must be included amongst the nations who saw in the universe a tree whose summit was the sky, and whose foot or trunk was the earth." Failing to discern its im-aginary *élan*, d'Alviella finds this a "puerile" concept, and indicates that it "seems to have been early thrown into the shade, in Meso-potamia," with the advance of more refined cosmogonic systems. The power passes to the mountain. But—and this is a very strange remark —the metaphors of the tree have such fundamental power that— defying all reason—they endow the sacred mountain with their own imaginary life: "O thou who givest shade, Lord who casteth thy shadow over the land, great mount . . . ." Along these same lines, we read in the *Rig Veda*: "In the bottomless abyss, King Varuna has erected the crown of the celestial tree." It seems that the tree holds the whole earth in the grasp of its roots and that its rising toward the sky has the strength to uphold the world. . . . Elsewhere we find: "Which is the tree in which they have chiseled the heavens and the earth?" And Goblet d'Alviella answers:

> It is the tree of the starry firmament whose fruits are precious stones, at other times it is the tree of the cloudy sky whose roots or branches shoot out over the canopy of heaven, like those sheaves of long and finespun clouds which, in the popular meteorology of our country, have been named Trees of Abraham.

Thus, the powerful tree reaches the sky, establishes its domain, and lives on forever. It becomes the firmament itself. Only those who are unaware that dream lives its end rather than its means will be surprised by this. When the reverie of the vegetable world takes hold of a dreamer, it takes him back to that night in Judea when Boaz saw an oak:

> Which, when it came out of his belly, rose up to the sky.

Cosmogony based on the tree gives an impression of nobility. R. B. Anderson express this very well:

> Ygdrasil, the ash tree, is one of the most noble ideas ever conceived in any system of cosmogony or human existence. It is, in fact, the great tree of life, wonderfully elaborated and extending over the whole universe. Its branches furnish the human race with bodies; its roots extend through all the worlds, while its life-giving arms spread in the skies. All life is sustained by it; even that of serpents who devour its roots and try to destroy it.

By tracing the life of this tree, we will understand better how someone can think that animals "come out" of the vegetable world and that the tree is truly their "family tree." "Animals move in and around it; every species of animal has its place and its destination." The eagle, the falcon, and the squirrel are not the only ones to benefit from it; four fowls are fed on its buds. Anderson concludes: "The particular nature of the myth of Ygdrasil is its expressive brevity. How beautiful the sight of a great tree is! Its far-flung branches; its moss-covered trunk; its deep roots remind us of the infinity of time; it has seen centuries pass before we were born." And, subsequently:

Nothing less than an infinite soul is needed to understand it; no brush can paint it; no color can express it. Nothing is tranquil; nothing is at rest; everything is in motion. This tree constitutes a whole world, and it can be understood only by the spirit of man or by the poet's soul. Only the constant flux of language can express it symbolically. This is not a subject for the painter or sculptor, but rather for the poet. Ygdrasil is the tree of the poetic experience of the Gothic race.

What better way is there to say that myth is not animated in response only to visual images and that it can reveal a direct, spoken imagination?

Sometimes an imagination that is too filled with facile fantasy can discover unknowingly and unintentionally some characteristics of the anthropogonic tree, the tree of life that produces human beings. Thus, Saintine relates the following dream:

> A few feet away, there arose an immense tree, glowing red like all the other trees, but, because of its gigantic seed pods, most of which hung down to the ground, it stood out from all of the rest. I went nearer and opened one. To my great surprise, I found on the satin-like parchment of the pod, separated from one another by a thin partition, gracefully folded up and arranged in rows like beans in their pod, yes, I found . . . I'll give you three guesses . . . women, my dear friend, charming young women. . . . Bewildered, dumbfounded, I began to back away, almost terrified by the sight of the marvel that I had just discovered, when all of the seed pods that were hanging over the ground opened spontaneously, by dehiscence, as we botanists say: the lovely fruits of the enchanted tree, freeing themselves from their covering, tossed left and right, jumped and fell back like balsamine seeds when their pod bursts.[26]

And recorded by Gubernatis reports that the *tree of Adam* reaches hell with its roots and heaven with its branches.[27] But one who dreams of the vertical tree has no need for such a legend in order to understand how oneirically natural are La Fontaine's wonderful lines which tell us about the oak:

> Whose head was neighbor to the heavens,
> And whose feet touched the realm of the dead.

26. X.-B. Saintine, *La Seconde vie* (Paris, 1864), 81-82. Psychoanalysts will have no trouble seeing into the dream of the innocent botanist.
27. Cf. Vergil, *Georgics*, Book II, lines 290-92.

Is this expanded image not, in fact, a natural image in the realm of dynamic imagination? The culture of ancient times will no doubt be evoked to explain La Fontaine's image. But that is no reason to underestimate personal reverie. It seems, as a matter of fact, that culture, by making us aware of ancient myths that resemble our reveries on certain subjects, grants us *permission to dream*. When I dream about an enormous tree, the tree of the world, the tree that gets its sustenance from the whole earth, the tree that speaks to all the winds and that holds up the stars . . . I am not, after all, a simple dreamer, a daydreamer, a living illusion! My folly is an ancient dream. There is a dreaming force within me, a force that has dreamed before in very distant times, and that comes back tonight to live again in a receptive imagination! *De te fabula narratur*. A knowledge of myths will show that certain reveries, so seemingly subjective, are really objective. They bind souls together in the way that concepts link minds. They categorize imaginations in the way that ideas categorize types of intelligence. Not everything can be explained by an association of ideas and shapes. We must also study the association of dreams. In this respect, knowledge of myth should be a healthy reaction against classic explanations of poetry, and we should be surprised at the absence of a serious study of myth in contemporary education.

Thus, after reading myths of the cosmogonic tree, it seems as though we should read with greater sensitivity certain passages from Paul Gadenne's *Siloé* in which the imagination of the tree is amplified. Here, for example, is a meditation on a gigantic walnut tree:

> It was a huge and profound being which had worked the earth year after year with all its roots, and which had likewise worked the sky, and which from this earth and this sky had woven an unyielding substance and tied these knots against which no axe could have prevailed. Its upward thrust was so great, the movement of its branches was so noble and aimed so high that it forced you to experience its rhythm and to follow it with your eyes to the very top.

And the dreamer, "leaning with his whole body against the tree, back to back, breast to breast . . . felt pass into his body a little of the thought and the strength that gave this giant, this marvelous being, its life."

IX

When the imaginary vegetable world is experienced in a very personal way, curious inversions can occur. Instead of idly experiencing the objective image of a tree renewed by the springtime sun and denuded by the autumn winds, an enthusiastic participation in the vegetable world will allow us to imagine the different seasons as though they were primitive vegetable forces. We experience the reverie of a tree *that produces the seasons*, that commands the whole forest to produce buds, that gives its sap to all of nature, that calls up the breezes, that forces the sun to rise earlier so that it can gild the new leaves. In short, we dream of a tree that constantly renews its cosmogonic power. To experience personally the springing to life of the vegetable world is to feel the same arborescent power in the whole universe and to become conscious of the imperious wood nymph that is the sum of the infinite world's vegetable will to power. We must, as a matter of fact, realize that for a decidedly mythic life, *there are no minor gods*. Whoever lives as a wood nymph commands a whole universe with the inner will of an oak tree. He projects *the vegetable world*. For such a reverie, the cosmogonic tree is not a more or less symbolic figure in which can be grouped some particular images. It is the *primary image*, the active image that produces all others.

Some will tell me that I am confusing the sign and the cause in a facile paradox. They will say that the botanist from Candolle, in his floral fantasies, was satisfied to plant "a floral clock" in his garden. Every plant opens out at a specific time, obeying the rhythmic call of the sun. Am I going to think that the slave is the master and that the flower bed commands the light? How the rationalists will laugh! But the dream does not follow reason. The stronger the reason that opposes a dream, the more profound the dream makes its images. When reverie truly yields to a beloved image with all its strength, then that image governs everything. Thus the absurd is governed by a law. As long as we judge dream from the outside, we will see in it only an illogical absurdity, which is very easy to imitate in works that are only parodies of oneiric life. Then dreams are explained by nightmares without the realization that a nightmare is an unhealthy dream. It disrupts and distorts oneiric powers; it is a poorly formed mixture of elemental oneiric substances. But dream, on the contrary, gives to us a unity that is beneficial. The life of the vegetable world, if it is a part of us, produces the peace that comes from slow movement, its own great, peaceful rhythm. The tree is at one with this great rhythm; it epitomizes annual rhythm. Its rhythm is the clearest, the most precise, the most dependable, the richest, and the most exuberant of all. There are no contradictions in vegetable life. Clouds come and cover up the sun at the solstice. No storm prevents the tree from turning green when its time has come. If we educate ourselves poetically by dreaming of a phylomorphism or a xylomorphism, we will understand, in their fullest meaning, statements like those made by D. H. Lawrence in *Fantasia of the Unconscious*. After quoting a phrase "from this already out-of-fashion book, *The Golden Bough*": "it must have appeared to the ancient Aryan that the sun was periodically recruited from the fire which resided in the sacred oak," Lawrence adds: "Exactly. The fire which resided in the Tree of Life. That is, life itself. So we must read: 'It must have appeared to the ancient Aryan that the sun was periodically recruited from life. . . . Instead of life being drawn from the sun, it is the emanation from life itself, that is, from all the living plants and creatures which nourish the sun.' "

Also, by going to the furthest limit of dreams and by giving ourselves body and soul to a particular oneiric power in the vegetable world, we have a better understanding of the calendar tree. Let me recall just one example of it. Terrien de la Couperie cites a Chinese tradition "that speaks of a marvelous plant that grew a pod on every day of the month up to the fifteenth and then had one fall off on every day up to the thirtieth."[28] In its exaggerated precision, such a legend shows rather clearly the will to make the day itself a part of vegetable activity. We will see its true meaning if we really dream of the power of the bud, if we go into the garden or walk along a hedge every morning to look at a bud, the same bud, and if we measure a day's activity by it. And when a flower is about to open, when the apple tree is about to produce light, its very own pink and white light, then we will really know that a single tree is a whole world.

28. Goblet d'Alviella, 160.

11

The Wind

> But I am not the sea nor the red sun,
> I am not the wind with girlish laughter
> Not the immense wind which strengthens,
>   not the wind that lashes,
> Not the spirit that ever lashes its own body
>   to terror and death.
>   WALT WHITMAN, *Leaves of Grass*

I

IF WE MOVE immediately to the most dynamic of all images of violent air, into a world of storms, we find images accumulating that are extremely clear psychologically. It seems that the immense void, in suddenly discovering an action, becomes a particularly clear image of cosmic anger. We could say that the raging wind is the symbol of *pure anger*, anger without purpose or pretext. Great writers of the storm, like Joseph Conrad in *Typhoon*, have loved one particular aspect of it: the unexpected storm, the unexplained physical tragedy. Little by little the cliché has worn out the image; we speak of the fury of the elements without experiencing its elemental force. The forest and the sea, thrown into upheaval by the storm, sometimes over-embellish the great but dynamically simple image of the hurricane. With violent air, we can grasp elemental fury, which is entirely motion and nothing but motion. In it we can find some very important images in which *will* and *imagination* are united. On the one hand, a strong will that is attached to nothing, and on the other, an imagination with *no* shape sustain each other. Experiencing personally the images of the hurricane, we learn what furious and vain will is. The wind, in its excess, is anger that is everywhere and nowhere, that is born and reborn out of itself, that twists and turns. The wind threatens and howls but has no shape unless it encounters dust; once visible, it becomes a mere annoyance. It has power over the imagination only in an essentially dynamic participation. Formed images would give it rather a derisory appearance.

We will see numerous examples of this essentially dynamic participation in the works of Jacob Boehme and William Blake. Besides expressions in which anger is expressed in fire or in bile, we find in Boehme images in which the dreamer sees the wrath of the heavens form in the "choleric region of the stars."[1]

Moreover, if we follow the great dreamers of cosmogony in their imaginary work, we can often discover a true valorization of anger. An initial anger is a sign of fundamental will. It *attacks* the work to be done. And the first thing to be created by this *creative anger* is the *whirlwind*. The primary object of *homo faber* dynamized by anger is the *vortex*.

Besides the whirlwind imagined by an even-tempered intellectual like Descartes, it is interesting to participate, through the dynamic imagination, in the angry and creative whirlwind of Blake. The image gets off to a weak start: "Urizens sons here labour also; & here are seen the Mills/Of Theotormon, on the verge of the Lake of Udan-Adan . . ."[2] We should not be put off by this image of the mills of Theotormon; they are there only to make a creative force "hum." By following the lessons of the dynamic imagination, we will find the explanation of this image, which remains obscure in the realm of forms, for barely has the poet spoken about the mills of Theotormon when whirlwinds fill the sky and carry it along with them. In the realm of the imaginary, it is not impossible for the mill to make the winds turn. Any reader who refuses to accept this reversal is not in tune with the principles of oneirism. Perhaps he can understand things that represent *reality*, but how can he understand a *creation*? A creation must be imagined. How can someone imagine if he does not understand the fundamental laws of the *imaginary*?

The imagination, for which the mill prepared the way, spreads out across the universe: these whirlwinds, says Blake, are "the starry voids of night & the depths & caverns of earth."

> These Mills are oceans, clouds & waters ungovernable in their fury
> Here are the stars created & the seeds of all things planted
> And here the Sun & Moon recieve their fixed destinations.

1. Jacob Boehme, *Concerning Three Principles of the Divine Essence*, cf. 396.
2. Blake, "Milton," Plate 27, lines 49-50, 124.

We do not perceive the cosmogonic whirlwind, the creative tempest or the wind of anger and creation in their geometrical forms, but rather as sources of power. Nothing can stop the whirling motion. In dynamic imagination, everything becomes active; nothing comes to rest. Motion creates being; whirling air creates the stars; the cry produces images, speech, and thought. As by a provocation, the world is created through anger. Anger lays the foundations for dynamic being. Anger is the act by which being begins. However prudent an action may be and however insidious it promises to be, it must first cross over a small threshold of anger. Anger is the acid without which no impression will be etched on our being. It creates an active impression.

In the reading of certain passages of Elémir Bourges' *The Ship*, it also seems that the noise of angry winds actually produces aerial monsters. They can be heard crying out "beneath the thunder's iron wheel." In the storm, "the Gorgon is multiplied by aerial apparitions that are monstrous images of herself," in a kind of sound mirage that *projects* terror to the four corners of the sky. As it bellows, the north wind multiplies the gaping jaws of flying monsters. For Bourges, the Medusa is a storm bird. She is simply a flying head "resembling a strange bird." Are not evil birds—far removed from any memory relating to the practive of augury, but as we hear them in reveries filled with sadness—creatures born out of the piercing cries of the wind? Hearing is more dramatic than seeing.

In reverie on the storm, it is not the eye that produces images, but rather the *startled ear*. We participate directly in the drama of violent air. Sights belonging to earth will no doubt enrich this horror of sound. Thus in *The Ship*, the scream born in the air gathers smoke and shadows: "A mountain of vapors invades the depths of heaven. Already the gelludes, with their brazen feathers, appear as couriers, hideous, boneless bodies that resemble ashes . . . A whirlwind of iron wings, manes, and flashing eyes fill the blazing cloud." A few pages later, Bourges is still talking about "winged she-wolves, gelludes, harpies, and stymphalides." This is the way that monstrous and discordant beings come together in the whirling winds of the hurricane. But anyone who is willing to investigate how these imaginary beings are created will soon recognize that the power that creates them is a cry of anger. Not a cry that comes out of an animal's throat, but the cry emanating from a storm. The *ouranide* is first the immense sound of angry winds. By following its genesis in cosmological accounts, we can be present when a cosmology of the scream is formed, that is to say, a cosmology that groups creatures around a scream. The scream is the primary verbal and cosmogonic reality.

Examples can be found in which dreams form images around a sound, or around a scream. How could the common image of "winged serpents" have meaning if man had not undergone the anxiety caused by the "whistling of the wind"? Victor Hugo, making a rapid ellipsis, writes: "The wind was like a snake." In the folklore of many countries, we can detect a crossover between images of wind and serpent. Griaule tells us that in Abyssinia it is forbidden to whistle at night, "because that is how serpents and demons may be attracted."[3] The very fact that demons can be called in the same way as snakes makes it imperative to add its cosmic resonances to the taboo. This suggestion will be easily accepted if we compare the Abyssinian taboo with the following interdictions: among the Yakuts no one is allowed to "whistle in the mountains and disturb the sleeping winds."[4] In the same way "the Kanakas whistle or not depending on the time of the year when trade winds are to be summoned or feared." Such legends bring us to the very heart of imaginary activity. The following note can be considered axiomatic: the imagination is at work whenever there is a tendency to rise to the cosmic level. Valorized images are not formed from the details of everyday life. Primitive man fears the world more than things. Cosmic terror can be focused secondarily on a particular object, but the terror exists primarily in a universe filled with anxiety before any object is designated. The violent whistling of the wind is what shakes the dreamer, or the listener. . . . By day, the Abyssinian can whistle. Day has dispersed the reserve of nocturnal terrors. Serpents and demons have lost their power.

Under these conditions, if we were to construct a phenomenology of the cry, still respecting the hierarchy of the imaginary, we would have to start out with a phenomenology of the storm. Next we would seek to compare it to a phenomenology of the animal cry. We would be very surprised, moreover, at the lifeless nature of animal voices. The imagination of voices listens almost exclusively to the

3. Marcel Griaule, *Jeux et divertissements abyssins* (Paris, 1935), 21n.
4. André Schaeffner, *Origine des instruments de musique* (Paris, 1936), 217.

great natural voices. At this point we would have proof, complete with details, that the howling wind heads a phenomenology of the scream. In a way, the wind howls before the animal, packs of wind before the packs of dogs. The thunder growls before the bear. A great master of waking dreams like Blake makes no mistake on this score.

> The Bleat the Bark Bellow & Roar
> Are Waves that Beat on Heavens Shore.[5]

Laforgue, too, hears the "bellowing" of "all the Walkyries of the wind."[6] Victor Hugo's Djinns are the "visions" of a "listener."

We could cite many poems whose primary power and voice is the storm. What would Ossian be without the life of his storms? Is it not by the attraction of the storm that Ossian's songs are vivid for so many people?[7]

Listening to the storm with all our sense alert is communicating in Fear and Anger alternately—or at the same time—with an enraged universe. In his wonderful thesis on Maurice de Guérin, M. E. Decahors notes this strange attitude in which our imagination in the face of the storm calls forth the very drama that it fears, "in which the soul and nature rise up to their full height face to face with each other." In this simple confrontation, even a person as gentle as de Guérin is aware of feelings of creative anger: "When I enjoy this kind of well-being in my irritation, I can compare my thought (it's almost madness) only to a light in the sky flickering on the horizon between two worlds." This is a very aerial anger that will break nothing on earth but that causes one to tremble in the very fibers of his being, quite apart from any reason for being angry.

In the somber reverie that Poe entitles "Silence" we can trace a feeling of resentment that he takes out on air instead of on water, as he would in a Xerxes complex. It is possible then to speak of a *Xerxes of the air*: "Then I cursed the elements with the curse of tumult; and a frightful tempest gathered in the heaven, where, before, there had been no wind. And the heaven became livid with the violence of the tempest. . . . "

The curse of the tumult is soon followed in Poe's tale by the curse of

5. Blake, "Auguries of Innocence," lines 71-72, 482.
6. Jules Laforgue, *Derniers Vers*, eds. Michael Collie and J. M. l'Heureux (Toronto, 1965), 24.
7. Cf. Etienne Pivert de Sénancour, *Obermann* (Paris, 1965), 340-41.

silence, but this very dialectic brings out more clearly the aerial dreamer's desire to be the master of storms. He commands the winds, flings them out, and takes them back again. Tumult and silence are two very characteristic forms of the will to power in Poe.

II

Each phase of the wind has its own psychology. The wind stirs itself up and becomes discouraged. It howls and groans. It goes from violence to distress. The very nature of the curtailed and useless gusts can give an image of anxious melancholy that is very different from oppressed melancholy. This nuance can be seen in a passage from Gabriele d'Annunzio: "And the wind was like the regret for what is no more, like the anxiety of creatures not yet formed, laden with memories, swollen with forebodings, made up of wounded souls and useless wings."[8]

The same impressions of a painful and desperate life can be found in the lines that Saint-Pol Roux has written in "The Mystery of the Wind." In a cosmic feeling that is excessive because it is not well enough worked out, the poet has the wind born out of a dream by Earth: "When the future's desires or the memory's regrets are awakened in some part of this giant skull, the Globe, the wind rises."[9] Then, as if the earth's dream was to be buffeted by opposing gusts, the poet calls up all of the wind's dissensions: "Space is made up of scattered souls, in expected or else irremediable exile from matter, whose diverse movements inspire branches, sails, and clouds." For the Breton poet, every breath of air is brought to life. It is a scrap of air's flesh that had at one time been alive, an aerial fabric that will clothe a soul. Another Breton writes, in a poem noteworthy for its being concentrated on the poetic core of impressions:

> There is someone
> In the wind.[10]

Roux's poem continues the reverie of memory and of the will to live:

8. Gabriele d'Annunzio, *Contemplazione della morte*, 111-12.
9. Saint-Pol Roux, "Le mystère du Vent," in *La Rose et les épines du chemin* (Paris, 1980), 71.
10. Guillévic, *Terraqué* (Paris, 1968), 76.

As theoreticians either of becoming or of a second becoming, these souls, past or imminent—some soon to be born and others soon to die from an earthly point of view—foster their potential for a former or future joy in living. They are non-persons in search of a value that they can grasp. Then the cavalcades come rushing, outdoing themselves amid collisions in which the skin and bones of their ambition are torn or broken, climbing mountains, filling valleys in their dizzying impatience to exist.

The wind is blowing.

III

Roux's passage suffers, it must be admitted, from excessive imagery, which was one of the failings of symbolism. But the dream behind it is genuine in the sense of the violent animism of the wind, an animism that is divided, hurried, and jostled, which creates a multitude of creatures in a storm. The poet, as if unconsciously, has rediscovered in his verse the oneiric core of many legends. How can we fail to recognize in it, in its movement alone, the theme of the *infernal hunt*, the ride, invisible and violent, with no slowing and no relief? If this theme can impose itself with no advance preparation, it is only because the infernal hunt is a natural reverie rather than a tradition. I would put it forth as an example of a *natural tale*; it is the *natural tale* of the howling wind, the wind of a thousand voices, plaintive and aggressive voices. Color and shapes will be added, but not according to any law. The tale of the infernal hunt is not a tale about things visible. It is the tale of the wind. Ménéchet talks of Welsh legends about the

> hounds of hell that are sometimes called the hounds of heaven . . . They are often heard in pursuit through the air . . . Some say that these animals are white with red ears; others claim that, on the contrary, they are all black. Perhaps they are like the chameleon, who is nourished by the air, as they are.[11]

Colin de Plancy recalls, moreover, the Arab legend about the creation of the horse:

> When God decided to create the horse, he called the South wind and said: "I want to make a new creature from your belly; make

11. Quoted by Colin de Plancy, *Dictionnaire infernal* (Geneva, 1980), 167 (s.v. *chien*).

> yourself denser by getting rid of your excess moisture." And he was
> obeyed. Then he took a handful of this element, breathed on it,
> and the horse appeared. [12]

Horses of the wind can be found in many other creation accounts,
which, if they are less picturesque, are more properly oneiric. This is
how we come to realize that dynamic characteristics rather than formal ones are responsible for creation. Thus Schwartz speaks of what
can be seen in the cloud hunt (*Wolkenjagd*), and some might believe
that the shapes of the clouds are the inspiring forms. But upon
reading more carefully the documents Schwartz has collected, we
realize that the dynamics of the storm, the hurricane hunt (*Gewitter-
jagd*), is what inspires the dreamer. [13] Schwartz tells of many other images in which the winds fight. It is a strange fight that often shows
vigorous action *with no opponent*. Nevertheless, we can see in it, as
does naturalistic mythology, an episode of the struggle between night
and light. [14] The battle of the clouds against the sky is thus
represented as the giants' assault on the Olympian gods.

Gerhardt Hauptmann, in *The Sunken Bell*, has also tried to make
the synthesis between the menacing cloud and the cries of the wind:

> Black goblins ready for the savage hunt assemble on the precipices
> and in the abysses. Soon the baying of the pack is heard. In the
> clear sky, fog giants build somber fog castles with their menacing
> towers and terrible walls, and, slowly, they come toward your
> mountain to crush you.

Schwartz associates images of the infernal hunt with the image of
"huntresses with snakes for hair." The "imaginary" analysis of the
Erinyes can come from this contrast. This analysis must catch the
image as it is forming, when it has as yet only a very small number of
features—and, naturally, it must keep at bay everything that has been

12. The Dauphin in Shakespeare's *Henry V* (Act III, sc. 7) speaks of his steed in
these terms: "When I bestride him, I soar, I am a hawk: he trots the air; the earth sings
when he touches it; the basest horn of his hoof is more musical than the pipe of
Hermes . . . he is pure air and fire; and the dull elements of earth and water never appear in him, but only in patient stillness while his rider mounts him." We see from
this that in the realm of the imaginary all four elements are needed to "explain" the
horse.

13. F. L. W. Schwartz, *Wolken und Wind, Blitz und Donner* (Berlin, 1879), cf.
52-153.

14. Cf. Charles Ploix, *Le Surnaturel dans les contes populaires* (Paris, 1891), 41.

added by tradition—while the galloping fury is still only a furious wind. What is it chasing? What is the wind pursuing? This is a meaningless question for the purely dynamic imagination of fury. A writer has Orestes say: "You don't see them . . . but *I* see them . . . they are pursuing me." Like the infernal hunt, the Erinyes embody both the hunter and the hunted. This synthesis, incarnated in a primary dynamic image, is far-reaching. So great is the wind's misfortune that it appears that it can embody both remorse and vengeance.

IV

How can we register the ambivalence of the wind, which is both gentleness and violence, purity and delirium, better than by reliving with Shelley its dual fervor for the destruction and the preservation of life:

> O wild West Wind, thou breath of Autumn's being,
>
> . . . .
>
> Wild Spirit, which art moving everywhere;
> Destroyer and preserver; hear, oh, hear!
>
> . . . .
>
> . . . O uncontrollable! If even
> I were as in my boyhood, and could be
>
> The comrade of thy wanderings over Heaven,
> As then, when to outstrip thy skiey speed
> Scarce seemed a vision; I would ne'er have striven
>
> As thus with thee in prayer in my sore need.
> Oh, lift me as a wave, a leaf, a cloud!
> I fall upon the thorns of life! I bleed!
>
> A heavy weight of hours has chained and bowed
> One too like thee: tameless, and swift, and proud.

V

> Make me thy lyre, even as the forest is:
> What if my leaves are falling like its own!
> The tumult of thy mighty harmonies
>
> Will take from both a deep, autumnal tone,
> Sweet though in sadness. Be thou, Spirit fierce,
> My spirit! Be thou me, impetuous one![15]

15. Shelley, "Ode to the West Wind," lines 1, 13-14, 47-62, p. 577ff.

The same vitality of the blowing wind will be found in a poem by Pierre Guéguen, "On the Mountain":

> The West Wind with its great fierce body
> Prodded me with its impetuous fingers.
> It pressed its mouth to my mouth
> And breathed its rude spirit into me.

In his commentary on the "Ode to the West Wind," M. Cazamian underscores the "prodigious feeling for the profound links between the great physical forces and human life" in Shelley's poetics. Chevrillon also notes: "*The soul in motion*, that is what Shelley sees everywhere." But everywhere the renewed soul of the world has a profound individuality. The gust is wild and pure. It dies and is born again. And the poet pursues the very life of the cosmic breath. In the west wind there breathes an oceanic soul, a virgin soul untainted by anything terrestrial. And life is so great that even autumn has a future.

Need I even mention the fact that for the imagination the origin of the wind is more important than its destination? A rationalist will smile as he reads René Vivien's poem "The Four Winds" in *Prose Poems*. He will be amazed that the north wind can say to a dreamer: "Let me carry you off to the snows," and the south wind: "Let me carry you off toward the blue."[16] He will think that the west wind is the one that can help us travel to the Orient. But dream has nothing but contempt for this learned "orientation." It attributes to the north wind, to Boreas, King of the Winds as Pindar says, all the powers of a Hyperborean beyond. And, in the same way, the south wind brings with it all the allurements of the sunny climates and the nostalgia for an eternal spring.

The soul that loves the wind is animated by the four winds of the sky. For many dreamers, the four cardinal points are above all the lands belonging to the four great winds. In many respects, these four great winds seem to me to be the foundation of the *Cosmic Four*. They yield the dual dialectics of hot and cold, dry and moist. Poets instinctively rediscover this dynamic and primitive orientation:

16. Renée Vivien, "Les Quatre vents," in *Poèmes en prose* (Paris, 1923-24), 7.

> The South, the West, the East, the North
> With their golden palms
> And icy fists,
> Dodge the blowing wind.[17]

On the plains of Flanders, Verhaeren has truly experienced the dynamism of all the different kinds of gusts of air:

> If I love, admire and madly sing the praises of
> The wind,
> And if I drink its fluid, living wine
> To the dregs,
> It is because it swells my whole being and because before
> It filters through my lungs and through my pores
> Into the blood that sustains my body,
> With its rude strength or its great gentleness
> Expansively, it has embraced the world.

If we read this poem with the same vitality with which it was written, we will very quickly realize that it is actually a way of breathing. It could serve as an example of poems that we breathe—the subject of the next chapter. The effect of this breathing will be better appreciated if we compare it to another poem which is every bit as beautiful, but which belongs to poetry to which we are intended to listen. I will take this example from *The Wings of Wieland*, written by the symbolist poet Viellé-Griffin:

> He is listening: the wind blows; he is listening:
> The wind is blowing, crying, moaning
> Like a horn
> That sobs and dies away
> Far away,
> Or so close!
> An arrow that whistles by my ear . . . [18]

V

A study that included all the details of the dynamic impressions that form the basis of poets' images should pay a great deal of

17. Emile Verhaeren,"A la Gloire du Vent," in *La Multiple splendeur*, 80.
18. Viellé-Griffin, *La légende ailée de Wieland* (Paris, 1900), 70.

attention to the psychology of the forehead. It should be noted that the forehead is sensitive to the slightest breath of air, that its recognition of the wind is due to a basic feeling. Pierre Villey relates it to the "sense of obstacles" in the blind. The blind "ordinarily perceive the sensations" sent out through the air by "face-high objects as localized on their foreheads or temples . . . Everyone who has studied the blind has noted this fact. It is mentioned as early as Diderot's *Letter of the Blind*."[19] A person need only play with a fan to become aware of the extraordinary sensitivity of the forehead, something we totally ignore in everyday life.

Poets who celebrate the breezes and the spring air sometimes tell us about this attraction:

> We were alone and walked along dreaming
> She and I, hair and thoughts blowing in the wind.[20]

The stronger the wind becomes, of course, the more clearly do the dynamic elements of the poetry of the forehead appear. When winds, as Shelley puts it, "blow health and renewal and the joy of youthful courage," then it seems as though the forehead becomes lofty. Instead of a halo of light, the face seems to be surrounded by a halo of energy. To face up to difficulty is not to struggle doggedly with some terrestrial chore; nor is it to maneuver obliquely on the waters. It is to truly turn your face to the wind and defy its force. All of the great forces of the universe inspire different forms of courage. They determine their own metaphors.

No one will be surprised then that, through its natural process of inversions, poetry attributes a face and a forehead to the wind:

> The wind's forehead appears
> Like dawn in the forest.[21]

VI

The relationship between the wind and breath would deserve a long study. It would need to include the aerial physiology that is so important in Indian thought. Breathing exercises, as we know, take

19. Pierre Villey, *Le Monde des aveugles* (Paris, 1914), 84.
20. Paul Verlaine, "Nevermore," in *Poems*, trans. Jacques Leclercq (New York, 1961), 41.
21. Emile Verhaeren, "Le Vent," in *Les Visages de la vie* (Paris, 1913), 124.

on a moral value in this system. They are actual rites that put man in contact with the universe. Wind for the world, and breath for man, demonstrate "the expansion of infinite things." In the *Chandoya-Upanishad* we read:

> When fire takes leave, it leaves on the wind. When the sun takes leave, it leaves on the wind. When the moon takes leave, it leaves on the wind. Thus the wind consumes all things. . . . When man goes to sleep, his voice takes leave on a puff of breath, and the same is true of his sight, his hearing, and his thought. Thus his breath consumes all things.

Only by experiencing the similarities of the wind and breath within ourselves are we able really to prepare for the health-giving synthesis of breathing exercises. An evaluation of the enlargement of the thoracic cavity is just an outer indication of a superficial exercise program which denies its eminently salutary effect on the life of the unconscious. The cosmic nature of breathing is the normal basis for the most lasting unconscious valorizations. A being has everything to gain by continuing to participate in cosmic forces.

It would be interesting, moreover, to follow in detail the imaginary syntheses in the practices of a psychology of breathing and those of a psychology of ascension. For example, height, light, and a breath of pure air can be associated dynamically by the imagination. To ascend while breathing better, breathing directly not only air but also light, participating in the summit's winds, are all feelings and images that constantly exchange their values and that are mutually supportive. An alchemist speaks of astral gold in these terms:

> It is an igneous substance and a continuous emanation of solar corpuscles that fill the whole universe because of the motion of the sun and the stars which are in a perpetual state of flux and reflux. Everything in the expanse of the skies, the earth, and its bowels is imbued with them. We continually breathe this astral gold; its solar particles are constantly entering our bodies and being exhaled.[22]

Balmy air and pleasant scents are experienced in such images. They are formed in a reverie about *sun-filled wind.*

22. Anon., "Entretiens d'Eudoxe et de Pyrophile," in *Bibliothèque des philosophes chimiques*, new ed. (Paris, 1740), III: 231.

In connection with the syntheses of air, height, and light, we will find a valuable notation in the work and the thesis of a young physician, Francis Lefébure.[23] A complete psychology of air should examine all of this work in detail. My subject is limited to the imagination of air, and within this area I want to limit myself further to a study of literary metaphors of air. I need only mention that these metaphors have deep roots in material life. Well-made metaphors are normally associated with air, height, light, and gentle, powerful wind, as well as pure, strong gusts of air. Such a synthesis gives life to our whole being. In the next chapter I am going to give some emphasis to this aspect of the imagination of air.

23. Francis Lefébure, *La respiration rythmique et la concentration mentale en éducation physique, en thérapeutique et en psychiatrie*, 2nd ed. (Paris, 1953).

12

Silent Speech[1]

> Breathing is the cradle of rhythm.
> *Cited by Kippenberg in
> her book on Rilke*

I

IN ITS SIMPLE, natural, primitive form, far from any aesthetic ambition or any metaphysics, poetry is an exhalation of joy, the outward expression of the joy of breathing. Before it is ever expressed metaphorically, *poetic breath* is a reality that can be found in the life of a poem if we are willing to follow the lessons of the *aerial material imagination*. And if we were to pay more attention to *poetic exuberance* and to all the forms that the joy of speaking takes—speaking quietly, rapidly, shouting, whispering, intoning—we would discover an incredible multiplicity of poetic breathing. In its strength as in its gentleness, in its poetic wrath as in its poetic tenderness, we would see an economy of breathing at work. We would find a wonderful control of word-bearing air. Such, at least, is poetry *that breathes well*; such are the poems that are the lovely, dynamic forms created by the act of breathing.

There are words that soothe all the tumult within us as soon as they are said or murmured. When it is able to bring these words together in a way that expresses aerial truth, a poem is sometimes a wonderful tranquilizer. Fierce, heroic verse is also able to hold breath in reserve. It gives to the brief utterance a resonant duration; to the excess of energy, a continuity. Thus it adds continuity to excessive force. A tonic air, material of courage, flows through the poem. All poetry—not only recited, but even read silently, as I will suggest in a minute—comes under the influence of this basic economy of breath. The most varied imaginary types, whether they belong to air, water,

---

1. The beginning of this chapter appeared in a collection of *Messages* (1942) under the title *Exercice du silence*.

fire, or earth, necessarily participate in aerial imagination as soon as they pass from reverie to a poem because of the way they are made. Man is a "sound chamber." Man is a "speaking reed."

II

Charles Nodier, my good mentor, succumbed several times to the temptation of establishing, on the fringes of historical knowledge, an etymology based on the vocal organs, an up-to-date one that would allow us to grasp the phonetic movements as they produce sound in our mouths. In its ontogenesis, this active phonetics repeats the phylogenesis taught in erudite books. In his *Critique of French Dictionaries* (1828), Nodier puts forth as an idea, which is "more ingenious than well-founded," an imaginary etymology of the word *âme* (soul). He looks for its "mimologism," that is, the whole group of oral and respiratory conditions that must be discovered by physiognomic imitation of *facial expressions* as we speak.[2] We will see through the single example of the word *âme* how this mimetic etymology yields a profound aerial valorization of *vocal movement*.

We will let the experts tell us that the word *âme* is a contraction of the Latin word *anima*, which has been caused by lax pronunciation, a tendency which, in many respects, is the determinant in phonetic evolution. Let us live the word, as we live it when we swear to love someone "with all our soul," to love "'til our last breath." Let us live it by "breathing" it. Then it will seem to us like a *mimologism of total exhalation.* If we pronounce the word *âme* in all of its aerial quality and with the conviction that comes from the life of the imaginary at just the right moment, when word and breath are one, then we will understand that the word takes on its proper sound value only when we have completed the breath. To express the word *âme* from within the depths of the imagination, our last reserves of air must be expended. It is one of those rare words that end as our breath ends. A purely aerial imagination would always prefer that this word come at the end of a phrase. In the imaginary life of breath, our soul is always our *last sigh.* A bit of our soul joins a universal soul.

---

2. Charles Nodier no longer speaks with the authority that his mind and wit earned him a century ago. Already in 1850, scholars were taking his theory of "mimologism" for a phenomenon of a "paradoxical and obscurantist mind." Cf. F. Génin, *Récréations philologiques* (Paris, 1856), 1:15n. But paradox should not be disdained by a psychologist of the poetic imagination.

To get a better feeling for it, let us try to establish silence in our entire being—let us listen to nothing but our own breathing—let us become as aerial as our breath—let us make no noise but our breathing, taking only shallow breaths—let us imagine only those words that form as we breathe . . . As this soul of a breath leaves us, we hear it say its name, we hear it say *âme*. The broad "â" is a vowel that is pronounced with a sigh—the word *âme* gives a bit of sonority to the aspirated vowel, a little liquid substance that gives realism to the last sigh. . . .

But this place that mimology has assigned to the word *âme*, that is, as the breath is completed, will perhaps be better understood if we are willing to participate in the odd respiratory dialectics of the words "*vie*" (life) and "*âme*" (soul).

Let us try again to attune our ear, our dream ear, to that unvoiced inner voice, the voice that is totally aerial, the voice that would fall silent at once should it stir our vocal cords and needs only breath in order to speak. By such total submission to aerial imagination, we will hear these two words pronounced *as we breathe, before we even think about them: vie* and *âme—vie* as we breathe in; *âme* as we breathe out. *Vie* is a word that shows aspiration, *âme*, expiration.

In the intoxication of aerial imagination raised to its cosmic role, we can discover, in the dual mimology of the words *vie* and *âme*, the imaginary theme of *breathing exercises*. Instead of breathing in undefined air, we will fill our lungs with the word *vie*; *âme* is what we will quietly give back to the world. Breathing exercises, far from being the setting in motion of a machinery that is watched over by a hygienist, is thus a function of universal life. A day whose rhythm is marked by the breathing of *vie-âme, vie-âme, vie-âme,* is one that will be in tune with the universe. The truly aerial being lives in a healthy universe. Between the universe and the breather there is the relationship of the healthy and the healthful. Beautiful aerial images vitalize us.

If we are willing at this stage to give primacy, as I never hesitate to do, to the imaginary over the real, we will be better prepared to understand Nodier's mimological phonetics in detail. Thus, on the subject of the word *âme*, Nodier writes: "In the formation of this word, the lips, when they are scarcely opened to allow the air to escape, quietly close again." On the word *vie*, the mimology is exactly the opposite: "then the lips gently separate and seem to aspirate the air."

In my own commentary, I have limited myself to moving one step further in the development of Nodier's paradox. One more step along this path, and we can understand that in the rhythmic *vie-âme*, the lips can remain motionless. Then it is really breath that speaks, and the breath that is the primary phenomenon of our silence. Listening to this barely audible breath, we can understand how different this is from the taciturn silence characterized by pinched lips. The moment that aerial imagination is awakened, the reign of *closed silence* is ended. Then there begins a silence that breathes. Then there begins the reign of "open silence. . . ."

III

If we could generalize on these remarks on the imagination of breathing, they would lead, it seems to me, to requirements for poems dictated by breath that would be very different from those dictated by scansion. More precisely, these two kinds of requirements would be shown to be complementary. Scansion would be expressed as a number, the pneumatology of lines would be expressed as a volume. The line would have both a certain quantity and a certain bulk. An aerial reality that swells and shrinks would govern its life along with a sound pattern that speeds up and slows down. Aerial matter will penetrate and live within a verbal form. Its light consistency would suffice to group the many verses and to correct the inferior cadence of poems with too regular a beat.

A reader destroys a poem if he takes no interest in this aerial matter, this breath. Moreover, he will not be conscious of the role of aerial matter if he examines a poem from a strictly phonetic point of view, because there the breath is worked, hammered, throttled, jarred, speeded up, caught up, and trapped in words. Aerial imagination requires more primitive intuitions. It demands the truths known through breath, the very life of audible air. Aerial matter necessarily flows in all poetry; it is not materialized time, nor is it a living duration. It has the same concrete value as the air we breathe. A line of poetry is a pneumatic reality. It must bow to aerial imagination. It is the creation of the joy of breathing:

Words bound together, tender or fierce words

. . . .

By pronouncing you, man breathes more easily.[3]

With this we can see everything that underlies the profound thought of Paul Valéry, who writes: "A poem is a continuity during which, reader, I breathe in accordance with a pre-established law. What I contribute is my breathing and the mechanics of my voice, or simply their potential, which can be reconciled with silence."[4] To find this *potential*, as we shall demonstrate, we must transpose the laws of governing poetry to those that govern will. Valéry's poetry reveals a power, an omnipotence regulated by will.

IV

In point of fact, wherever imagination is omnipotent, reality becomes useless. I am going to push my paradox to the point of proposing a kind of unaspirated breathing in silent speech. In this way, I will provide an outline for a metaphysics of speech.

To do this, I must seize the *will to speak*, and I must do it at the point where there is as yet not a single sound impression or a need to translate the delights acquired by sight, in short, before any impulse is received from representation or sensibility. Nowhere in the whole area of will is there a place where the distance between will and its manifestation is shorter. The will, if we catch it in the act of speaking, reveals its natural self. This is where we must seek the meaning of poetic ontogenesis, the bridge between those two radical powers, will and imagination. It is with reference to the will to speak that we can say that will *wills* the image or that the imagination *imagines* will. There is a synthesis between the word that orders and the one that imagines. Through speech, imagination orders and will imagines.

This metaphysical aspect, which I will develop elsewhere, will immediately be clear if we reflect on the primacy of *speech* over *sound*. All this comes down to becoming conscious of the speaker, who experiences feelings in a throat that is rich in nerve endings. The poet helps us to become conscious of this. Paul Claudel tells us in *Positions*

3. Emile Verhaeren, "Le Verbe," in *La Multiple splendeur*, 21.
4. Paul Valéry, "The Lover of Poems," in *The Collected Works*, ed. Matthew Jackson, trans. David Paul, Bollingen Series (Princeton, N. J., 1971), 3.

et Propositions that "we inform the reader, we make him a participant in our creative or *poetic* act; we put in the secret mouth of his mind the enunciation of an object or a feeling that appeals both to his thought and to his vocal cords."

In a throat that has been thus attuned by poetry, we feel a thousand forces of evolution and speech at work. And these forces are so sudden, so numerous, so revitalizing, so unexpected, that we are constantly occupied with keeping watch over them. Will that desires to speak is hard to hide, disguise, or hold back. Classical poetry and rhetoric, as taught in schools under inspection and with traditions and rules, stifle thousands of ways of speaking. Already established language patterns also act as censors in our nervous system, which constantly restricts to fixed norms the resonances permitted the vocal cords. But despite reason and despite language, vocal imagination, as soon as its freedom to breathe is restored, still suggests new verbal images.

Yet there are indications of the primacy of speech over sound that are more radical and closer to pure will. I appeal to the experience of all those who can feel *vocal pleasure* without having to speak, to all those who are stimulated by silent reading and who lay on the threshold of their morning the verbal dawn of a beautiful poem.

A preliminary classification of poems by their value for silent reading, by their power for silent speech, will place in an unrivaled position all those that do not cause vocal fatigue and that induce unexpressed vocal dreams. These dreams are perfect from a vocal point of view, and in them the form of the words contains exactly the right amount of aerial matter. They will be sur-rhythmed, and they will benefit from a surrealism of rhythm in the sense that they will derive their rhythm directly from aerial substance, from the material of breath. It is not for the ear to judge, but it is rather for the *poetic will*, which projects well-blended phonemes, to make judgments on this matter. The spoken word is, as far as we can determine, projected before being heard. According to the principle of projection, the word is willed before it is spoken. In this way, pure poetry is formed in the realm of the will before appearing on the emotional level. For this reason it is all the more true that pure poetry is far from being the art of representation. Created in the silence and solitude of being, with no connection to hearing or sight, poetry seems to me to be the primary phenomenon of the human aesthetic will.

Willed and re-willed, the origins of poetry's vocal values are cherished in their essential expressions of will. As they join together, these values give rise to symphonies in our nervous system that animate even the most silent being. These are the most lively and playful of all dynamic values. The will finds them in the silence and emptiness of being, at a time when it does not have to set our muscles in motion, but rather when it indulges in the irrationality of an innocent word. And thus appears, on the vocal cords, the splendid phenomena of a will that is specifically human, one that could be termed the *will to logos*. These first phenomena of the will to logos quickly assume the dialectics of *reason* and *speech*, the dialectics of reflection and expression. It is curious, we note, that reason and speech, by merging into the same verbalism, can degenerate into a lifeless tradition of thought and language. They can also be hardened through stubbornness and stentorian blustering. This hardening and degeneration can be avoided by returning to silence, by joining reflective silence to attentive silence, and by reviving the will to speak in its nascent state while it is yet a primary, potential, unuttered vocalization. Voiceless reason and silent speech will appear as primary factors in human development. Before any act, we need to say to ourselves, in the silence of our own being, what it is we *will* to become; we need to *convince ourselves* of our own becoming and to *exalt* it for ourselves. This is the function that poetry plays in questions of will. The *poetry of will* must then be put in touch with the tenacity and courage of a silent being.

V

It seems to me that the debate over pure poetry should be reintroduced, this time beginning with the problem of willed poetry, that is, a poetry that speaks directly to the will and occurs as a necessary expression of the will. To put it another way, I propose judging pure poetry not by what results from it, but by its élan at the moment when it was poetic will. Pleasant, relaxing poetry is certainly the most common kind. But describing it as an absence or a denial of will demonstrates our misunderstanding of its nature. If we look more closely, we can grasp the veiled presence of a will that seeks this pleasantness. Contemplation and will are antithetical only in their general aspects. The will to contemplate is manifest in all great poetic souls.

It has been said that the poetic work of Paul Valéry bears the stamp of *thought re-thought*. It would be better, I think, to speak of a thought *willed and re-willed*. A great deal of evidence pointing to this can be found if readers are willing to re-establish, as I am suggesting, the *primacy* of what is said over what is heard. For example, let us reread the first two stanzas of "The Graveyard by the Sea":

> Quiet the roof, where the doves are walking,
> Quivers between the pines, between the tombs;
> Justicer Noon out there compounds with fires
> The sea, the sea, perpetually renewed!
> Ah what a recompense, after a thought,
> A prolonged gazing on the calm of gods!
> What lucid toil of pure lightings consumes
> Many a diamond of imperceptible foams,
> And what a stillness seems to beget itself.
> For while a sun hangs over the abyss
> Pure workings of an eternal cause
> Time scintillates; and the Dream is knowledge.

The hard *c*'s that proliferate in this passage are phonemes of will, and, more specifically, phonemes of a will for calm. And still they are much more beautiful to will than to say. They are willed and re-willed. In them the will wills its poem, the very human will for calm. In a poetic universe that is limited to auditory values, they could determine motions that are much too angular. In a truly nascent poetic universe, the vocal universe, they appear as wonderful occasions for breathing, occasions on which strength and calm can assert themselves. When placed in each line of the poem with suitable space between, they dynamize silent speech. They fix their volume with astonishing exactness, one which shows the true quantity of poetic *matter*. Here the laws of scansion are done away with. Here the laws of speech are found. We can, I believe, cite these two stanzas as one of the most outstanding examples of a "mass of calm" contained in the vocal patterns of a poem.

Conclusion

Part I: The Literary Image

> Heard melodies are sweet, but those unheard
> Are sweeter; therefore, ye soft pipes, play on;
> Not to the sensual ear, but, more endear'd,
> Pipe to the spirit ditties of no tone . . .
> KEATS, *Ode on a Grecian Urn*

I

THERE ARE MUSICIANS who compose on blank paper, in silence and immobility. Their eyes wide open, they create, by a gaze that stretches into emptiness, a kind of visual silence, a silent gaze that effaces the world in order to silence its noises; they *write* music. They do not move their lips; even the rhythm of their blood has stopped its drumming; life waits; harmony is about to come. Then they hear what they are creating in the creative act itself. They no longer belong to a world of echoes or resonances. They hear the black quarter notes, the eighth notes, the half notes fall, tremble, glide, bounce back on the staff. For them, the staff is an abstract lyre that is already sonorous. There, on the blank page, they take pleasure in conscious counterpoint. In a live performance, some voices may get lost, be too low, or be drowned out; the blend may not work well. But creators of written music have ten ears and one hand. The hand wrapped around a pen draws together the world of harmony: ten ears, ten powers of concentration, ten chronometers to listen, reach out, and regulate the onrush of symphonic sounds.

There are also silent poets, silencers who start by quieting an overly noisy universe and all the hubbub caused by its thunderous sound. They also hear what they write at the same time as they are writing it, in the slow cadence of written language. They do not transcribe poetry; they write it. Let others "execute" what they have created there on the blank page. Let others use the megaphone of solemn public "recitals." As for them, they savor the harmony of the written page on which thought speaks and the word thinks. They know before they scan and before they hear it that the rhythm that they have written is certain. They know that their pen would stop of its own accord if it encountered a hiatus, that it would refuse to write unnecessary alliterations since it would no more want to repeat sounds than thoughts. How pleasant it is to write this way, mulling over the depths of reflective thoughts! How free we can feel from these absurd, bustling, wretched times! By virtue of written poetry's slow pace, verbs rediscover the fine points of their original movement. Each verb is accorded, not the time of its expression, but the true time of its action. No longer will the motion of verbs that turn be confused with those that thrust. And when an adjective makes its object blossom, written poetry, the literary image, allows us to live slowly the time of its blooming. Thus is poetry truly the first manifestation of silence. Poetry leaves attentive silence alive beneath the images. It constructs a poem based on silent time, on a time which is not labored, rushed, or controlled by anything, on a time that is open to everything spiritual, on the time of our freedom. How poor are moments lived compared to the moments created in poems! Poem: a beautiful temporal thing that creates its own tempo. Baudelaire dreamed of this plurality of temporal modes:

> Who among us has not, on days when he is ambitious, dreamed of the miracle of a poetic, musical prose, without rhythm or rhyme, and both supple and abrupt enough to adapt to the soul's lyrical movements, the undulations of reverie and the rude shocks of consciousness?

Need I emphasize that in three lines Baudelaire has pointed out all of the basic attractions of prosody's dynamism with its continuity, its undulations, and its sudden accents? But it is especially its counterpoint that makes *written poetry* surpass any diction. It is in writing or reflection that counterpoint awakens as the echo of a kind of epilogue. True poetry always has several registers. Thought runs sometimes above and sometimes below the singing voice. At least three levels are discernable in this multipronged polylogism, and they must find the place where words, symbols, and thoughts are in accord. Hearing does not allow the dreaming of images in depth. I have always thought that an ordinary reader appreciated poems more by copying them rather than by reciting them. Pen in hand, we have some possibility of doing away with the unfair advantage of sounds. We can teach ourselves to relive one of the most all-inclusive of associations, that of dream and meaning, by allowing dream the time to find its sign and to form its meaning slowly.

How, in fact, to forget the signifying role of the poetic image? The sign is not, in this case, a recall, a memory, the indelible stamp of a distant past. To deserve the title *literary image*, it must have the virtue of originality. A literary image is a nascent *meaning*. From it, the word—the old word—gets a new meaning. But that is still not enough: the *literary image* must be enriched with a new *oneirism*. Such is the dual function of the literary image: to mean something different and to make readers dream another way. Poetry does not express something alien to itself. Even a kind of purely poetic didactic function, which might express what poetry is, would not reveal the true function of poetry. There is no *poetry* that precedes the action of the poetic verb. There is no reality that precedes the literary image. The literary image does not clothe a naked image, nor does it grant speech to a mute image. Within us, imagination speaks; our dreams speak; our thoughts speak. Every human activity wants to speak. When this speech becomes conscious of itself, then human activity wants to write, that is, to organize dreams and thoughts. The imagination is delighted by the literary image. Literature is not merely a substitute for some other activity. It brings a human desire to fruition. It represents an *emergence* of the imagination.

The literary image emits sounds that must be called, in a barely metaphorical mode, *written sounds*. A kind of abstract ear, capable of distinguishing silent voices, is activated by writing; it lays down the canons that define literary genres. Through a lovingly written language is developed a kind of projective hearing, one that is in no way passive. *Natura audiens* takes precedence over *Natura audita*. The pen sings! If we could accept this notion of a *Natura audiens*, we would understand the value of reveries like those of Jacob Boehme:

> Now what is it that maketh the hearing, that you can hear that which stirreth and maketh a noise? Wilt thou say that it is caused by the noise of that outward thing which giveth the sound? No!

there must also be something that must receive the sound, and qualify or mix with the sound, and distinguish the sound of what is played or sung.[1]

One more step and the person who is writing hears the written Word, the Word created for men.

Reality is so distant for anyone who knows written reverie, for anyone who can live and live to the full with the flow of the pen! What he had intended to say is so quickly replaced by what he discovers himself writing that he feels clearly that the written language is creating its own universe. A universe of sentences arranges itself on the blank page with a coherence among its images that often has very diverse laws, but which always keeps the great laws of the imaginary. Revolutions that bring about modifications in written universes bring about more natural, less affected, universes, but they never efface the functions of imaginary universes. The most revolutionary manifestos are always new literary *constitutions*. They may cause us to change universes, but they always shelter us in an imaginary one.

Moreover, even in isolated literary images, we feel the cosmic functions of literature at work. Sometimes one literary image is enough to transport us from one world to another. It is in that respect that literary images appear to be the most innovative function of language. Language evolves through its images much more than through its semantic efforts. In an alchemical meditation, Boehme hears "voices of substances" after their explosion, when the explosion has destroyed the "Gehenna of astringency" and has "crossed the threshold of the land of the shades." In the same way a literary image is an explosive. It suddenly bursts open familiar phrases, it breaks open proverbs that have rolled on from age to age; it lets us hear the substantives after their explosion when they have left the Gehenna of their root and have crossed the threshold of the land of the shades, when they have transmuted their matter. In short, the literary image puts words in motion; it restores them to their imaginative function.

The written word has an enormous advantage over a spoken one, because it can call forth abstract echoes in which thoughts and dreams reverberate. The spoken word requires too much effort on our part; it requires too much presence; it does not allow us total

1. Jacob Boehme, 335-36.

mastery over our slow pace. There are literary images that involve us in vague, silent reflections. Then we become aware that a deep silence is incorporated into the image itself. If we want to study this integration of silence into a poem, we must not make it a simple linear dialectic of pauses and sudden starts through a recitation of the poem. We must understand that the element of silence in poetry is a hidden, secret thought. The moment that a thought, cleverly hiding beneath its images, lies in the shadow waiting for a reader, noises are muffled, the reading begins, and it is a slow, dreaming reading. In the search for a thought hidden under expressive sediments, a geology of silence is developed. In Rilke's work we can find many examples of this textually profound silence, in which the poet forces the reader to hear thought, far from noises perceived by the senses, and far from the old murmur of bygone words. And when this silence has fallen, then we can understand the strange expressive burst, the *élan vital* of a confession:

> No, loving is nothing, young man, even if your voice forces your mouth, —but learn to forget the sudden lurch of your outcry. It passes.
>
> Really sing, ah! that is another breath
> A breath around nothing. A flight into God. A Wind.[2]

In this way, this advice to attain silence is expressed by a will to become aerial and to break with an overly rich matter, or to impose upon material abundance the different forms of sublimation, liberation, and mobility. Through dreams of air, all images become elevated, free, and mobile.

The fact that the most beautiful literary images are not understood in one reading, that they are revealed little by little, both in an actual becoming of the imagination and in an enrichment of their meanings, is proof that an epilogism is possible which might designate the literary image as a very particular psychological function, one which I should like to emphasize.

Taken as a will to refine an expression, the literary image is a physical reality that has a particular relief, or, to put it more precisely, it is psychic relief, the multileveled psyche. It engraves or it raises. It

2. Rainer-Maria Rilke, "Un Dieu le peut," in *Poésie*, trans. Maurice Betz (Paris, 1938), 226.

discovers a depth or it suggests an elevation. It rises or falls between sky and earth. It is polyphonic because it is polysemantic. If it takes on too many meanings, it can degenerate into a "play on words." If it is restricted to a single meaning, it can degenerate into didacticism. The true poet avoids both dangers. He plays and he instructs. Within him, the word reflects and flows back. Within him, time begins to wait. The true poem awakens an unconquerable desire to be reread. A reader has the immediate impression that the second reading will reveal more than the first. And the second reading—very different from an intellectualized reading—is slower than the first. It is contemplative. No one ever finishes dreaming or thinking about a poem. And sometimes we discover a great line of poetry, one that contains such suffering or such a great thought that the reader—the solitary reader—murmurs: and that day, I shall read no further.

Through the inner workings of its poetic values, the literary image reveals that the formation of a doublet is a normal, fruitful linguistic activity. Even when erudite language is not available to incorporate the new idea, a linguistic sensibility is sufficient to demonstrate the reality of double meanings. It is these double and triple meanings that are exchanged in "correspondences." Doublets, triplets, and quadruplets can take form better if we can strengthen and prolong our impressions by following the reveries of material imagination on two, three, or four imaginary elements.

But let us take an example of a literary image where we can feel the work of a poetic triplet. It is found, incidentally, in the middle of one of Poe's tales. It was for me precisely one of those occasions when I stopped reading, and I have never stopped dreaming about it.

In his tale, "The Man of the Crowd," Poe dreams at nightfall about the milling crowd of people in a large city. As the night grows deeper, the crowd becomes more criminal. As honest people go home, night "[brings] forth every species of infamy from its den." And little by little, the evil of the dying day, as it grows blacker, takes on a tonality of moral evil. The gaslight, which is artificial and tainted, casts "over every thing a fitful and garish lustre." And then, with no further preparation, the many transpositions of this strange image, to which I should like to draw the reader's attention, are thrust upon us: "All was dark yet splendid—as that ebony to which has been likened the style of Tertullian."[3]

3. Poe, *The Complete Tales and Poems of Edgar Allan Poem*, 478.

If, having experienced the beloved image of ebony in Poe's other poems, you will remember that for him ebony is melancholy water—heavy and black—then you will feel an initial material transposition at work when the twilight, which was still aerial a moment ago, becomes nocturnal matter, compact, splendid, and, under the gaslight, enlivened by evil reflections. And scarcely have these first reveries been formed than the image looms larger: the dreamer remembers the style of Tertullian, as though it were a gloomy prophecy. This, then, is the triplet: night, ebony, style. And with greater depth and greater breadth, air that is growing darker—water—perhaps even metallic wood—then a written voice—a harsh voice, moving as a mass—emphasized like a black prophecy—the feeling of misfortune, sin, remorse. . . . What dreams in two lines! What exchanges of imaginary matter! After slowly dwelling in the land of reveries which has just been opened up to him, does not the reader's imagination reveal itself as a pure mobility of images? From that point on, radical shortcuts are possible. Yes, one night is black like an implacable style; another one is black and sticky like a mournful chant. Images have style. Cosmic images are literary styles. Literature is a world of values. Its images are primary. They are the images of the dream speaking, of the dream which lives in the fervor of nocturnal motionlessness between silence and a whisper. Imaginary life—true life!—is animated by a pure literary image. About the literary image we must say with O. V. de L. Milosz:

> But those are things
> Whose name is neither sound nor silence.

How unjust criticism is when it sees in language only an ossified form of an inner experience! On the contrary, language is always a little ahead of thought and a little more impetuous than love. It is the beautiful function of human imprudence and the dynamogenic boasting of will which exaggerates strength. In this study I have stressed in several ways the dynamic nature of imaginative exaggeration. Without this exaggeration, life cannot develop. Life always takes too much of everything in order to have enough. The imagination must take too much for thought to have enough. The will must imagine too much in order to realize enough.

Conclusion

Part II: Cinematic Philosophy and Dynamic Philosophy

> Endowed with a more discerning vision,
> you would see all moving things.
> NIETZSCHE, *The Will to Power*

I

IN ITS REVOLUTION against conceptual philosophy, Bergsonian thought has rightly advocated the study of change as one of the most urgent tasks of metaphysics. Only a direct study of change can enlighten us on the principle of evolution of concrete and living beings; it alone can teach us the essence of quality. Explaining change by movement and quality by vibrations is taking the part for the whole and the effect for the cause. If metaphysics is going to explain movement, then it will have to examine beings for whom an inner change is truly the cause of their movement. Bergson showed that the scientific study of movement, by concentrating principally on spatial referents, led to putting all phenomena of motion in geometrical terms without ever coming into direct contact with the power of becoming which is expressed in movement. Motion, examined objectively as in a study of mechanics, becomes simply the transporting of an unchanging object through space. If we were to study objects that move in order to change, objects whose movement manifests a will to change, we would have to recognize the fact that the objective and visual study of movement—that is, an entirely kinematic study—does not prepare the integration of the will to move and the experience of motion. Bergson has often shown that mechanics—actually, classical mechanics—gave us only linear graphs of many very different phenomena. These lines are static, always perceived as completed, and never really experienced as they develop in a certain set of circumstances. Consequently, we never grasp their full potential.

We understand, of course, that the abstraction produced by mechanics is completely justified from the particular point of view from which scientific research sets out when it studies physical move-ment. But if we want to study objects that truly *produce* motion and that are truly the initial causes of movement, we may find it useful to replace a philosophy that deals with kinematic description with one that studies dynamic production.

When making this shift it will be helpful, I believe, to include ex-periences of dynamic and material imagination. Le Senne has pointed out that by going from psychology to ethics, Bergson's work has gone from water to fire images. Still, it seems to me that there are other images whose material and dynamic aspects could provide even more appropriate means of clarifying Bergsonian thought. The im-ages that I will propose would lend themselves to upholding Bergson's intuition—which is often put forth only as a means of expanding knowledge—by means of positive experiences of will and imagination. Moreover, isn't it surprising that a work of such great scope has not envisioned the problems posed by imagination and will? Because there is not strong attachment in its images to the matter itself, it seems to me that Bergsonism has often remained kinematic in many respects, and that it has not always acceded to the potential dyna-mism that it possesses. Bergsonian thought could, I believe, be made more versatile if we could tie it more closely to its own rich images by examining the matter and dynamics of these images. In this way, images would no longer be seen as simple metaphors added simply to make up for the insufficiencies of conceptual language. Images of life would be at one with life itself. Life could be known no better than by the production of its images. The imagination, then, would be the best possible standpoint for meditating on life. What seems to be ex-cessive in this paradox, moreover, can be corrected with one word. We need only say that any meditation on life is a meditation on psychic life. Then everything becomes clear at once: it is the psyche's drive that possesses the continuity of duration. Life is content to swing back and forth. It swings between need and the satisfaction of need. And if we must show in what way the psyche has duration, we need only put our trust in *intuition as it imagines*.

II

Let me begin by giving an example of criticism based on images, that is, of an "imaginary" criticism.

To explain the dynamic value of a duration that is to unite past and future, there are no images in Bergsonian thought more common than drive and aspiration. But are these two images truly connected? In exposition, do they not play the role of image-filled concepts rather than active image? They become separated in any analysis which, all things considered, remains conceptual and engaged in logical dialectics. The imagination will resist this facile dialectics: it quietly effects a union of opposites. I would be willing to formulate my objection by quoting these verses from Rilke's *Groves*:

> Thus we live in a most strange dilemma
> between the distant bow and the too piercing arrow.

The bow—the past that impels us—is too distant, too old, too out-of-date. The arrow—the future that entices us—is too fleeting, too isolated, too ephemeral. The will needs more vivid designs of the future, and more compelling ones of the past. To use the double meaning which Claudel enjoys, the will is "design" in two senses: it is both *dessein* (purpose or intention) and *dessin* (plan or drawing). Past and future are not carefully integrated in Bergsonian duration for the very reason that the *dessein* of the present has been underestimated. The past is organized hierarchically in the present by the form of the intention, the *dessein*. In this *dessein*, memories that are unquestionably out-of-date are eliminated. The intention projects onto the future a preconceived, predesigned will. An enduring being has, then, at the very moment he decides to accomplish a given purpose, the benefit of a true presence. The past is no longer merely a slackened bow and the future simply a flying arrow, because the present is an immanent reality. The present is the sum both of a drive and an aspiration. And we understand the words of a great poet, Hugo von Hofmannsthal: "In the moment there is everything, counsel and action."[1] A wonderful thought in which we recognize the human being in all his grandeur, displaying his will. He is a creature who consults both his own past and his brother's wisdom. He groups his personal thoughts and advice from others by engaging a polymorphous psyche in a carefully chosen action.

Faced with such complexity, it seems to me that we cannot integrate drive and aspiration if we limit ourselves to the dynamic images

1. Hugo von Hofmannsthal, *Die Frau ohne Schatten* (Berlin, 1920), 162.

suggested by communal life and common efforts which are too closely bound up with managing concrete things. But to describe a duration that takes over our whole being, why not take those images in which we dream of being carried away by a movement that originates within ourselves? Aerial imagination provides us with such an image in the lived experience of oneiric flight. Why not put our trust in it? Why not experience all of its themes and their variations?

Some will no doubt object that I am making too much of a very restricted image. They may also claim that my desire to think through images could easily be satisfied by the flight of a bird which is also completely carried away by its *élan* and which is also master of its own flight path. But are these winged lines in the blue sky really anything more to us than a chalk line on a blackboard whose abstraction is so often criticized? From my particular point of view, they bear the mark of their own inadequacy: they are visual, they are drawn, simply drawn. They are not lived as acts of will. No matter where we look, there is really nothing but oneiric flight that allows us to define ourselves, in our whole being, as mobile, as a mobility that is conscious of its unity, experiencing complete and total mobility from within.[2]

III

Therefore, the essential problem for a meditation that is to give us images of living duration is, as I see it, to constitute being as both *moved* and *moving*, as mobility and motion, drive and aspiration.[3]

2. It is perhaps interesting to see a poet make the effort to group together all the experiences of the airplane, skiing, flying, jumping, and children's reveries, in order to arrive at the dynamic image of the *élan vital*. Francis Jammes, in *La légende de l'aile, ou Marie-Elisabeth* (p. 61-62) imagines the following scene: "A single visitor, who was strolling along, passed by quite close to her and then stood for a long time watching a chicken who was pecking outside the farm. She knew very little about this gentleman, except that his name was Henri Bergson, that he spoke gently, and that he usually kept his hands thrust into his coat pockets right up to his thumbs. She had heard him questioning her father about the mechanical aspects of the airplane. The king of the air and the philosopher had exchanged views on the way in which a clown, whom she had much admired in Medrano, did a dangerous double somersault. 'I wonder,' Monsieur Bergson said, 'whether man could fly without wings if he had enough will to power.' Mary Elizabeth had smiled inside herself, because she knew, down to the smallest details, how to skim along the top of the snow, both on the level with skis and going uphill."

3. It is within this synthesis of *moved* and *moving* that Saint-Exupéry forms a *bond* between plane and pilot at the moment of take-off. Here is how he describes the

On this point we return to the very precise thesis that I have been defending throughout this essay: in order to set ourselves up as the moving force that synthesizes from within both being and becoming, we must experience within ourselves the actual feeling of growing light. To move with a motion that involves the whole being in the developing stages of lightness, is already the transformation of any moving being. We must be an imaginary mass in order to feel ourselves the autonomous creator of our own becoming. There is no better way to accomplish this than to become conscious of the power within us that allows us to transform imaginary mass and to become in our imagination matter suitable for the development of our present duration. In more general terms, we can make either lead or light air flow into us. We can make ourselves be the mobility of a fall or the mobility of an *élan*. We thus give substance to our duration, in the two larger senses of duration: that which saddens and that which elates. Specifically, it is impossible to live the intuition of an *élan* unless we engage in this process of lightening our inmost being. To think force without thinking matter is to be the victim of analytic idols. The operation of a force within us is necessarily the consciousness within us of an inner transformation.

---

departure of a hydroplane in *Terre des Hommes*: "Air and water, and not machinery, are the concern of the hydroplane pilot about to take off. The motors are running free and the plane is already ploughing the surface of the sea. Under the dizzying whirl of the scythe-like propellers, clusters of silvery water bloom and drown the flotation gear. The element smacks the sides of the hull with a sound like a gong, and the pilot can sense this tumult in the quivering of his body. He feels the ship charging itself with power as from second to second it picks up speed. He feels the development, in these fifteen tons of matter, of a maturity that is about to make flight possible. He closes his hands over the controls, and little by little in his bare palms he receives the gift of this power. The metal organs of the controls, progressively as this gift is made him, become the messengers of the power in his hands. And when his power is ripe, then, in a gentler gesture than the culling of a flower, the pilot severs the ship from the water and establishes it in the air." Trans. Lewis Galantière (New York, 1940), 72-73.

Need I stress that this *participation* of the pilot in the complex act of flight is a participation accomplished by means of *dynamic imagination*? The passenger gets very little from it. He has not lived through the preparation for becoming lighter by means of the dynamism in the fifteen tons of matter behind the pilot involved in this act. The master of flight, dynamically intoxicated, becomes one with his machine. It makes a reality of the synthesis of what is *moved* and what is *moving*. With its images, the imagination gives him support. Cf. Gabriele d'Annunzio, *Forse che sì forse che no*, 45th ed. (Paris, 1910), 102-03.

The poet is not misled when he sings of his *self* becoming aerial:

> I, this animated body, so light for itself
> . . . .
> Some secret ether in my bones
> Makes me light, like a bird.[4]

Active meditation, meditated action, is necessarily a task of the imaginary matter of our being. The awareness of being a force puts our being to the test. Within this crucible we are a substance which is crystallized or refined, which falls or rises, grows richer or grows lighter, is collected or exalted. If we pay some attention to the substance of our meditating being, we will discover two directions for the dynamic *cogito*, depending on whether our being is searching for richness or for freedom. Every valorization must take this dialectic into account. We must first ascribe value to our own being before we can judge the value of others. That is why the image of the weigher is so important in Nietzsche's philosophy. "*Je pense*" (*I think*), therefore "*je pèse*" (*I weigh*): it is not by coincidence that these two terms have a profound etymological link. The *cogito* that weighs is the first of the dynamic *cogitos*. It is to this weighty *cogito* that all our dynamic values must be referred. This imagined value judgment on our own being is where the primary images of value are to be discovered. Finally, if we remember that every value is essentially a valorization and therefore a change of values, we realize that the images of dynamic values are the basis for all valorization.

To study this *cogito* that ascribes value, the dialectic of these two extremes, enrichment and liberation, is useful, as suggested by the terrestrial and aerial imagination—the one dreams of losing nothing and the other of giving everything! The second type is less common. Anyone trying to describe it always runs the risk of writing a frivolous book; opposed to him is everyone who limits realism to the terrestrial imagination. For the terrestrial imagination, giving always seems to be the equivalent of giving up, and becoming light always implies losing substance and gravity. But everything depends on one's point of view: what is rich in matter is often lacking in motion. Although terrestrial matter, with its rocks, salts, crystals, clays, minerals, and metals, may be the mainstay of infinite imaginary

4. Pierre Guéguen, "Sensation de soi," in *Jeux cosmiques*, 59-62.

riches, it is, dynamically speaking, the most static of dreams. Dynamic exuberance, on the other hand, belongs to air and fire—the light elements. The realism of psychic becoming needs ethereal lessons. It even seems that, without aerial discipline, without apprenticeship in lightness, the human psyche cannot evolve. At least, without aerial evolution, the human psyche understands only the evolution that creates a past. Establishing a future always requires the values of flight. It is in this sense that I want to meditate upon a wonderful expression that Jean-Paul writes in *Hesperus*, the most aerial of all his books: "Man . . . must be *lifted up* in order to be *transformed*."[5]

IV

In the realm of images, there is no way to separate the normative and the descriptive, as some would like to do. The imagination is necessarily valorization. As long as an image does not reveal its value by beauty, or, to speak more dynamically, feeling the value of beauty, as long as it does not have a pancalist and pancalizing function or find a place for one who imagines in a world of beauty, then it is not fulfilling its dynamic function. If it does not lift up the psyche, it does not transform it. For this reason, a philosophy that expresses itself in images must put absolute trust in them, or else it will lose a part of its force. A doctrine on the psyche that posits it as essentially expressive, imaginative, and valorizing in nature will always, in any circumstance, associate image and value. Belief in images is the secret of psychic dynamism. But even though images are fundamental psychic realities, they have a hierarchy. A doctrine of the imaginary must work on the task of defining this hierarchy. Basic images, especially those involving the way we imagine life, must be linked with elementary matters and fundamental movements. Going up and going down —air and earth—will always be associated with vital values, with the expression of life, with life itself.

For example, if we need to measure the amount of resistance caused by a matter that is weighing down a life that seeks to surge upward, we must find the images that truly involve the material imagination, images that link air and earth. If, on the other hand, we put the

5. Jean-Paul Richter, *Hespérus*, in *Sämtliche Werke* (Weimar, 1929), IV:74.

dialectics of ascent and descent, progress and habit, into more subtle, more purely dynamic themes, in such a way as to recognize in matter an *élan* that regresses, a motion that loses impetus, then we will have to animate the great impulses of the dynamic imagination.

The image of a water fountain that falls and stops the *élan* of the spray can serve only as a partially conceptualized illustration. It is visual—the kind of motion whose design can be described, not the kind that is experienced. It does not awake any participation in us. As far as temporal psychology is concerned, such an image sums up two moments that are remote from each other. The falling of the water has no part in the fountain's function. The drama of matter and of *élan* which we wish to represent is not really involved in this image. The philosopher-poet has not discovered in it the great contradiction of life, that it both rises and falls, springs forth and hesitates, that it is both changing and resisting. To experience the drama of life's progress, we must have other material and dynamic dreams. Moreover, if life is valorization, how can an image that is totally devoid of value express it? The water fountain is only a cold vertical line, a figure in the garden and a very monotonous one that is virtually static. It symbolizes motion without destiny.

Since it is both the valorization of life and the devalorization of matter that are involved here, we must give ourselves over, body and soul, to material imagination. We must look for our images in the work of those who have longest dreamed and valorized matter. Let us turn then to the alchemists. For them, to transmute is to perfect. Gold is metallic matter raised to the highest degree of perfection. Lead and iron are base metals that are inert so long as they remain impure. Theirs is an incomplete life. They have not yet ripened in the earth long enough. Clearly, the scale of perfection that rises from lead to gold involves not only metallic values, but the values of life itself. The producer of philosopher's gold, the philosopher's stone, will also know the secret of health and youth, and of life. The nature of values is to proliferate.

Having very briefly described the profound oneiric quality of alchemical thought, let us see how images of the *élan* of minerals will be formed in the process of simple distillation. I will show how this image, which for the modern mind is completely rationalized and consequently devoid of oneiric values, gives us, if experienced alchemically, all the dreams of the thwarted *élan*.

For an alchemist, distillation is a purification that elevates the substance by lightening its impurities. But it is here that the simultaneous rising and falling action that was lacking in the water fountain image comes into play: rising and lightening are accomplished in accordance with the profound Novalisian dictum of *uno actu*. As the ascension progresses, there is a consequent "descent," as the alchemists expressed it. Everywhere and in a single act something ascends *because* something descends. The converse reverie in which the imagination can say that something descends because something else ascends is less common. It is indicative of an alchemist who is more aerial than terrestrial. But, in any case, alchemical distillation like sublimation is born out of the dual material imagination of earth and air.

From this point on, to attain *purity* through distillation or sublimation, an alchemist will not rely solely on an aerial power. He will find it necessary to call up a terrestrial power so that terrestrial impurities will be drawn down toward the earth. The descent that is activated in this way will promote ascent. To help this terrestrial action along, many alchemists add impurities to the matter to be purified. They soil it, the better to cleanse it.[6] Weighted down by extra-terrestrial matter, the substance to be purified will follow a more normal distillation process. If an earthy substance, a mass of impurities, actively draws these impurities downward, then the pure substance, attracted by aerial purity, will rise more easily, bringing with it fewer impurities.[7] This is a state of mind, or state of dream, that a modern distiller finds very static! We might say that modern processes of distillation and sublimation are operations with a single arrow ↑ whereas, to the alchemists' way of thinking, both of them are operations with two arrows ↑↓, two arrows loosely joined like two opposite attractions.

These two arrows, joined in order to diverge, represent a kind of participation that only dreams can live perfectly: active participation in two opposite characteristics. This double participation in one act corresponds to a true Manicheism of motion. The flower, with its

6. It seems that a really dirty substance allows the cleansing action to take hold better. The will to cleanse is aroused by a filthy object. This is one of the principles of dynamic material imagination.
7. Guillaume Salmon, "La somme de Geber," in *Bibliothèque des philosophes chimiques* (Paris, 1741), I:178.

aerial perfume, the seed with its terrestrial weight, are formed in opposite ways, but together. Every evolution is marked by a dual
destiny. Angry and peaceable forces work on minerals as well as on
the human heart. All of Jacob Boehme's work is composed of reveries
that are torn between aerial and terrestrial forces. Thus Boehme is a
moralist of metal. This metallic realism of good and evil provides a
way of measuring the universality of images. It helps us understand
that the image commands both heart and mind.

It seems to me, then, that the image of material sublimation, as it
was experienced by generations of alchemists, can account for a dynamic duality in which matter and impetus act in opposite directions
while still retaining close ties to each other. If the evolving action
deposits sediments in order to rise upward, while at the same time re-
jecting the already materialized result of a previous impetus, then it is
an act that points in two directions. To imagine it well, there must be
a dual participation. Only material imagination, the imagination
that dreams of the matter beneath forms, can, by uniting terrestrial
and aerial images, supply imaginary substances in which the two
dynamic processes of life are animated: that dynamism which pre-
serves and that which transforms. We come again, as always, to the
same conclusions: to imagine motion we must imagine matter. To the
purely kinematic description of a movement—even a metaphorical
one—must always be added a dynamic consideration of matter that is
affected by movement.

V

The metaphysics of freedom could also be based on the same
alchemical image. In fact, a linear destiny in which someone finds
himself at a crossroads and imagines himself free to choose between
the left or the right-hand paths will not suffice for this metaphysics.
Scarcely has the choice been made when the course followed reveals
its inner unity. To think about such an image is to establish the
psychology of hesitation rather than the psychology of freedom. Here
again, we must go beyond a descriptive and kinematic study of free
movement to get to the dynamics of liberation. We must become involved in our images. It is precisely a dynamics of liberation that
animated alchemical reveries during the long process of sublimation.
In alchemical literature, there are countless images of a metallic soul

caught in impure matter! Pure substance is a being in flight: it is necessary to help it use its wings. At all stages of the purification process can be added images of liberation in which the aerial being frees itself from the terrestrial and vice versa. In alchemy, the processes of freeing and purifying are in complete accord. These are two values, or better, two ways of expressing the same value. For this reason, they can explain each other all along the vertical axis of values that we sense at work in fine images. And the alchemical image of active and continuous sublimation truly makes available to us the differential of freedom, the close duel of the aerial and the terrestrial. In this image two things happen at the very same time. Aerial matter becomes free air, and terrestrial matter becomes unmoving earth. No one has ever sensed better than in alchemy how closely linked are these two divergent processes. We cannot describe one without reference to the other. But once again, geometrical references, references to figures are not enough. We must involve ourselves in the really material relationship between yeast and its rising, between *pâte* and smoke. How we can come to know and love qualitative life as, with the soul of an alchemist, we watch the appearance of a new color! When matter is still black, we already imagine, or foretell, a bright whitening. A dawn, a sense of freedom, is on the rise. Then, the slightest shade of something lighter is truly a moment of hope. Similarly, hoping for light actively pushes darkness away. Everywhere, in all images, the dynamic dialectics of air and earth reverberate. As Baudelaire writes on the first page of *My Heart Laid Bare*: "Evaporation and concentration of the *Self*. That is the crux."

VI

I could tie my two conclusions together and pose the problem of freedom on the plane of the literary image. As a matter of fact, in the active language of literature the psyche wishes to unite change and security as it does in all its other operations. It organizes habits of knowing—concepts—which will serve and capture it. So much for security, sad state of security. But the psyche renews its images, and it is through images that change comes about. If we examine the act by which the image goes beyond and changes the concept, we will sense a bi-directional evolution at work. In fact, the newly formed literary image adapts to the antecedent language and is inscribed like a new crystal in the soil of language. But the moment before, in its conception, the literary image satisfied needs for expansion, exuberance, and expression. And these two developments are connected, for it seems that to express the ineffable, the evasive, the aerial, every writer needs to develop themes of inner wealth, wealth that bears the weight of inner certainty. From that moment on, the literary image presents itself from two perspectives: expansion and intimacy. In their rough form, the two perspectives are contradictory. But when one experiences his language genetically, giving himself over to literary activity, to speaking the imagination with all his heart and soul, the two perspectives of expansion and intimacy manifest themselves as curiously homographic. The image is as shining, as beautiful, and as lively in expressing the universe as in expressing the heart. Expansion and depth are dynamically linked from the moment that a person exuberantly discovers himself. Each infers the other. Experienced in the sincerity of its images, the exuberance of the being reveals its depth. Reciprocally, it seems that the depth of the inner being is like an expansion with regard to oneself.

As soon as we put language in its proper place, at the height of human evolution, it is revealed in its double effectiveness: it bestows on us the virtues of clarity and the powers of dream. Really knowing the images of words, the images that exist beneath our thoughts and upon which our thoughts live, would advance our thinking in a natural manner. A philosophy concerned with human destiny must not only admit its images, but adapt to them and continue their flow. It must be an openly living language. It must study the *literary man* candidly, because the literary man is the culmination of meditation and expression, the culmination of thought and of dream.

Dijon
2 May 1943

Endnotes

Like many of his contemporaries in France, Gaston Bachelard documented his sources in a rather desultory fashion, footnoting or not at his discretion. This practice, so disconcerting to American readers accustomed to stricter conventions, was exacerbated by wartime conditions. Yet the very casualness of Bachelard's documentation may well contribute to the characteristic flow of his prose. For this reason, the author's original notes, corrected when necessary, have been kept in place at the bottom of the page. All other information or commentary has been assembled in these endnotes. They are referenced neither by means of superscripts in the text nor by page and line numbers but by page number and keyword or phrase.

The reader can locate a keyword in the text by scanning the left margin. For instance, bibliographical information for the citations on pages twenty-two and twenty-three—from Spencer and Brillat-Savarin—is listed after the respective keys: "attempt" and "make this discovery." If the quotation occupies more than one line, the final line is the one referenced.

P. 1   **poets:** Joseph Joubert, *Pensées* (Paris, 1866), 266.

P. 4   **one who inspires:** Paul Valéry. Could not be verified.

P. 6   **precursory . . . *Water and Dreams*:** Gaston Bachelard, *Water and Dreams*, trans. Edith R. Farrell (Dallas, 1983).

P. 9   **"non-dimensional space":** Joé Bousquet. Could not be verified.

P. 10   *tial in* . . . **Bergson:** Henri Bergson, *La Pensée et le mouvant* (Paris, 1946), 29.

P. 16   **as in my book:** Bachelard, Chapter 8.

P. 19   **can trace:** Gabriele d'Annunzio, "Undulna," in *Textes inédites* (Paris, 1942), 20.

P. 22   **attempt.:** Herbert Spencer, *The Study of Sociology*, cited in Havelock Ellis, *The World of Dreams* (Boston, 1911), 130.

P. 23   **make this discovery:** Jean Anthelème Brillat-Savarin, *Physiologie du goût* (Belley, France, 1867), 179.

P. 23   **awake for:** Joseph de Maistre, *Les Soirées de Saint-Pétersbourg* (Brussels, 1837), II:200-01.

P. 24   **we already knew it:** Denis Saurat, *La fin de la peur* (London, 1938), 43.

P. 24   **influence of some:** Havelock Ellis, *The World of Dreams*, 134-35.

P. 25   **progress in his:** Charles Nodier, "Palingénésie humaine et la résurrection" ("Human Regeneration and Resurrection"), in *Rêveries* (Paris, 1799), 235.

P. 26   shell of an: Ibid., 234.

P. 26   dreams: Ibid., 235.

P. 27   does . . . in Nodier's: Ibid.

P. 28   attempted to: Havelock Ellis, 130.

P. 30   the help of: Jules Duhem. Could not be verified.

P. 30   the good . . . petasus: a petasus is a broad-brimmed, low-crowned hat.

P. 30   ing boots: Gustave Flaubert, La Première Tentation de Saint Antoine (1848-1856), unedited work published by Louis Bertrand (Paris, 1908), 219.

P. 31   from either heel: John Milton, Paradise Lost, Book V, lines 283-85, in The Complete Poetical Works of John Milton, ed. Douglas Bush (Boston, 1965), 305.

P. 33   there passes: Rilke, Poèmes, trans. Mme Lou Albert-Lasard (Paris, 1937), 5.

P. 34   above the inner: Ibid.

P. 34   more than the: Rainer Maria Rilke, Selected Works I: Prose, trans. G. Craig Houston (New York, 1967), 24.

P. 36   light as I: Cyrano de Bergerac, Préface à l'histoire comique des Etats et Empires du Soleil. None of the editions available contained a preface.

P. 36   wind.": Duhem. Could not be verified.

P. 36   cause birds: De Maistre, Les Soirées, II:199.

P. 36   ears, ventricles: Cited by Giuseppe Boffito, Biblioteca Aeronautica Italiana (Florence, 1929), xlix.

P. 37   pression must: Editor of Les Soirées. Could not be verified.

P. 37   the sky: Cf. Berthold Laufer, The Prehistory of Aviation (Chicago, 1928), 68.

P. 37   Ethereal, as we . . . : Milton, Paradise Lost, Book V, lines 479-87, 493-99, p. 310.

P. 38   Vico has said: Vico. Could not be verified.

P. 38   and your wings: Percy Bysshe Shelley, "Prometheus Unbound" IV, lines 89-91, in The Complete Poetical Works of Percy Bysshe Shelley, ed. Thomas Hutchinson (London, 1905), 256.

P. 39   were less aethereally: Shelley, "Epipsychidon," lines 75-77, 413.

P. 40   glades . . . : Shelley, "Prometheus Unbound," preface, 205.

P. 40   "poetry is a: Ibid., 206.

P. 41   analyzing the "operations: Ibid., 205.

P. 42   and Dreams: Bachelard, Chapter 3.

P. 43   and Sea: Shelley, "Epipsychidon," lines 457-58, 421.

P. 43   poet . . . aëry dew": Shelley, "The Witch of Atlas," line 474, 383.

P. 43   "fragments of: Shelley, "Epipsychidon," lines 505-06, 422.

P. 44   **Read in their:** Ibid., lines 508-12, 422.

P. 44   **Seem silent summits:** Rilke, *Vergers* (Paris, 1926), 41.

P. 45   **thou wilt:** Shelley, "Epipsychidon," line 388, 420.

P. 46   **And bears me:** Shelley, "Prometheus," IV, line 321, 261.

P. 46   **wings. They "drink:** Shelley, "Prometheus," II, lines 135-36, 239.

P. 46   **"I change:** Shelley, "The Cloud," line 76, 602.

P. 46   **Piaget noted:** Jean Piaget, *The Child's Conception of Physical Causality* (Ottowa, New Jersey, 1972), 23.

P. 47   **To let her:** Shelley, "The Witch of Atlas," lines 489ff, 383.

P. 48   **and snow:** Ibid., lines 321-23, 379.

P. 49   **And gaze upon:** Shelley, "Prometheus," IV, lines 189-93, 259.

P. 50   **Out of the:** Ibid., lines 504-5, 266.

P. 50   **Of their aëreal:** Ibid., II, lines 171-72, 230.

P. 50   **unembodied:** André Chevrillon, "La nature dans la poésie de Shelley," in *Etudes Anglaises* (Paris, 1910), 135.

P. 51   **transformed into:** Ibid., 120.

P. 51   **Of planetary music:** Shelley, "Epipsychidon," lines 83-86, 413.

P. 51   **really . . . "light is:** Ibid., line 336, 419.

P. 52   **Whose soft step:** Shelley, "The Witch of Atlas," lines 521-22, 384.

P. 52   **space like a shot:** Louis-Claude de Saint-Martin, *L'Homme du désir* (Monaco, 1979), 83.

P. 52   **of the regions":** Ibid.

P. 52   **reward.":** Ibid.

P. 53   **sphere to another,":** Honoré de Balzac, "Les Proscrits," in *La Comédie Humaine*, ed. Marcel Bouteron, Bibliothèque de la Pléiade (Paris, 1962), 10:322ff.

P. 54   **when we want:** Ibid., 338.

P. 54   **passed as if:** Ibid., 348.

P. 55   **as a fish:** Victor-Emile Michelet, *L'Amour et la magie* (Paris, 1909), 68.

P. 56   **suffering and understanding:** Balzac, 338-39.

P. 56   **word *fall*:** Ibid., 339.

P. 56   **tion, the constant:** Ibid.

P. 58   **were protecting:** August Strindberg, *Inferno, Alone, and Other Writings* (New York, Garden City, 1968), 150.

P. 58   **ing up his:** Balzac, 550.

P. 59   **skier . . . "like:** Ibid., 475.

P. 59   **prey . . . "to grind:** Ibid., 466.

P. 59   **more immense:** Ibid., 467.

P. 59   **clouds were:** Ibid.

P. 60   **of clouds, and:** Ibid., 468.

P. 60   **everything was:** Ibid., 584.

P. 61   does," a reader: Edgar Quinet, *Merlin l'enchanteur* (Geneva, 1977), II:9.

P. 62   she is as: Ibid., I:291.

P. 62   top.' ": Ibid., II:24.

P. 63   Like the Son: Johann Wolfgang von Goethe, *The Second Faust*, trans. Charles E. Passage (New York, 1965), 327.

P. 63   Into its grip: Ibid., 331.

P. 63   are left behind.": Ibid., 337.

P. 63   perhaps the original: André Schaeffner, *Origine des instruments de musique* (Paris, 1936), 217. While Bachelard cites Schaeffner, the quotation is attributed in Schaeffner to Maurice Leenhardt.

P. 64   Of luxuries: Keats, "I stood tiptoe upon a little hill," in *The Complete Poetical Works and Letters* (Boston and New York, 1899), 14.

P. 65   Every virgin: D'Annunzio, *The Dead City*, act III, sc. 2, trans. Prof. G. Mantellini (Chicago, 1902), 185.

P. 67   by unseen powers": Alphonse Toussenel, *L'Esprit des Bêtes: le monde des oiseaux* (Paris, 1884-1889), I:3.

P. 67   you of the: Ibid.

P. 67   the ability: Ibid.

P. 68   carnate in: Ibid., 2.

P. 68   nature of the: *Phaedrus*, in *Plato in Twelve Volumes*, trans. Harold North Fowler (Cambridge, 1977), 1:473.

P. 68   phrase . . . "I have: Ibid., 3.

P. 68   ages of love: Ibid., 4.

P. 69   glorious of all: Ibid., 5.

P. 70   with a bird.: Pierre Emmanuel, "Le Jeune Mort" in *Messages*, Cahier I (1942), 4.

P. 70   and sky; come: La comtesse Mathieu (Anna) de Noailles, *La Domination* (Paris, n.d.), 265. Ellipses are Noailles'.

P. 70   the summit: Ibid., 267-68. Ellipses are Noailles'.

P. 70   Made of: Victor Hugo, "La Fin de Satan: Le Cantique de Bethphagé" in *La Légende des siècles, La Fin de Satan-Dieu*, ed. Jacques H. Truchet, Bibliothèque de la Pléiade (Paris, 1950), 840.

P. 70n *Le témoin invisible:* Could not be verified.

P. 71   faithful, aerial: Toussenel, 5.

P. 72   regions of the air: Duhem, *Histoire des idées aéronautiques avant Montgolfier* (Paris, 1943), 306.

P. 72   looked upon: Author unknown.

P. 73   Something blue: Hugo, "La Légende des siècles: Booz endormi," op. cit., 36.

P. 73   when put: Maurice Maeterlinck, *L'Oiseau bleu* (Paris, 1910), 145.

P. 74   nonetheless functions: Jules Michelet, 99.

P. 74   and the eagle: Victor Hugo, "Dieu," passim, 943ff.
P. 74   credulous mortals.": Toussenel, *Les Bêtes.* Could not be verified.
P. 75   stand in his: J. Villette, *L'Ange dans l'art occidental du XIIème au XVIème siècle* (Paris, 1940), 26.
P. 75   to direct their: Ibid., 164.
P. 76   strengthen this illusion.": Ibid., 162.
P. 76   the . . . page 80: Ibid., 80xii.
P. 76   follow these: Ibid., 20.
P. 77   cov'ring: William Blake, "Visions of the Daughters of Albion," Plate 8, line 6, in *The Poetry and Prose of William Blake*, ed. David V. Erdman (Garden City, New York, 1965), 49.
P. 77   Puts all: Blake, "Auguries of Innocence," lines 5-6, 481.
P. 78   Or poison: Blake, "Daughters of Albion," Plate 4, lines 8-11, 47.
P. 78   substance is: Ibid., Plate 3, line 23, 46.
P. 78   is holy!": Ibid., Plate 8, lines 9-10, 50.
P. 78   length.": Blake, "Tiriel," 8, line 21, 282.
P. 79   And a state: Blake, "The Book of Urizen," Ch. IV(b), line 35-43, 74.
P. 79   Round Enitharmons: Ibid., Ch. VI, 5, lines 24-28, 78.
P. 80   Where was a worm: Ibid., 6, lines 29-36.
P. 80   The meshes: Ibid., Ch. VIII, Plate 25, 8, lines 20-21, 81.
P. 80   Bind around: Blake, "The Kid," 467, 468.
P. 80   wake! expand!: Blake, "Jerusalem," Plate 4,line 6, 145.
P. 81   see does not: Blake, (Blake's Exhibition and Catalogue of 1809, P. 37), 532.
P. 83   the bird "so: Jules Michelet, 258.
P. 83   lark." . . . "is now: Ibid., 8.
P. 83   most unappreciated: Toussenel, II:256.
P. 84   singing . . . : Adolphe Retté, "La Légende du Bon Pauvre," in *Passantes* in *Oeuvres complètes*, I:30. A typographical error identified this author as "Ressé" in the original text.
P. 84   axiom . . . "You sing: Jean-Paul Richter, *Der Jubelsenior in Sämtliche Werke* (Weimar, 1930), 5th band, 401.
P. 84   final act: Tristan Tzara, *Grains et Issues* in *Oeuvres complètes* (Paris, 1979), III:58-59.
P. 84   the dawn: Eichendorff, 51.
P. 85   to console: Jules Michelet, 90.
P. 85   Like an unbodied: Shelley, "To a Skylark," line 15, 602.
P. 85   form . . . "hidden: Ibid., lines 36-37, 602.
P. 85   sky": Toussenel, 248.
P. 85   What thou: Shelley, "To a Skylark," line 31, 602.
P. 85   That panted: Ibid., lines 61-65, 603.

P. 85   noyance": Ibid., line 78, 603.

P. 86   **What love:** Ibid., lines 71-75, 603.

P. 86   **The world:** Ibid, lines 101-105, 603.

P. 86   **blithe Spirit:** Ibid., lines 1-2, 602.

P. 86   **" . . . carries:** Jules Michelet, 256.

P. 87   **sickness is relieved:** Leonardo da Vinci, *Les Carnets de Léonard de Vinci*, trans. Louise Servicen, preface by Paul Valéry (Paris, 1942), II:377.

P. 87n   **Ballades Francaises inédites:** This title could not be verified through the Bibliothèque Nationale.

P. 88   **much joy:** D'Annunzio, *The Dead City*, 52-53.

P. 88   **pleasures, of:** Lucien Wolff, *Georges Meredith, Poète et Romancier*, 37.

P. 88   **in . . . "moves what:** Ibid., 40.

P. 91   **enough strength:** Paul Claudel, *Positions et Propositions*, II:237. Could not be verified.

P. 91   **point . . . "racial memory":** Jack London, *Before Adam* (London, 1974), 73.

P. 91   **our dreams:** Ibid., 13-14.

P. 92   **day personality:** Ibid., 14-15.

P. 92   **through space.":** Ibid., 15.

P. 92   **Imagination in Me:** Blake, "Annotations to Wordsworth's Poems," Page 44, 655.

P. 96   **tinguish its:** Edgar Allan Poe, "The Pit and the Pendulum," in *The Complete Tales and Poems of Edgar Allan Poe* (New York, 1938), 247. All references to Poe are to this volume unless otherwise noted.

P. 96   **slumber, and:** Poe, *Marginalia*, (Charlottesville, 1981), 77.

P. 97   **of success.":** Poe, 247.

P. 97   **madness of a:** Ibid.

P. 97   **can imagine . . . "eyes closed":** Ibid.

P. 98   **cadence:** Ibid.

P. 98   **pulse on the:** Poe, "The Power of Words," 442.

P. 99   **degrees, seventeen:** Charles George Thomas Garnier, "Relation d'un voyage du pôle arctique au pôle antarctique par le centre du monde," in *Voyages imaginaires, songes, visions et romans cabbalistiques*, trans. M. de Mauvillon (Amsterdam, 1787; Paris, 1787-95), 369.

P. 99   **coast—in:** Poe, "A Descent into the Maelström," 127.

P. 100   **danger from:** Ibid.

P. 101   **dizzy, as if:** Ibid., 134-35.

P. 102   **text the image:** Hugo von Hofmannsthal, "Entretien sur la poésie" in *Ecrits en prose*, 160.

P. 102   *soft* . . . *"soft and:* Poe, "The Pit and the Pendulum," 246.

P. 102   **heavy folds:** Poe, "The Masque of the Red Death," 270.

P. 102   **tains which:** Poe, "Ligeia," 661.

P. 103   **Comes down:** Poe, "The Conqueror Worm," 961.

P. 103   **pressively low:** Poe, "The Fall of the House of Usher," 231.

P. 103   **that "paradoxical:** Ibid., 232.

P. 104   **ible, and:** Ibid., 233.

P. 104   **all,":** Ibid., 234.

P. 105   **mained burning:** Poe, "Shadow," 457-58.

P. 105   **to its feet.":** Cyrano de Bergerac, *Oeuvres*, I:400. Could not be verified.

P. 105   **that is, toward:** Victor-Emile Michelet, *L'Amour et la Magie*, 49.

P. 106   **of time!:** O. V. de L. Milosz, "Psaume du roi de beauté," *Derniers poèmes*, in *Poésies II* (Paris, 1960), 178.

P. 107   **From life to:** Milosz, "La Confession de Lemuel," in *Poésies II*, 158.

P. 107   **other of light.":** Albert Béguin, *L'Ame romantique et le rêve* (Paris, 1946), 121.

P. 107   **nature.":** Ricarda Ruch. Could not be verified.

P. 109   **flight toward:** Novalis, *Journal intime suivi de Hymnes de la nuit et de Maximes inédites*, trans. G. Clarette (Paris, 1927), 98.

P. 109   **invisible bond:** Ibid.

P. 112   **complexes "by":** Robert Desoille, *Exploration de l'affectivité subconsciente par la méthode du rêve éveillé. Sublimation et acquisitions psychologiques* (Paris, 1938), 55.

P. 112   **does . . . "having:** Ibid.

P. 116   **a state incompatible:** Ibid., 37.

P. 116   **future.":** René Crevel, *Mon corps et moi* (Paris, 1974 rpt.), 75.

P. 117   **Desoille asks:** Desoille, 40.

P. 117n   *Poétique du ciel:* This edition was "out of circulation" in the Bibliothèque Nationale in 1985. A 1927 edition also exists, but the quotation was not found in it.

P. 119   **you do?:** Jacob Boehme, *Concerning Three Principles of the Divine Essence*, trans. John Sparrow (London, 1910), 44.

P. 119   **earth. . . . :** Ibid., 73.

P. 119n   **Stilling's remarks:** Page reference could not be verified.

P. 120   **darkness.":** Elémir Bourges, *La Nef* (Paris, 1922), 297.

P. 120   **ing, if possible:** Desoille, 189-90.

P. 120   **Desoilles' comparative:** Ibid., 192-93.

P. 121   **evidence of a:** E. Caslant, *Méthode de développement des facultés supra-normales*, 2nd ed. (Paris, 1927), 132.

P. 122   **by lightning . . . :** O. V. de L. Milosz, "Epître à Storge" in *Oeuvres complètes* (Paris, 1960), 7:28.

P. 122   **ultimate Rhythm:** Ibid., 29.

P. 122   **Affirmation.":** Ibid., 37.

P. 122   **an old mirror.":** Ibid., 29.

P. 122   **head of the:** Ibid., 40.

P. 123   **sufficiently sublimated:** Desoille, 177.

P. 123   **state.:** Ibid., 178.

P. 123   **story.:** Ibid., 181.

P. 123   **he has . . . new knowledge:** Cf. Pierre Janet, *Acquisitions Psychologiques*, 187.

P. 125   **"Today you:** Hofmannsthal, "Entretien sur la Poésie," 91-92.

P. 127   **Malchut, is:** O. V. de L. Milosz, "Psaume du roi de beauté," in *Oeuvres complètes* (Paris, 1960), II:178.

P. 128   **cavernous, compressed.":** "On Great Events," *Thus Spoke Zarathustra*, in *The Portable Nietzsche*, trans. and ed. Walter Kaufmann (New York, 1954), 243. All subsequent quotations from *Thus Spoke Zarathustra* are taken from this edition, unless otherwise noted.

P. 130   **To immortal life:** *Fragments of Dionysus-Dithyrambs*, 75, trans. Paul V. Cohn in *The Complete Works of Friedrich Nietzsche*, ed. Dr. Oscar Levy (New York, 1964), XVII:202.

P. 130   **I flow:** translated by Philip Grundlehner in Philip Grundlehner, *The Poetry of Friedrich Nietzsche* (New York, 1986), 277.

P. 130   **Mythology, Poseidon:** Cf. *Water and Dreams*, 154-55.

P. 131   **cloudy, moist:** "Among Daughters of the Wilderness," *Thus Spoke Zarathustra*, 416.

P. 131   **swamp-blood:** "On Passing By," Ibid., 289.

P. 131   **these cows are:** *Bruckstocke zu den Dionysos-Dithyramben*, in *Nietzsches Werke Band 1* (Salzburg Stuttgart, n.d.), 285.

P. 132   **quite different:** *Nietzsche contra Wagner*, in *The Portable Nietzsche*, 666.

P. 132   **walking, striding:** Ibid., 664.

P. 133   **With sword of:** *Fragments of Dionysus-Dithyrambs*, 17, 194.

P. 134   **And their mouths:** Ibid., 99, 205.

P. 134   **You would surely:** *The Gay Science*, trans. Walter Kaufmann (New York, 1974), 55.

P. 134   **fire idols:** "Upon the Mount of Olives," *Thus Spoke Zarathustra*, 285.

P. 134   **a snake:** *The Poetry of Friedrich Nietzsche*, 259.

P. 135   **comb honey:** *Thus Spoke Zarathustra*, 350.

P. 135   **new honey:** Ibid., 383.

P. 135   **their coldness.":** Ibid., 219.

P. 135   **for us, the:** *Werke*, 282.

P. 136   **one who is:** Could not be verified.

P. 137 tastes the new: "Among Daughters of the Wilderness," *Thus Spoke Zarathustra*, 417.

P. 138 cut off: Rudolf Kassner, *Buch der Erinnerung*, 2nd Aufl. (Erlenbach Zürich, 1954), 14-15.

P. 138 —the great: *Werke*, 288.

P. 139 greatest pleasure: "Among Daughters of the Wilderness," *Thus Spoke Zarathustra*, 416.

P. 139 mountains, barely: *Werke*, 243.

P. 139 and the wind: "Drei Bruchstücke," Ibid., 249.

P. 139 Attacked . . . "a higher: "On the Afterworldly," *Thus Spoke Zarathustra*, 145.

P. 139 which "often: "Upon the Mount of Olives," Ibid., 285.

P. 139 wonders . . . "the long: Ibid.

P. 139 clean air!": *Thus Spoke Zarathustra*, 296.

P. 140 oneself!: *Basic Writings of Nietzsche*, trans. and ed. Walter Kaufmann (New York, 1966), 674.

P. 141 beyond the world: *Thus Spake Zarathustra*, in *The Complete Works of Friedrich Nietzsche*, XI:227. Bachelard in French also reads "promontory," while Kaufmann translates this as "foothills."

P. 141 . . . thus did: Ibid., 228.

P. 142 how had it: Ibid.

P. 142 him, and he: *Thus Spoke Zarathustra*, 304.

P. 142 Meredith also says: Could not be verified.

P. 143 and dance: "On the Spirit of Gravity," *Thus Spoke Zarathustra*, 307.

P. 143 Divine is the: *Fragments of Dionysus-Dithyrambs*, 67, 201.

P. 143 psyche . . . regenerated by: Cf. *Water and Dreams*, Chapter 6.

P. 144 It seems . . . *thyself:* however, thyself is not italicized in the Levy edition.

P. 144 Sank into: "The Sun Sinks," in *The Poetry of Friedrich Nietzsche*, 291.

P. 144 "now I see: *Thus Spoke Zarathustra*, 153.

P. 144 how can . . . words like: All of these word mean "now" or "from now on."

P. 145 azure bell: "Before Sunrise," *Thus Spoke Zarathustra*, 277.

P. 145 close, my: "At Noon," Ibid., 388.

P. 146 and even annoyed: "The Wanderer," Ibid., 266.

P. 146 of the loneliest.": Ibid., 267.

P. 146 comfort even: Ibid., 266.

P. 146 lie to those: *Thus Spoke Zarathustra*, 343.

P. 147 at the depths—: "Between Birds of Prey," in *The Poetry of Friedrich Nietzsche*, 203.

P. 147 lonely . . . : Ibid.

P. 148   reassures and: *Thus Spoke Zarathustra*, 392-3.

P. 149   into evil.": "On the Tree on the Mountainside," Ibid., 154.

P. 149   the highest: "The Wanderer," Ibid., 266.

P. 149   ing lame: "On the Vision and the Riddle," Ibid., 268.

P. 150   become air: "On the Immaculate Perception," Ibid., 236.

P. 150   he searchingly: "The Beacon," in *The Poetry of Friedrich Nietzsche*, 259.

P. 150   green and yellow . . . ": "The Honey Sacrifice," *Thus Spoke Zarathustra*, 351.

P. 151   stillest cove: "At Noon," Ibid., 388.

P. 151   leap . . . ": "On the Great Longing," Ibid., 335.

P. 151   smooth lie: "The Sun Sinks," in *The Poetry of Friedrich Nietzsche*, 292.

P. 152   Tablet of: "Fame and Eternity," Ibid., 269.

P. 153   bird—and: *Thus Spoke Zarathustra*, 342.

P. 153   Up high: *Songs of Prince Vogelfrei*, in *The Gay Science*, 359-61.

P. 153   not "flown: *Thus Spoke Zarathustra*, 432.

P. 153   . . . is no: Ibid.

P. 153   delight . . . ": "On Old and New Tablets," Ibid., 309.

P. 153   light.": "The Sign," Ibid., ´437.

P. 154   fly—woe: "On Old and New Tablets," Ibid., 322.

P. 154   laughter . . . ": Ibid., 309.

P. 154   flight we . . . "wild wisdom.": Ibid.

P. 154   warm breath, a: "The Wanderer," Ibid., 267.

P. 155   vibrate . . . : "Fame and Eternity," in *The Poetry of Friedrich Nietzsche*, 267.

P. 155   is *my:* "Before Sunrise," *Thus Spoke Zarathustra*, 276.

P. 155   to my insight?": Ibid.

P. 155   trivance and: Ibid.

P. 156   lessness:: Ibid.

P. 156   only a long: Could not be verified.

P. 157   fall. . . . ": "On the Vision and the Riddle," *Thus Spoke Zarathustra*, 268.

P. 157   heart becomes: "On Human Prudence," Ibid., 254.

P. 157   greatness!: *Thus Spoke Zarathustra*, 264.

P. 158   faster.": "On Old and New Tablets," Ibid., 321.

P. 158   their sweep: Ibid.

P. 158   ing as on: *The Joyful Wisdom* in *The Complete Works of Friedrich Nietzsche*, X:222.

P. 158   around us.": Ibid., 229.

P. 159   Do ye not: *Fragments of Dionysus-Dithyrambs*, 54, 199.

P. 159   electrified atmosphere,": *The Joyful Wisdom*, 229.

P. 159 **time!"**: Introduction, *Thus Spake Zarathustra*, in *The Complete Works of Friedrich Nietzsche*, xv. The French reads: "6000 feet above sea-level and even higher above all things human." The German reads "above men and time," as does the English (cf. *Werke*, 292).

P. 159 **Nice"**: Ibid., xxiii.

P. 159 **as those . . . "even**: Ibid.

P. 160 **speaks, I**: "The Convalescent," *Thus Spoke Zarathustra*, 328.

P. 160 **not burden himself**: *The Dawn of Day*, 475, trans. J. M. Kennedy in *The Complete Works of Friedrich Nietzsche*, IX:336.

P. 160 **And in the**: *The Complete Works of Friedrich Nietzsche*, XVII:168. The French, which means "Thou art the depth of all the heights," is closer to the original German (cf. *Werke*, 244) than is the official English translation.

P. 161 **purest things.**: André Gide, *Journal*, in *Oeuvres complètes d'André Gide*, ed. L. Martin-Chauffier (Paris, 1932-39), I:491.

P. 161 **flame—"searing"**: Noailles, *Les Forces éternelles* (Paris, 1920), 119.

P. 161 **painted vault—"compact**: Ibid., 155.

P. 162 **with arrows**: Noailles, *La Domination*, 303. Ellipses are Noailles'.

P. 164 **horizon, made.**: Emile Zola, "La faute de l'abbé Mouret," in *Les Rougon-Macquart* (Paris, 1960), I:1323-24.

P. 165 **that the limitation**: Charpentier, *Coleridge, The Sublime Somnambulist*, trans. M. V. Nugent (New York, 1929), 210. Nugent's version of Coleridge's original text is defective. We have cited the correct text from *Anima Poetae from the Unpublished Notebooks of Samuel Taylor Coleridge*, edited by Ernest Hartley Coleridge (Boston and New York, 1895), 85. Charpentier's French translation alters and expands the last part of the passage, "the eye feels . . . in the object," to "the eye feels that the limitation is in its own power to transcend, in the presence of this unlimitedness, what it sees."

P. 166 **ible for me**: Paul Eluard, *Donner à voir* (Paris, 1939), 11.

P. 170 **the Eastern sky**: Claudel. None of the quotations from Claudel in Section IV could be located.

P. 170 **blue."**: D'Annunzio, *Léda sans cygne* (Paris, 1922), 67.

P. 171 **a property of**: Hofmannsthal, *Ecrits en prose*, 152-53.

P. 172 **Milosz writes: "Pure**: Milosz, "La Terre," in *Les Eléments*, in *Oeuvres complètes*, II:35.

P. 173 **me wherever I**: Friedrich Hölderlin, "Hypérion," in *Poèmes/ Gedichte*, trans. and intro. Geneviève Bianquis (Paris, 1943), 16-17.

P. 173 **itself and as**: Alphonse de Lamartine, "Les Confidences" in *Oeuvres d'Alphonse de Lamartine* (Paris, n.d.), II:142.

P. 175 **The soul imposes**: Paul Valéry, "Odes secrètes," *Charmes*, in *Poems*, 222(Fr.) and 223(Eng.)

P. 175   **kind.:** Louis Nicholas et Albert Bescherelle, *Dictionnaire National ou Grand Dictionnaire de la langue française* (Paris, 1843-46).

P. 177n   **Poétique du ciel:** The 1930 edition was "out of circulation" in the Bibliothèque Nationale in 1985, and the quotation was not found in the 1927 edition.

P. 178   **in the endless:** Bourges, 271.

P. 179   **viting each:** George Sand, *Lélia* (Paris, 1960), 496.

P. 179   **Awake in the:** Charles van Lerberghe, *Entrevisions* (Paris, 1923), 47.

P. 180   **woods.":** Maurice de Guérin, "La Bacchante," in *Maurice de Guérin* (Paris, 1947), II:18.

P. 181   **the night, immobile:** Ibid.

P. 181   **dressed her:** Ibid., 21.

P. 182   **the shadows, she:** Ibid., 24.

P. 182   **carnage and terror:** Bourges, 38.

P. 182   **start out of:** Ibid., 39.

P. 183   **other evening . . . moth:** A double meaning is lost in the English word, "moth." The French word means literally "butterfly of the night."

P. 185   **poetic game . . . :** Novalis, *Journal intime*, 132.

P. 186   **Sénéchal . . . asks literary criticism:** Sénéchal, *Jules Supervielle, poète de l'univers intérieur* (Paris, 1939), 53.

P. 187   **end of the:** Supervielle, "Miracle des aveugles"; see Sénéchal, 54.

P. 187   **I shall:** Supervielle, "L'Amour et les mains"; see Sénéchal, 60.

P. 188   **Called the:** Supervielle, "Matins du Monde: Le Matin du Monde," in *Gravitations* (Paris, 1966), 109.

P. 188   **that see further:** D'Annunzio, "Sera su i Colli d'Alba," in *Versi d'Amore e di Gloria* (1964), 318.

P. 189   **Vowing the splendid:** Valéry, "La Fileuse," 2(Fr.) and 3(Eng.).

P. 189   **honor of living:** Eluard, *Donner à voir*, 97.

P. 190   **knives, birds:** Ibid., 102.

P. 190   **(Gemütserregungskunst).":** Novalis, cited by Spenlé in *Essai sur l'Idéalisme romantique en Allemagne* (Paris, 1903), 356.

P. 190   **Nothing seems:** Supervielle, *Gravitations*, 214.

P. 191   **And the barks:** Ibid.

P. 191   **wave, the earth:** Noailles, "Pour un jardin de Savoie," "Vers écrits en Alsace," in *Les Forces Eternelles*, 139.

P. 191   **the wishes and:** Angelo de Gubernatis, *La Mythologie des plantes* (Paris, 1878), I:240.

P. 191   **"Everything is a:** Supervielle; see Sénéchal, 142.

P. 194   **cracking his "lightning whip.":** Nicholas Franz Niembsch von Strehdenau Lenau, "L'Auberge de la lande," in *Poèmes et poésies*, trans. V. Descreux (Paris, 1892), stanzas 10-11, 151.

P. 194 **it occur:** Charles Baudelaire, *Curiosités esthétiques* (Lausanne, 1956), 369.

P. 195 **speed of eagles.":** Edgar Quinet, *Merlin l'Enchanteur*, 23.

P. 195 **Across the ether:** Goethe, *Second Faust*, act III, lines 9950-53.

P. 196 **heavenly cows:** Michel Bréal, *Hercules et Cacus* (Paris, 1863), 108.

P. 196 **clouds *gavas*:** Ibid.

P. 196 **nyms.":** Ibid., 109.

P. 197 **Mother Nebula?:** Jules Laforgue, "Préludes Autobiographiques," in *Oeuvres complètes*, II:60.

P. 198 **Herdsman's oar.:** Lafcadio Hearn, "The Romance of the Milky Way," in *The Romance of the Milky Way and Other Studies and Stories* (Freeport, New York, n.d.), 48-49.

P. 198 **Milky Way seems:** D'Annunzio, *The Dead City*, act III, sc. 2, 185.

P. 198 **Victor Hugo called:** Could not be verified.

P. 199 **living in the:** Laforgue, *Lettres à un ami* (Paris, 1941), 79.

P. 199 **accountable to:** Laforgue, "Complainte-placet de Faust fils," in *Oeuvres complètes*, 65.

P. 199 **An incandescent:** Laforgue, "Litanies de Misère," Ibid., 30.

P. 199 **From whom emerged:** Laforgue, "Crépuscule de dimanche d'été," Ibid., 37.

P. 200 **"dream machine":** Ibid., 58.

P. 200 **the stars themselves:** Ibid., 58-59.

P. 200 **again.":** Ibid., 59.

P. 200 **eagle, the bull:** Bourges, *La Nef*, 5.

P. 200 **"The whole ether:** Ibid.

P. 203 **wings.:** André Suarès, *Rêves de l'Ombre* (Paris, 1937), 62.

P. 205 **essential . . . "aerial, suspended":** Paul Claudel, *Oeuvres poétique*, Bibliothèque de la Pléiade (Paris, 1962), 80.

P. 208 **other side of:** Rilke, *Fragments en prose*, 109.

P. 208 **least, for standing:** Ibid., 110.

P. 209 **what tree metamorphosis.":** Charles A. Sainte-Beuve, in Maurice de Guérin's *Journal, Lettres et Poèmes* (Paris, 1862), xx-xv. Ellipses are Bachelard's.

P. 209 **for a Laprade's:** Ibid.

P. 209n **A book published anonymously:** This book is now listed under Le Chevalier de Mailly.

P. 210 **around me.":** D. H. Lawrence, *Fantasia of the Unconscious* (Melbourne, London, Toronto, 1961), 38-39.

P. 210 **anybody?":** Ibid., 39.

P. 210n **you.":** Ibid., 38-39 and 76.

P. 213 **seven kingdoms.":** Strindberg, *Swanwhite, A Fairy Dream*, trans. Francis J. Ziegler (Philadelphia, 1909), 14.

P. 213 **hold thyself high:** Ibid., 18.
P. 213 **to the tree:** Lawrence, 146.
P. 214 **maternal duties.:** Guérin, 171.
P. 214 **are all moved:** Ibid., 158.
P. 215 **found a secret:** Félix Rabbe, *Shelley: The Man and the Poet* (London, 1888, rpt. 1978), 45.
P. 216 **scale as the:** Paul Gadenne, *Siloé* (Paris, 1974), 397-98.
P. 216 **brought them face:** D'Annunzio, *The Triumph of Death*, trans. Arthur Hornblow (New York, 1897), 34.
P. 217 **other unhappy:** Théodore Simon Jouffroy. Could not be verified.
P. 218 **velops and darkens:** Charles Ploix, *Le surnaturel dans les contes populaires* (Paris, 1891), 21.
P. 219 **the earth, the:** Goblet d'Alviella, 141.
P. 219 **and whose foot:** Ibid., 155.
P. 219 **potamia,":** Ibid., 156.
P. 219 **shadow over:** Ibid.
P. 220 **erected the crown:** *Rig Veda*. Could not be verified.
P. 220 **our country:** Goblet d'Alviella, 161.
P. 220 **Which, when it:** Hugo, "Booz endormi," in *La Légende des siècles*, 35.
P. 220 **who devour:** Rasmus Bjorn Anderson, *La Mythologie scandinave: légendes des Eddas*, trans. Jules Leclerc (Paris, 1886), 34.
P. 220 **around it:** Ibid., 54.
P. 220 **seen centuries pass:** Ibid., 53.
P. 221 **the Gothic race.:** Ibid., 55.
P. 221 **hell with its:** De Gubernatis, I:18.
P. 222 **perience its:** Gadenne, 270.
P. 225 **to terror and:** Walt Whitman, *Leaves of Grass*, eds. Harold W. Blodgett and Sculley Bradley (New York, 1965), 286.
P. 226 **And here the Sun:** Blake, "Milton," Plate 27, lines 51-54, 124.
P. 227 **wheel.":** Bourges, 26.
P. 227 **that are monstrous:** Ibid.
P. 227 **strange bird.":** Ibid.
P. 227 **wings, manes:** Ibid., 69.
P. 227 **harpies, and stymphalides.":** Ibid., 71.
P. 228 **anxiety caused . . . "whistling:** In French the same verb, *siffler*, is used for both "whistling" and "hissing."
P. 228 **a rapid . . . "The wind:** Hugo, "Les Paysans au bord de la mer," in *Légende des siècles*, 518.
P. 228 **feared.":** André Schaeffner, *Origine des instruments de musique* (Paris, 1936), 217. Bachelard cites Schaeffner as the source, but in a footnote, Schaeffner attributes this quote to Wencelas Sieroszewski

in his "Chamanisme d'après les croyances des Yakoutes" in *Revue de l'histoire des religions*, vol. XLVI (University of Denver, 1902).

P. 229   **other.":** (M. E. Decahors, thesis on Maurice de Guérin. Could not be verified.

P. 229   **two worlds.":** Guérin, *Morceaux choisis* (Paris, 1923), 247.

P. 229   **tempest. . . . ":** Poe, "Silence," 460.

P. 231   **The wind is blowing.:** Saint-Pol Roux, "Le Mystère du Vent," in *La Rose et les épines du chemin* (Paris, 1980), 71.

P. 232   **and the horse:** Colin de Plancy, s.v. *Cheval*.

P. 232   **mountain to crush:** Hauptmann, *The Sunken Bell*, trans. and ed. Montrose J. Moses (Boston, 1924), 86-87.

P. 232   **"huntresses with snakes:** Schwartz, cf. 229ff.

P. 233   **pursuing me.":** Could not be verified.

P. 234   **And breathed:** Pierre Guéguen, "Sur la montagne," in *Jeux cosmiques* (Paris, 1929), 57.

P. 234   **the great physical:** Cazamian, 61.

P. 234   **everywhere.":** Chevrillon, 111.

P. 235   **Expansively, it:** Verhaeren, "A la Gloire du Vent," in *La Multiple splendeur*, 80.

P. 236   **the Blind.":** Denis Diderot, *Lettre sur les aveugles*, in *Oeuvres philosophiques de Diderot* (Paris, 1964), 90.

P. 236   **courage,":** Shelley. Could not be verified.

P. 237   **consumes all things.:** Swami Swahananda explains that "air" refers to a force that causes movement; "prana" is the "vital breath." *The Chandogya Upanishad*(4.3.3), 2nd ed. (Mylapore, Madras, 1965), 268, 270.

P. 237n   **Anon., "Entretiens d'Eudoxe et de Pyrophile":** Author is Guillaume Salmon.

P. 239   **Breathing is the:** Katarina Kippenberg, *Rainer Maria Rilke: Un Témoignage* (Paris, 1942), 219.

P. 240   **Man is a:** "speaking reed" is a play on Blaise Pascal's famous formula that man is a "thinking reed."

P. 240   **genious than:** Charles Nodier, *Examen critique des Dictionnaires de la langue française* (Brussels, 1829), 8.

P. 242   **air.":** Ibid.

P. 243   **thought of . . . "A poem:** Emphasis has been lost, for whereas the French word "UN" before poem is capitalized, this cannot be reflected by the single letter "A" in English.

P. 244   **thought and to:** Paul Claudel, *Positions et Propositions*, in *Oeuvres en Prose*, ed. Charles Galpérine, Bibliothèque de la Pléiade (Paris, 1965), 4.

P. 246   **Time scintillates:** Valéry, "Cimitière marin," 213.

P. 247   **Pipe to the spirit:** Keats, "Ode on a Grecian Urn," 135.

P. 248   **consciousness?:** Baudelaire, *Petits poèmes en prose*, Bibliothèque de la Pléîade (Paris, 1968), 311.

P. 250   **threshold of the:** Boehme, cf. 330.

P. 253   **Whose name is:** Milosz, "La Confession de Lemuel," in *Poésie II*, 155.

P. 255   **you would see:** Bachelard cites Geneviève Bianquis' translation, *Volonté de puissance*, I:217: "Doué d'une vue plus subtile, tu verras toutes choses mouvantes." This appears to correspond to Fragment 386: "Mit einem überlegnen Auge, wunscht man gerade umgekehrt," which Kaufmann translates as: "From a superior viewpoint one desires the contrary." *The Will to Power*, trans. Walter Kaufmann and R. J. Hollingdale (New York, 1967), 208.

P. 257   **between the distant:** Rilke, *Vergers*, 52, 56.

P. 265   **tion of the *Self.*:** Baudelaire, *Mon Coeur mis à nu*, Bibliothèque de la Pléîade (Paris, 1968), 1271.

Author / Title Index

Subject Index

35; life, 29, 35, 36, 48, 56, 92, 178, 206; peace, 141; realism, 35

O

oneirism, 14, 30, 31, 140, 146, 150, 166, 176, 177, 213, 226, 249; oneiric, 19-36, 38, 39, 42, 48, 53, 54, 57, 61-64, 66-71, 75, 77, 79, 91, 100, 108, 112, 118, 153, 168, 182, 185, 189, 190, 195, 206, 209, 212, 219, 231, 232, 258, 262
ornipsychology, 77

P

pancalism, 82, pancalistic, 49, 166
Philemon and Baucis, 209
Plato, 68
Platonic ideas, 44; participation, 68; reminiscence, 143
poetics, aerial, 47; Blake's, 80; Nietzsche's, 127, 128, 150; of anger, 16; of flight, 66; of the storm, 16; of wings, 14, 65; Poe's, 102, 103, 105; Shelley's, 41, 43-45, 48, 86, 234
poetry, 10, 73, 86, 98, 121, 122, 161, 175, 178, 179, 190, 201, 203, 211, 222, 236, 239, 242-245, 247-249, 251, 252; telepoetry, 124
Poseidon, 130
power, creative, 49; graceful, 20; imaginary, 201, 207; imaginative, 61-63; of becoming, 255; of words, 98, 61; oneiric, 223, 224
Prometheus, 39, 81; Promethean, 40, 41
psychagogy, 111
psyche, 1-6, 21, 22, 24, 96, 98, 111, 113, 124, 143, 167, 176, 251, 256, 257, 261, 265; aerial, 6, 8, 42, 43, 158; ascensional, 12, 127, 160
psychic destiny, 10, 35, 39; forces, 39, 41; life, 107, 123, 256; operation, 40
psychoanalysis, 19-22, 24, 48, 68, 112-116, 123, 143, 176, 177
psychology, 6, 44, 61, 77, 93, 97, 115, 121, 152, 156, 165, 183, 230, 236-238, 256, 262, 264; ascensional, 9, 11, 13, 15, 22, 57, 59, 111, 141, 192; of air, 8, 17, 21, 238; of ethics, 158; of literary imagination, 203; of the

imagination, 2, 13, 21, 28, 71, 99; of the moment, 144; of the worker, 206; of vertical life, 214; of verticality, 92; ornipsychology, 77; projective, 54; Pteropsychology, 67, 68; vertical, 205
purity, 68, 69, 71-73, 88, 136, 164, 166, 173, 233, 263

R-S-T

reverie, 65, 67, 69, 166-169, 175-177, 183, 185, 186, 192-195, 197-200, 206, 210-214, 222; ascensional, 111; dynamic, 3, 52, 130, 204, 210, 213; vegetable, 203
silence, 26, 49, 51, 139, 140, 201, 230, 241-245, 247, 248, 251, 253
sleep, 11, 26, 28, 29, 31, 35, 36, 43, 44, 52, 56, 67, 70, 73, 100, 118, 140-143, 145, 148, 180, 181, 197, 206, 237
sound, 49-52, 60, 61, 74, 227-229, 242-244, 249, 253
sublimation, 9, 51, 72, 73, 88, 107, 108, 111-113, 120, 123-125, 165, 174, 192, 251, 263-265; aerial, 8, 50; autonomous, 116; complex, 54; dialectical, 6, 8; discursive, 6, 8, 11, 13, dynamic, 8; induced, 123; material, 264; rational, 116; Shelleyan, 84; vegetal, 37
symbol, 16, 19, 21, 35, 61, 63, 68, 93, 102, 106, 128, 144, 160, 163, 165, 173, 195, 197, 219, 225, 248
symbolism, 22, 39, 83, 93, 231
telepoetry, 124
terror, 34, 35, 92, 96, 100, 101, 103, 104, 227, 228
transparency, 60, 61, 74, 166, 169, 173

U-V

unconscious, 19, 28, 31, 33, 36, 42, 57, 68, 91, 101, 111, 112, 123, 176, 180, 237
uno actu, 107-109, 144, 263
Uranotropism, 182
valorization, 11, 67, 69, 74, 152, 158, 226, 240, 260-262; human, 10; oneiric, 66; poetic, 134; Promethean, 41; vertical, 10